GIFTS THAT SAVE THE ANIMALS

1001 GREAT GIFTS SOLD BY NONPROFITS THAT PROTECT ANIMALS

D0877992

Ellen Berry
Foxglove Publishing

GIFTS THAT
SAVE THE ANIMALS

1001 GREAT GIFTS SOLD BY
NONPROFITS THAT PROTECT ANIMALS

Copyright © 1995 by Ellen Berry
All rights reserved.
Printed in the United States of America
First printing September 1995

Cover design: Kay Selke ◆ Cover illustration: Mohammed Masoor
Text design/typography: Phyllis McDermitt ◆ Illustrations: Tom Kenney

Publisher's Cataloging in Publication
(Prepared by *Quality Books Inc.*)

Berry, Ellen, 1947–
  Gifts that save the animals: 1001 great gifts sold by
nonprofits that protect animals / Ellen Berry. – Dayton, Ohio:
Foxglove Pub., 1995
    p.cm
  Includes bibliographical references and index.
  Preassigned LCCN: 95-060918.
  ISBN 0-9633126-4-2

  1. Gifts. 2. Animal welfare–Societies. etc. 3. Nonprofit
  organizations. I. Title
GT3050.B47 1995   394
                                      QB195-20379

Library of Congress Card #95-060918
ISBN# 0-9633126-4-2 $9.95 Softcover

Foxglove Publishing
P.O. Box 292500
Dayton, Ohio 45429-0500
513-293-5649
USA

Printed on recycled paper.

To Sam and Dave,
the animals who inspire
me to care about the rest

CENTER FOR
MARINE
CONSERVATION
shell oil lamps
pink or blue
♦ $36.00

THE
PEREGRINE
FUND
Silk scarf
♦ $95.00

WILD CANID SURVIVAL
& RESEARCH CENTER
Wolf in sheep's
clothing
stuffed toy
♦ $100.00

TABLE OF CONTENTS

TABLE OF CONTENTS

SECTION FOUR

TABLE OF CONTENTS

SECTION FIVE

CENTER FOR
MARINE
CONSERVATION
Orca mug
♦ $13.50

CENTER FOR
MARINE
CONSERVATION
Dolphin glasses
♦ 4/$28.00

CENTER FOR
MARINE
CONSERVATION
Dolphin music box
♦ $32.95

CENTER FOR
MARINE
CONSERVATION
Whale video
♦ $29.95

ACKNOWLEDGMENTS

I owe thanks to many people as I finish the production of this book.

First, my husband, John, who has been patient, supportive and encouraging and who remains my best friend in the world.

Also, I thank the people who did all of my other life's work while I was sequestered with this project. Marlene, Pam and Rhonda, my guardian angels, thanks for taking care of me, my home and my precious animals.

Robin Cohen, thank you for the many, many hours spent calling, faxing, working at the computer and otherwise looking after my interests in my absence.

Billie Bosser, my dear sweet sister, who is the most "good" person I have ever known, thanks for taking care of Florida, researching, and continuing to be a special friend to me.

Phyllis McDermitt, my typographer and graphic designer, I appreciate your excellent skills and patient grace in an always ASAP project.

Kay Selke, thanks for your astute perception in designing the cover of this second book.

Finally, I must thank the YPO Forum C friends who championed me on as I worked on this book: Jody Akers, Barbara Bushman, Jane Dewey, Kerry Dicke, Vicky Herche, Marty Humes, Carolyn Neff, Loes Van Melle, and Judy Voet.

CENTER FOR
MARINE
CONSERVATION
Turtle magnets
♦ 3/$17.50

CENTER FOR MARINE
CONSERVATION
Penguin insulated
carrier
♦ $7.95

DOLPHIN
RESEARCH
CENTER
Baseball shirt
♦ $28.00

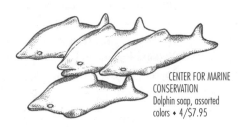

CENTER FOR MARINE
CONSERVATION
Dolphin soap, assorted
colors ♦ 4/$7.95

This book is a sequel to *Gifts That Make A Difference: How To Buy Hundreds Of Great Gifts Sold Through Nonprofits*. The response was almost unanimously "What a great idea!" Many people enjoyed the idea that one could buy holiday gifts and at the same time support worthwhile causes.

The largest category of gifts in *Gifts That Make A Difference* came from organizations that protect animals. So this book was a natural first sequel.

I started out being just a researcher, but the more I found out about the lives of animals, the more I sympathized with their plight. There are so many things that I did not know about happening in the animal world. My eyes are open! I hope that this book will not only serve as an instrument for veteran animal lovers to further their interests but also for people who had no idea what kinds of peril the animals face.

There are many worthwhile animal protection organizations. I have included those that I could find that also have gift merchandise as a way to raise money for their causes. There are also many animal protection nonprofits who do not have gift items for sale as a part of their fund-raising efforts. They are just as viable as those included in this book.

It is satisfying for me to know that many animals may have a chance to live on this Earth while they help make the world a better place for all. They are as necessary in the chain of nature as we are.

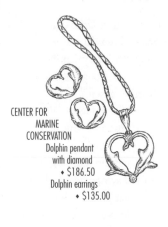

CENTER FOR
MARINE
CONSERVATION
Dolphin pendant
with diamond
♦ $186.50
Dolphin earrings
♦ $135.00

CENTER FOR
MARINE
CONSERVATION
Verdigris pelican wind
chime
♦ $32.95

FRIENDS OF
CONSERVATION
Glassware
♦ $50.–$290.00

I have tried to make this resource
user-friendly. The following are a few
suggestions to help you find the perfect gift:

- **If there is a particular organization you would like to support,** look in Section One (192 animal nonprofits) and Section Two (78 zoos and aquariums) to see if it is among the animal nonprofits with gifts available by mail.

- **If you have an area of interest you would like to support,** look in Section Three to find the organizations that protect whales, dolphins, wolves, chimpanzees, cats, dogs, etc. or those that promote vegetarianism, anti-fur, anti-hunting, education, etc.

- **If you would like to support an organization close to your home,** look in Section Four to locate the organizations near your home.

- **If you have a category of gift in mind,** look in Section Five to find jewelry, stationery, toys, clothing, gift baskets, etc.

- **The index is extensive and will help you further locate the perfect gift for that special someone while helping the animals at the same time!**

- Unless you are in a particular hurry for a gift, it is always best to **call or write for a brochure or catalog of gifts** rather than order an item unseen over the telephone. You will then be able to see pictures and prices and ordering information.

- You may want to **send a number of postcards to selected organizations** requesting information on merchandise available. You will be pleasantly surprised to see how many great gifts you can buy especially from organizations who have large catalogs, i.e., The Center for Marine Conservation, The World Wildlife Fund, Friends of the Sea Otter, etc.

If you would like more information about an organization:

- Ask for reports from the **National Charities Information Bureau** (19 Union Square W., 6th Floor, New York, NY 10003; 212-929-6300). Send a self-addressed stamped envelope (SASE) for the "Wise Giving Guide" and up to three reports on particular organizations per request.

- Request information on particular organizations from the **Philanthropic Advisory Service (PAS) of the Council of Better Business Bureaus** (4200 Wilson Bld., Suite 800, Arlington, VA 22203-1804; 703-276-0100). Send a SASE for "Tips on Charitable Giving" and up to three reports per request.

- Your local **Better Business Bureau** and your **State Attorney General's Office** can also help you with information on local charitable agencies.

If you would like to buy from local charities not listed in this book:

- Find them in the yellow pages under: **Humane Societies or Animal Shelters**. Local veterinarians and animal hospitals will also be able to refer you to area animal protection organizations. Most **zoos will have on-site gift shops** with many unique gifts.

The prices in this book do not generally reflect **charges for handling and shipping.** Therefore, please expect a nominal fee to be added when you order.

What to Get for Each Person
on Your Gift List

**Christmas
and Birthdays:**

Children: Adopt a whale, a wolf, a manatee, a mountain lion, a sea lion, a zoo animal, a farm animal or an injured bird. The child will receive an adoption certificate and other information on his animal. Children love connections to animals and will get an education in the species you adopt for him. I think this is an especially fun gift for godparents and grandparents to give. You can enjoy asking "Have you heard any news lately about your whale?" And the child will enjoy showing you what he has received. Toys and books are also welcome gifts.

Teenagers: Environmental or wildlife T-shirts and other articles of clothing, adopt-an-acre and adopt-an-animal programs, jewelry, books, calendars, posters, duffel bags.

7

Adults: Almost anything listed can be a suitable gift for an adult. If you don't know the recipient well, you may consider stationery, calendars, books, gift baskets or desk accessories.

Wedding and Anniversaries: There are many appropriate gifts to select from in the housewares and art categories. A novel gift for an anniversary might be rain forest-acreage adoptions for the number of years of the marriage.

Newborns: Adoptions of acreage in rain forests say to the child and his parents that you have hope for his future on this planet. The framed certificate will be an interesting addition to the nursery. Music boxes, children's training dishes, baby picture frames, stuffed toys, mobiles.

Housewarmings: Housewares, art and art objects, gift baskets, gourmet foods, wind chimes.

Father's Day: Key rings, mugs, duffel bags, money clips, books, belt buckles, hats, jackets, polo shirts, tie tacks, wallets, bolo ties, pens, bird houses and feeders.

Mother's Day: Stationery, figurines, cookbooks, aprons, carves, cross-stitch, nesting boxes, pewter, jewelry, totes, music boxes, wind chimes, trays.

Business (for employees or clients): Bronzes, sculptures, prints, original art, pens, books, bookends, handcrafts from around the world, tree ornaments, pewter, gift baskets, music boxes, etched glassware. There is added public relations value to a business gift accompanied by a gift card indicating that the item's sale helps support an organization making the world a better place.

DON'T FORGET YOURSELF! You deserve the satisfaction of knowing the merchandise you buy for yourself or your home is making the world a better place too. Also remember to buy the accessories to your gift-giving from the nonprofits: gift wrap, Christmas cards, greeting cards, note cards.

WORLD WILDLIFE
FUND
Frog sound alarm
clock ◆ $47.50

CENTER FOR
MARINE CONSERVATION
Dolphin Post-It® notes
◆ 10 pads/$13.50

FRIENDS OF THE SEA OTTER
Sea otter pillow ◆ $82.00

FRIENDS OF
THE SEA OTTER
Sea otter canister
◆ $72.00

An Alphabetical Listing of the Profiles of 192 Nonprofit Organizations

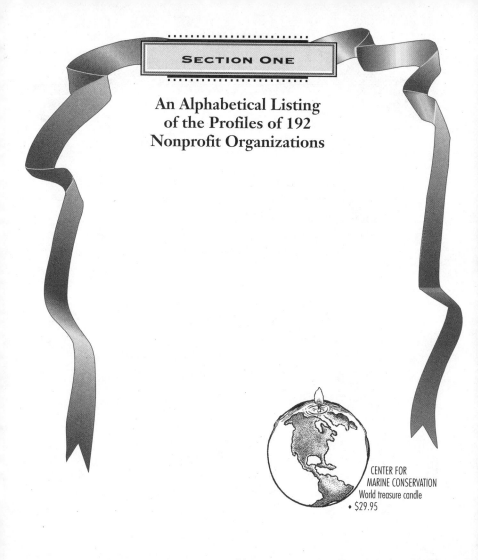

CENTER FOR
MARINE CONSERVATION
World treasure candle
• $29.95

ACTORS AND OTHERS FOR ANIMALS

⊸ PURPOSE ⊷
Promote the humane treatment of animals

⊸ ACTIVITIES ⊷
Help line and referral service; humane education;
legislation; spay/neuter program; pet assisted therapy
for elderly patients isolated in nursing homes, hospitals
and special treatment centers; pet placement

⊸ GIFTS ⊷
Celebrity-autographed T-shirts,
sweatshirts and mugs, "animal autographed" bandanas

"Helping all creatures great and small since 1971..."

Actors and Others for Animals
11523 Burbank Boulevard
North Hollywood CA 91601
818-386-5870 (merchandise orders) ♦ 818-368-4625 (fax orders)
818-755-6045 (agency info)

ADOPT-A-COW

⊸ PURPOSE ⊷
Cow protection

⊸ ACTIVITIES ⊷
Providing a cruelty-free life
for cows at the Village; education

⊸ GIFTS ⊷
Adopt-A-Cow: adoption certificate, photo of
your cow or ox, newsletter, updates–starting at $30 per month;
Vegetarian cookbooks, T-shirts, baseball caps, travel mugs

*"The most revolutionary cow
protection program in the world"*

Adopt-A-Cow
Gita-nagari Village
RD 1 Box 839
Port Royal PA 17082
717-527-2476

ADOPT A RABBIT

⤙ PURPOSE ⤚
Provide a permanent home for rabbits who
are fugitives from abusive situations, local shelters,
commercial breeders and laboratories

⤙ ACTIVITIES ⤚
Operate the rabbit sanctuary; education

⤙ GIFTS ⤚
Adopt A Rabbit: adoption certificate and individual history
of the rabbit adopted, a color photo, periodic sanctuary reports,
informative articles and rabbit stories–$20

"The rabbits need you."

Adopt A Rabbit Program
The Fund for Animals, Inc.
P.O. Box 554
Faith NC 28041

AFRICAN WILDLIFE FOUNDATION

⬦ PURPOSE ⬦
Protect the wildlife of Africa (elephants,
rhinos, gorillas, lions, cheetahs) and their habitats

⬦ ACTIVITIES ⬦
Conservation programs that focus on
education, wildlife parks and endangered species

⬦ GIFTS ⬦
Posters, books

"Only elephants should wear ivory."

African Wildlife Foundation
1717 Massachusettes Avenue, N.W.
Washington DC 20036
202-265-8393 ⬦ 202-265-2361 fax

ALASKA WILDLIFE ALLIANCE

⚊ PURPOSE ⚊
Protect Alaska's wildlife

⚊ ACTIVITIES ⚊
Fight predator-killing programs; represent
nonconsumptive use and protect threatened
and endangered species through legislation,
public education and policy forums

⚊ GIFTS ⚊
Calendars, prints, books, T-shirts,
sweatshirts, postcards, pins, note cards, watches

*"Please help us protect
Alaska's magnificent wildlife."*

**Wolf watch
♦ $59.95**

Alaska Wildlife Alliance
P.O. Box 202022
Anchorage AK 99520
907-277-0897 ♦ 907-277-7423 fax

ALLIANCE AGAINST ANIMAL ABUSE

⌐ PURPOSE ⌐
Advocate humane treatment for
animals with emphasis on equines and
otherwise provide for their welfare

⌐ ACTIVITIES ⌐
Work with local agencies to see that existing
laws concerning animal abuse are enforced;
spay/neuter programs

⌐ GIFTS ⌐
Calendars, T-shirts, sweatshirts, dog sweaters

"The Horse Force"

Alliance Against Animal Abuse, Inc.
P. O. Box 90601
Albuquerque NM 87199-0601
505-821-0393 ♦ 505-294-8358

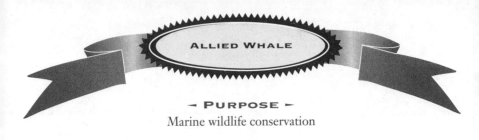

ALLIED WHALE

⊸ PURPOSE ⊱
Marine wildlife conservation

⊸ ACTIVITIES ⊱
Conduct population research on humpback,
finback and right whales; maintain catalogues of
photo-identified finback and humpback whales

⊸ GIFTS ⊱
Adopt A Finback Whale: adoption certificate,
color photo, a drawing detailing individual identifying
characteristics, fact sheets, newsletter–$30; adopt a mother
and her calf and receive 2 photos–$50; Videos, books

*"The finback whale is the second
largest mammal to inhabit the earth."*

Allied Whale
College of the Atlantic
105 Eden Street
Bar Harbor ME 04609
207-288-5644 ♦ 207-288-5015
207-288-2328

⚊ PURPOSE ⚊
Eliminate the use of animals in
research and testing; education

⚊ ACTIVITIES ⚊
Fund non-animal research, initiate
campaigns against vivisectors,
support grassroots activists throughout the
nation, educational programs

⚊ GIFTS ⚊
Mugs, T-shirts, animal rights bookshelf

"Animal experiments are a dying tradition."

The American Anti-Vivisection Society
801 Old York Road, #204
Jenkintown PA 19046-1685
215-887-0816 ♦ 215-887-2088 fax

AMERICAN CETACEAN SOCIETY

⚊ PURPOSE ⚊
Preserve and protect
dolphins and whales

⚊ ACTIVITIES ⚊
Education, research, conservation

⚊ GIFTS ⚊
Pendants, tie tacks, note cards,
postcards, T-shirts, sweatshirts, books

*"The oldest nonprofit whale
organization in the world"*

Silver fluke
pendant
♦ $24.00

American Cetacean Society
P .O. Box 2639
San Pedro CA 90731-0943
310-548-6279 ♦ 310-548-6950

AMERICAN HORSE PROTECTION ASSOCIATION

⌐ PURPOSE ¬

Protect the welfare of horses

⌐ ACTIVITIES ¬

Education, legislation, state volunteer
program, seminars, special projects and events

⌐ GIFTS ¬

Prints, T-shirts, sweatshirts,
baseball caps, mugs, books

"For the love of horses..."

American Horse Protection Association, Inc.
1000 29th Street, N.W., Suite T-100
Washington DC 20007
202-965-0500 ♦ 202-965-9621 fax

AMERICAN HUMANE ASSOCIATION

⊰ PURPOSE ⊱

Prevention of cruelty, neglect,
abuse and exploitation of animals

⊰ ACTIVITIES ⊱

Advocacy, education, extensive resources
and trainings for local animal shelters, emergency
animal relief, information and referral services;
L.A. office focused on protecting animals used in TV and
movies; Washington, D.C. office focused on helping
animals through legislation

⊰ GIFTS ⊱

T-shirts, sweatshirts, posters, bookmarks

"Be kind to animals."

American Humane Association
63 Inverness Drive East
Englewood CO 80112
303-792-9900

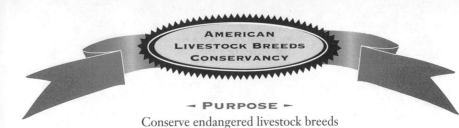

AMERICAN LIVESTOCK BREEDS CONSERVANCY

⊸ PURPOSE ⊶
Conserve endangered livestock breeds

⊸ ACTIVITIES ⊶
Provide technical support to breeders
and breed associations, operation of a semen
bank, clearinghouse, education

⊸ GIFTS ⊶
T-shirts, note cards, tote bags,
pins, earrings, tie tacks, books

"Saving rare farm animals for the future"

American Livestock Breeds Conservancy
P.O. Box 477
Pittsboro, NC 27312
919-542-5704

⊸ PURPOSE ⊶

Protection and preservation of
America's wild equine

⊸ ACTIVITIES ⊶

Rescue, rehabilitation and relocation services;
adoptions; education and service to adopters;
abuse and neglect hotline; educational programs,
shows, clinics and playdays; registry

⊸ GIFTS ⊶

Calendars, T-shirts, sweatshirts,
books, videos, limited edition prints

*"Symbols of the historic and pioneer
spirit of the West"*

Calendar
♦ $9.95

American Mustang & Burro Association
P.O. Box 788
Lincoln CA 95648
916-633-9271

AMERICAN RESCUE DOG ASSOCIATION

⊸ PURPOSE ⊶

Provide search and rescue response, share training
techniques, maintain uniform standards and a national
alerting system for major emergencies with various state
rescue dog associations in the U.S.

⊸ ACTIVITIES ⊶

Search response; training and education;
coordination of rescue dog associations

⊸ GIFTS ⊶

T-shirts, mugs, tiles, tie tack/lapel pins, key chains

"Dogs in search and rescue...that others may live"

American Rescue Dog Association
P.O. Box 151
Chester NY 10918
914-469-4173

AMERICAN SOCIETY FOR THE PREVENTION OF CRUELTY TO ANIMALS

⊸ PURPOSE ⊷

Alleviate fear, pain and suffering in the
animal world; promote spaying and neutering

⊸ ACTIVITIES ⊷

Pet adoptions, animal shelter, Bergh Animal Hospital,
humane education, companion animal services, humane
law enforcement, legislative activities, Animalport

⊸ GIFTS ⊷

T-shirts, caps, mugs, umbrellas, tote bags, cat bowls
and placemats, note cards, posters, coloring books, books

"The ASPCA is America's first humane society."

American Society for the Prevention of Cruelty to Animals
424 East 92nd Street
New York NY 10128
212-876-7700

AMERICAN VEGAN SOCIETY

⊸ PURPOSE ⊱

Teach a compassionate way of living

⊸ ACTIVITIES ⊱

Educational programs including live-in
weekend vegan cooking classes, lectures, conventions,
distribution of publications

⊸ GIFTS ⊱

Cookbooks, books, videos, audio tapes

*"The natural results of widespread veganism are not
only better human health and happier circumstances for the
animal kingdom, but also a tremendous alleviation of the
environmental burden placed upon this planet."*

The American Vegan Society
P.O. Box H
Malaga NJ 08328-0908
609-694-2887

⌐ PURPOSE ¬

Save injured, sick, abused and orphaned wild animals
and birds in Santa Cruz County and surrounding areas from
unnecessary suffering and death; provide permanent sanctuary
for wild and exotic animals and birds in need

⌐ ACTIVITIES ¬

Provide care, food and compassion for all wild
and exotic creatures brought to the wildlife center

⌐ GIFTS ¬

Adopt an Animal: photo and a history of the animal chosen (cougar,
bobcat, leopard, wolf, monkey, wild boar, hawk, owl, or miniature
goat)–$10/month; T-shirts, sweatshirts

"We are the <u>original</u> wildlife rescue organization – established in 1968."

American Wildlife Rescue Service, Inc.
1296 Conference Drive
Scotts Valley CA 95066-2901
408-335-3232 ♦ 408-438-7516 fax

ANIMAL ALLIES

⤙ PURPOSE ⤚
Animal welfare

⤙ ACTIVITIES ⤚
Find homes for unwanted animals, promote
spaying/neutering, maintain a wildlife sanctuary
for the less adoptable pets

⤙ GIFTS ⤚
Calendars

"We do not destroy animals PERIOD."

Animal Allies
P.O. Box 353
Fairfax Station VA 22039

ANIMAL PROTECTION INSTITUTE OF AMERICA

◄ PURPOSE ►

Educate, investigate and advocate
the humane treatment of all animals

◄ ACTIVITIES ►

Protect against animal abuse through enforcement/legislative actions,
investigations, advocacy campaigns and education; specific areas of concern are
companion animals, wildlife, animals used in entertainment, animals used in
laboratory research and humane education in schools

◄ GIFTS ►

T-shirts, mugs, tote bags, fanny packs,
lunch boxes, videos, license plate frames

"Stand up for animals."

Animal Protection Institute of America
2831 Fruitridge Road
P.O. Box 22505
Sacramento CA 95822
916-731-5521 ♦ 916-731-4467 fax

ANIMAL RESCUE

⊸ PURPOSE ⊳

Animal conservation

⊸ ACTIVITIES ⊳

Education, spay/neuter programs,
maintenance of an animal shelter

⊸ GIFTS ⊳

Foster Pet Program: photo and brief write-up
of the cat or dog sponsored–$5 per month; Calendars,
coloring books, photo mugs, key tags

"Have you hugged your pet today?"

Animal Rescue, Inc.
P. O. Box 35
Maryland Line MD 21105
717-993-3232

ANIMAL RIGHTS COALITION

⊸ PURPOSE ⊱
End all exploitation and
institutionalized cruelty to all animals

⊸ ACTIVITIES ⊱
Education; legislation; workshops; referrals;
networking with other animal, environmental and
civic groups; Speakers' Bureau

⊸ GIFTS ⊱
T-shirts, books

"We share the earth together; let them live in peace."

Animal Rights Coalition, Inc.
P.O. Box 20315
Bloomington MN 55420
612-822-6161 ♦ 612-822-0469 fax

ANIMAL WELFARE INSTITUTE

– PURPOSE –
Reduce the pain and fear inflicted on
animals by humans; protect endangered species

– ACTIVITIES –
Campaign against steel jaw leghold traps for capture of
fur-bearing animals and predators; campaign against commercial
killing of whales; campaign against factory farming practices that
cruelly confine veal calves and pigs to small crates and laying
hens to battery cages; publications

– GIFTS –
Books, videos, prints, T-shirts

"Help us stop this cruelty."

Animal Welfare Institute
P.O. Box 3650
Washington DC 20007
202-337-2332 ♦ 202-338-9478 fax

ANIMAL WELFARE SOCIETY OF SOUTHEASTERN MICHIGAN

⊸ PURPOSE ⊸
Protect the welfare of animals
throughout Southeastern Michigan

⊸ ACTIVITIES ⊸
Humane education in public schools; therapeutic visits
with cats or dogs to nursing homes, health care facilities and
schools for the mentally or physically challenged; free referral
and lost and found services; adoption placement

⊸ GIFTS ⊸
T-shirts, sweatshirts

"Everyone Needs A Second Chance."

Animal Welfare Society of Southeastern Michigan
29081 Dequindre, Suite E
Madison Heights MI 48071
810-548-1150 ♦ 810-548-1183 fax

ANTI-CRUELTY SOCIETY

➤ PURPOSE ➤
Promote humane
treatment of animals

➤ ACTIVITIES ➤
Educational resource center, mobile
vaccination clinic, animal shelter, spay/neuter
program, adoption placement, abuse investigations

➤ GIFTS ➤
Frisbees, T-shirts, caps, sweatshirts

*"The Anti-Cruelty Society will
never turn its back on an animal in need."*

The Anti-Cruelty Society
157 West Grand Avenue
Chicago IL 60610
312-644-8338 ◆ 312-644-3878 fax

ASSISI ANIMAL FOUNDATION

⊸ PURPOSE ⊸
Operate a no-kill shelter for cats and dogs

⊸ ACTIVITIES ⊸
Maintenance of the cageless shelter, spay/neuter
program, Pets for Patients visitation program, local
educational programs, Wildlife Education Outreach featuring
deep-discounted luxury safaris to Kenya and Tanzania

⊸ GIFTS ⊸
Armchair Adoptions: photos and regular news of the
companion you have adopted–$15 per month; T-shirts, sweatshirts

"One can make a difference. Together we can make a miracle."

Assisi Animal Foundation
P.O. Box 143
Crystal Lake IL 60039-0143
815-455-9411 ♦ 815-455-9417

ASSOCIATED HUMANE SOCIETIES

⤙ PURPOSE ⤚

Prevention of cruelty to animals throughout the
United States and specifically the state of New Jersey

⤙ ACTIVITIES ⤚

Adoption services, animal turn-in services, boarding, cremation, burial, cruelty
investigations, education programs, low cost spay/neuter clinics, maintenance of a
hospital clinic, tattooing, grooming, lost pet service, problem pet consultations, pet
retirement home, wildlife rescue and release service, maintenance of Popcorn Park Zoo

⤙ GIFTS ⤚

Popcorn Park Wildlife Club Animal Sponsorship: a report every four months and a
photo of the animal sponsored, Humane News monthly–starting at $2 per month;
Share-A-Pet Animal Sponsorship: color photo, a letter every four months on the
health and activities of the dog or cat sponsored, Humane News monthly, free
admission to Popcorn Park Zoo–$10 per month; Lunch boxes

"Help reduce the animal population...Have YOUR pet spayed or neutered."

Associated Humane Societies
124 Evergreen Avenue
Newark NJ 07114
201-824-7080 ◆ 201-824-2720 fax

**BACK TO NATURE
WILDLIFE REFUGE**

⊸ PURPOSE ⊷
Provide a wildlife rehabilitation facility for permanently
injured animals and a wildlife/environmental education center

⊸ ACTIVITIES ⊷
Rescue, raise, rehabilitate and release wild animals
and birds; provide a home for non-releasable animals

⊸ GIFTS ⊷
Wildlife adoptions: adoption certificate, 8x10 photo,
the chosen animal's special story, invitation to visit the
adopted critter–$30

"Rescue-Raise-Rehabilitate-Release"

Back To Nature Wildlife, Inc.
18515 East Colonial Drive
Orlando FL 32820
407-568-5138

BAT CONSERVATION INTERNATIONAL

◄ PURPOSE ►

Conservation of bats and their habitats worldwide

◄ ACTIVITIES ►

Through education, raise awareness about the importance of bats
and the ecosystems that depend on them; protect critical bat habitats through
conservation partnerships around the world; research

◄ GIFTS ►

Adopt-A-Bat: adoption certificate, color photo, information sheet,
"Batty About Bats" bumper sticker–$15; T-shirts, caps, stationery, note cards,
bat houses, bat detectors, posters, computer screen savers, card sets, videos, books

Stellaluna,
children's book
♦ $15.95

*"These gentle friends and essential allies
carry the seeds that make the rainforest
grow and the deserts bloom."*

Bat Conservation International, Inc.
P.O. Box 162603
Austin TX 78716-2603
800-538-BATS ♦ 512-327-9721
512-327-9724 fax

BEST FRIENDS ANIMAL SANCTUARY

⊶ PURPOSE ⊷
Provide sanctuary for homeless, abused
or neglected dogs, cats and other animals

⊶ ACTIVITIES ⊷
Operate an animal sanctuary; provide a low-cost
spay/neuter program; sponsor a national network
of animal lovers who take part in animal rescue,
foster care and humane education

⊶ GIFTS ⊷
Adopt A Pet Program: adoption certificate, photo of
your new friend, monthly letters with good news about the
animals you are helping to support, monthly magazine–$15;
T-shirts, greeting cards, pins, bean bag toys

"The largest no-kill shelter in the United States"

Best Friends Animal Sanctuary
P.O. Box G
Kanab UT 84741
801-644-2001

BIRDS OF PREY REHABILITATION FOUNDATION

⊣ PURPOSE ⊢
Rehabilitate injured and orphaned raptors
(eagles, owls, hawks, accipters, falcons)

⊣ ACTIVITIES ⊢
Treat and care for hurt birds at the
Sanctuary, return the rehabilitated birds to the place
of their recovery, educational programs

⊣ GIFTS ⊢
Adopt A Raptor: adoption certificate, life history
of the bird, photo–$120 to $240 per year; T-shirts,
sweatshirts, holiday cards, note cards

"The future of birds of prey depends on us."

Birds of Prey Rehabilitation Foundation
2290 S. 104th Street
Broomfield CO 80020
303-460-0674

CAMP FIRE CONSERVATION FUND

⌐ PURPOSE ⌐
Prevent the extinction of the
antelope of the Arizona Sonoran Desert

⌐ ACTIVITIES ⌐
Recover and enlarge the
dwindling population of the Sonoran antelope

⌐ GIFTS ⌐
Limited edition prints

Please help us save these phantoms of the desert."

Camp Fire Conservation Fund
230 Camp Fire Road
Chappaqua NY 10514
914-941-0199 ♦ 914-923-0977 fax

To order prints:
Fulfillment Services
1955 West Grant Road, Suite 230
Tuscon AZ 85745
602-798-1513 ♦ 602-798-1514 fax

⊸ PURPOSE ⊱

Manage and protect migrant bird and
butterfly populations and their habitats

⊸ ACTIVITIES ⊱

Butterfly tagging sanctioned by the
Monarch Migration Association of North America

⊸ GIFTS ⊱

Sponsor A Migrant: certificate with your Monarch butterfly's sex,
date tagged, tagging location and tagger's name. If your butterfly is recovered,
a second certificate will be sent telling where your butterfly was found,
by whom and under what circumstances–$25; for an extra $10, you will receive
a color photo of the species you sponsored

"A way to help protect open space for wildlife"

Cape May Bird Observatory
Project Wind Seine
P.O. Box 3
Cape May Point NJ 08212-0003
609-884-2736 ◆ 609-884-6052 fax

CARIBBEAN CONSERVATION CORPORATION

⊸ PURPOSE ⊷
Conservation of sea turtles and coastal
habitats throughout the Caribbean and Atlantic

⊸ ACTIVITIES ⊷
Habitat protection, education,
research, conservation, training

⊸ GIFTS ⊷
Adopt-A-Turtle: adoption certificate, profile of the adopted
turtle, sea turtle fact sheet, a year's subscription to the newsletter,
decal–$25; T-shirts, whistles, stuffed toys, note cards, mugs, earrings,
bracelets, pendants, charms, rings, pins, key chains, books

*"Sea turtle shell is the most frequent
contraband brought back from the Caribbean."*

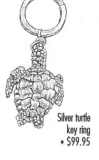

Silver turtle
key ring
♦ $99.95

Caribbean Conservation Corporation
P.O. Box 2866
Gainesville FL 32602
800-678-7853 ♦ 904-373-6441
904-375-2449 fax

CAT CARE SOCIETY

⊰ PURPOSE ⊱
Improve the quality of life for abandoned, injured,
abused and unwanted cats in the Denver metro area

⊰ ACTIVITIES ⊱
Operate a cageless adoption facility, educational programs
that promote responsible pet ownership, nursing home visitations,
lifetime care, spay/neuter assistance, behavior counseling, Sponsor A Cat

⊰ GIFTS ⊱
Note cards

"Help save lives..Please spay and neuter your pets."

Cat Care Society
5985 West 11th Avenue
Lakewood CO 80214-2105
303-239-9680

CENTER FOR MARINE CONSERVATION

⤙ PURPOSE ⤚

Conserve marine species, protect special marine habitats, prevent marine pollution

⤙ ACTIVITIES ⤚

Science-based advocacy, policy-oriented research, public awareness and education, support of domestic and international conservation programs, involve citizens in public policy decisions

⤙ GIFTS ⤚

T-shirts, sweatshirts, shirts, boxer shorts, jogging suits, sweat suits, jackets, neckties, belts, vests, socks, caps, suspenders, nightshirts, robes, toothbrushes, soaps, figurines, sculptures, ceramic boxes, nesting boxes, music boxes, sparkle globes, art bowls, candles, frames, lamps, vases, potpourri bowls, glasses, child's training dishes, mugs, teapots, salt-and-pepper sets, pendants, earrings, rings, bracelets, necklaces, pins, tie tacks, watches, telephones, clocks, cotton throws, rugs, pillows, door mats, door knockers, umbrellas, tote bags, duffel bags, backpacks, shower curtains, bath mats, towels, soap dispensers, tissue boxes, welcome plaques, switch plate covers, wallpaper borders, night-lights, magnets, coat hooks, wind chimes, stained glass, suncatchers, flags, mailboxes, chocolate eggs, prints, posters, notepads, stationery, calendars, stuffed toys, puzzles, games, rubber stamp sets, activity sets, videos, audio cassettes, CD's, books, money clips, letter openers, key rings, hair barrettes

"Wholly dedicated to protecting diversity and abundance of life in the sea"

Center for Marine Conservation
1725 Desales Street, N.W.
Washington DC 20036
800-227-1929 (catalog) ♦ 202-429-5609 (D.C. headquarters)

CENTER FOR WHALE RESEARCH

◄ PURPOSE ►

Promote, support and conduct benign scientific
research on marine mammals of the Order Cetacea–
whales, dolphins and porpoises

◄ ACTIVITIES ►

Photoidentification in population and behavioral studies

◄ GIFTS ►

Note cards, books

"Observe, study and portray cetaceans"

Center for Whale research
P.O. Box 1577
Friday Harbor WA 98250

◄ PURPOSE ►

Preservation of wildlife diversity and the environment which supports it

◄ ACTIVITIES ►

Dolphin conservation in the Bahamas; sea turtle survey in the
Gulf of Mexico; cheetah conservation in Namibia; bengal tiger tracking in
India; elephant research in Kenya; Peruvian rain forest protection; macaw parrot
research in Peru; porpoise protection in the Sea of Cortez, Mexico; gray and
Mexican wolf reintroduction program in Arizona and Yellowstone Park;
barrier reef protection in Belize; jaguar survey in Belize

◄ GIFTS ►

Coasters, porcelain boxes, posters, note cards

*"Stop habitat loss in areas of dense biodiversity
in order to protect the natural resources
of wild environments around the world."*

Chase Wildlife Foundation
38C Grove Street
Ridgefield CT 06877
203-438-9655 ♦ 203-431-6241 fax

Parrot
porcelain
coasters
♦ 4/$35.00

COLORADO
HORSE RESCUE

PURPOSE
Horse welfare

ACTIVITIES
Rescue abandoned, abused, unwanted
and neglected horses; operate a shelter for
horses; placement; educational programs

GIFTS
Sweatshirts, T-shirts, hats, visors, mugs

*"Dedicated to horses and
the people who love horses"*

Colorado Horse Rescue
P.O. Box 1510
Arvada CO 80001
303-439-9217 ♦ 303-439-9259 fax

COMMITTEE TO ABOLISH SPORT HUNTING

⊸ PURPOSE ⊱
Abolish sport hunting

⊸ ACTIVITIES ⊱
Protection of wildlife from hunting
and other harassment, education, exposés

⊸ GIFTS ⊱
Necklaces, pins, tote bags,
pillow covers, wall hangings, books, hats

"A nature preservationist organization"

Committee to Abolish Sport Hunting, Inc. (C.A.S.H.)
P.O. Box 44
Tomkins Cove NY 10986
914-429-8733 ♦ 914-429-1545

CONCERN FOR CRITTERS

‑ PURPOSE ‑
Raise awareness about animal
welfare and animal rights issues

‑ ACTIVITIES ‑
Public education, neuter/spay
program, pet food assistance program

‑ GIFTS ‑
T-shirts, sweatshirts

*"Animals have the right to
share our planet without being harmed."*

Concern for Critters
P.O. Box 990
Battle Creek MI 49016
616-965-4529 day ◆ 616-968-1540 evening
616-964-4879

CONCERN FOR HELPING ANIMALS IN ISRAEL

⊸ PURPOSE ⊷
Help the Israeli animal welfare community
improve the condition and treatment of Israel's animals

⊸ ACTIVITIES ⊷
Send funds, veterinary medical supplies and equipment to animal shelters;
promote humane education and animal protection legislation; promote humane
population control instead of strychnine poisoning; sponsor conferences on
various issues such as the child/animal abuse link and alternatives to animals in
laboratories; bring Jewish and Arab children together to learn about animals
and participate in projects that help them

⊸ GIFTS ⊷
Frames, note cards, T-shirts

*"We work to bring light into the darkness, to help
where the need is greatest and the resources fewest."*

Concern for Helping Animals in Israel
P.O. Box 3341
Alexandria VA 22302
703-658-9650

DAYS END FARM HORSE RESCUE

⊸ PURPOSE ⊱
Create a symbiotic relationship between
abused and neglected horses and caring human beings

⊸ ACTIVITIES ⊱
Provide shelter, rehabilitation, training
and qualified adoption of abused horses in Maryland

⊸ GIFTS ⊱
T-shirts, tank tops, sport cups

"Please..Help us help the horses."

Days End Farm Horse Rescue, Inc.
15856 Frederick Road
P.O. Box 309
Lisbon MD 21765
301-854-5037 phone/fax

DELAWARE VALLEY RAPTOR CENTER

⤙ PURPOSE ⤚
Conservation of birds of prey

⤙ ACTIVITIES ⤚
Treatment, rehabilitation and return to the wild
of injured, ill and orphaned raptors; public education

⤙ GIFTS ⤚
Adoption program: adoption certificate, color
photo of the bird sponsored, fact sheet, decal & sticker, DVRC
journal, starting at $15; T-shirts, sweatshirts, note cards

"The time has come to mother nature."

Delaware Valley Raptor Center
R.D. 2 Box 9335
Milford, PA 18337
717-296-6025

DELTA SOCIETY

⊸ PURPOSE ⊱
Promote better health, healing and independence
through companion, therapy and service animals

⊸ ACTIVITIES ⊱
Pet Partners Program® trains volunteers and their pets to work in hospitals
and nursing homes and trains health care professionals in animal-assisted
therapy; Service Dog Center links people with disabilities with dogs specially
trained to assist them and advocates for their right to be in public places;
People & Pets services provides an 800 Actionline and National Referral Center
for information and advocacy on the health benefits of animal compassion,
pet loss, pets in housing and other topics

⊸ GIFTS ⊱
Note cards, T-shirts, sweatshirts, pins

"Bringing people and animals together for companionship and healing"

Delta Society
P.O. Box 1080
Renton WA 98057-9906
800-869-6898 ♦ 206-235-1076 fax

DESERT TORTOISE PRESERVE COMMITTEE

⤙ PURPOSE ⤚
Protect the welfare of wild tortoise populations

⤙ ACTIVITIES ⤚
Maintenance of a 39 square mile
tortoise preserve, conservation education

⤙ GIFTS ⤚
Note cards, postcards, T-shirts, pin/tie tacks,
wind chimes, pendant/bolos, mugs, caps

"Do not release captive tortoises!"

**Bolo tie
♦ $2.35**

Desert Tortoise Preserve Committee, Inc.
P.O. Box 2910
San Bernardino CA 92406
800-525-2443

DIAN FOSSEY GORILLA FUND

⊸ PURPOSE ⊱

Protect mountain gorillas in Rwanda

⊸ ACTIVITIES ⊱

Maintenance of the Karisoke Research Center in Rwanda, provide anti-poaching patrols, education in Rwanda and the U.S., development of accurate maps of gorilla rain forest and volcano habitats, digitized database containing 28 years of mountain gorilla research, Scientific Advisory Committee invites research proposals for graduate and post-graduate students interested in conducting on-site mountain gorilla or bio-diversity research projects at Karisoke

⊸ GIFTS ⊱

Adopt A Gorilla: adoption certificate, Digit News quarterly, a photo of your gorilla, a field report on the gorilla's progress-starting at $1000; Journals, boxer shorts, coloring books, tote bags, sweatshirts, T-shirts, mugs, gorilla cookie cutter and recipe card gift sets, steins, pins, pewter gorilla figurines, posters, note cards, stuffed toys, luggage tags

Gorilla boxer shorts
◆ $20.00

"Digit was Dr. Fossey's favorite gorilla.
He was killed by poachers."

Dian Fossey Gorilla Fund
45 Inverness Drive East, Suite B
Englewood CO 80112-5480
800-851-0203 ◆ 303-790-2349
303-790-9460 fax

DOGS FOR THE DEAF

⁃ PURPOSE ⁃
Rescue unwanted dogs to supply
hearing and companion dogs to the
hearing impaired

⁃ ACTIVITIES ⁃
Choose and test dogs from adoption shelters,
intensive training of the dogs and the recipients,
dog placement and follow-up

⁃ GIFTS ⁃
Note cards, polo shirts, T-shirts,
sweatshirts, windbreakers, caps, pins,
tote bags, mugs, sport tumblers

"Rescuing dogs to help the deaf since 1977"

Dogs for the Deaf, Inc.
10175 Wheeler Road
Central Point OR 97502-9360
503-826-9220 Voice/TDD
503-826-6696 fax

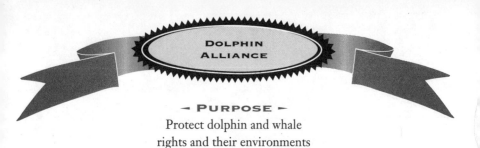

⊸ PURPOSE ⊱

Protect dolphin and whale
rights and their environments

⊸ ACTIVITIES ⊱

Education, legislation, rehabilitation and
release of currently held captive dolphins back into the wild

⊸ GIFTS ⊱

T-shirts, audio cassettes

*"Working to restore the ancient
friendship of humans and dolphins"*

Dolphin Alliance
P.O. Box 510273
Melbourne Beach FL 32951
407-951-1301 ◆ 407-724-5121 fax

DOLPHIN FREEDOM FOUNDATION

⤙ PURPOSE ⤚
Gain the freedom of all marine mammals
held in captivity for casual amusement or display; free the
oceans of drift nets, tuna nets and pollution

⤙ ACTIVITIES ⤚
Public education, establish a citizens watch group to visit
marine parks to report violations, establish a center to re-adapt captive
dolphins back to the wild, petition to ban the capture of wild dolphins inside
Florida state waters for the purpose of casual amusement

⤙ GIFTS ⤚
T-shirts

"Captivity is for a lifetime; freedom is forever."

Dolphin Freedom Foundation
824 SW 13 Street
Fort Lauderdale FL 33315
305-462-1817

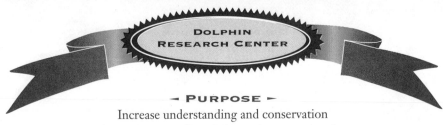

DOLPHIN RESEARCH CENTER

⊸ PURPOSE ⊸

Increase understanding and conservation
of marine mammals and the environment we share

⊸ ACTIVITIES ⊸

Rescue and rehabilitate stranded whales and dolphins and act as a critical care unit
for sick or injured marine mammals; Swim-With-The-Dolphins programs;
Dolphinlab, a week long college-accredited experiential program with the dolphins

⊸ GIFTS ⊸

Adopt-A-Dolphin: adoption certificate with your name and the dolphin's name and
photo, two Dolphin Parent T-shirts, bi-monthly newletter, four free passes for
tours–$200 per year; Be A Dolfriend: a certificate with your name and the dolphin's
name and photo, a year's free admission to any regularly scheduled tour at the
DRC, bi-monthly newsletter–$20 per year; Dolphin Encounter: swim with the
dolphins in an educational workshop, age 5 up–$90; Dolphin Insight: a half day
interactive program with the dolphins, age 12 up–$75 per person; DolphinLab:
spend an educational week at the dolphin research Center, age 18 up, includes room
and board and ground transportation–$1050; T-shirts, sweatshirts, baseball shirts,
shorts, hats, earrings, rings, charms, pendants, pins, tote bags, fanny packs, stuffed
toys, magnets, prints, posters, audio cassettes, CD's, videos, books, calendars

"Teaching...Learning...Caring...For marine mammals and our environment"

Dolphin Research Center
P.O. Box 522875
Marathon Shores FL 33052
305-289-1121 ♦ 305-743-7627 fax

DORIS DAY ANIMAL LEAGUE

⊸ PURPOSE ⊸
Focus public attention on the needless suffering of
many animals in commercial testing facilities and laboratories

⊸ ACTIVITIES ⊸
Encourage letter writing and petitions to representatives
and senators to help pass laws ending the suffering

⊸ GIFTS ⊸
T-shirts, sweatshirts, tote bags, books

*"The animals can't lobby Congress; they can't vote and
they can't speak out against the agonizing tortures being inflicted
upon them every day. We must do it for them."*

Pets-R-Permitted book
♦ $9.95

Doris Day Animal League
227 Massachusetts Avenue, N.E., Suite 100
Washington DC 20002
202-546-1761

DORIS DAY PET FOUNDATION

⊸ PURPOSE ⊹
Improve the lives of pets and the people who love them

⊸ ACTIVITIES ⊹
Educate people about the responsibilities of pet ownership,
spay/neuter program, rescue abused animals, pet food program

⊸ GIFTS ⊹
Cookbooks, books, posters, T-shirts, sweatshirts,
key racks, sports bottles, fanny packs, audio cassettes,
videos, aprons, note cards, memo pads, magnetic
memo pad holders, animal sculptures,
pet first aid kits

*"Dedicated to improving
the lives of our best friends"*

Apron
♦ $11.95

Doris Day Pet Foundation
P.O. Box 8509
Universal City CA 91608

EARTHTRUST

⊸ PURPOSE ⊸
Wildlife protection worldwide

⊸ ACTIVITIES ⊸
Education, research, investigation
and exposure of illegal wildlife trade

⊸ GIFTS ⊸
Adopt A Whale: adoption certificate with a color photo
and information about your whale, humpback whale fact sheet,
sticker, updates–$30; T-shirts, polo shirts, tote bags, videos

"Become an Earthtrustee."

Earthtrust
25 Kaneohe Bay Drive #205
Kailua HI 96734-1711
808-254-2866 ♦ 808-254-6409

ELEPHANT RESEARCH FOUNDATION

⊸ PURPOSE ⊷
Research and conservation
of elephants, living and extinct

⊸ ACTIVITIES ⊷
Education, research, information dissemination

⊸ GIFTS ⊷
T-shirts, foldover notes, pendants, key chains, books

"Elephants: The Super-Keystone-Species"

Elephant Research Foundation
106 East Hickey Grove Road
Bloomfield Hills MI 48304
810-540-3947

EQUINE RESCUE LEAGUE

⊸ PURPOSE ⊷
Promote the humane treatment
of horses in the greater Washington, D.C. area

⊸ ACTIVITIES ⊷
Operate a farm shelter for the rescue and rehabilitation of
abused and neglected horses, adoption program, education,
local investigations to reduce abuse and neglect, humane
euthanasia services for aged or ill horses, provide quarantine
facilities for horses rescued from auctions

⊸ GIFTS ⊷
T-shirts, sweatshirts, mugs

"Your purchases and contributions make a difference!"

Equine Rescue League
P.O. Box 4366
Leesburg VA 22075
703-771-1240

EVERGREEN WILDLIFE CONSERVATION SOCIETY

PURPOSE
Protect and aid all animals

ACTIVITIES
Acquire land for wildlife preservation,
educate to promote coexistence with animals, rehabilitate
injured and orphaned wildlife, hotline

GIFTS
Sponsor an orphaned animal: photo of the animal
you saved (deer, rabbit, bird, raccoon, opossum, skunk),
Feel The Magic-Save An Orphan T-shirt–$20

"Share the earth with wildlife."

Evergreen Wildlife Conservation Society
P.O. Box 805
McHenry IL 60051-0805
815-344-2111

FARM ANIMAL
REFORM MOVEMENT

◄ PURPOSE ►
Expose and stop animal abuse and
other destructive impacts of factory farming

◄ ACTIVITIES ►
The Great American Meatout, Veal Ban Day,
World Farm Animals Day, Industry Watch, Consumers
for Healthy Options in Children's Education, publications

◄ GIFTS ►
T-shirts, tote bags, aprons,
cookbooks, books, posters, videos

"Fight factory farming."

Farm Animal Reform Movement (FARM)
P.O. Box 30654
Bethesda MD 20897-1425
800-MEATOUT ♦ 301-530-1737

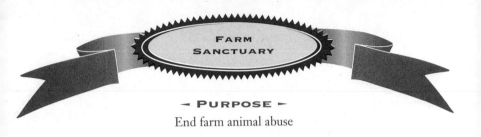

FARM SANCTUARY

⌐ PURPOSE ⌐
End farm animal abuse

⌐ ACTIVITIES ⌐
Rescue abused farm animals, shelter and feed the
animals at the Sanctuary, compel livestock facilities to adopt
humane care practices, vegetarian education

⌐ GIFTS ⌐
Adopt A Farm Animal: adoption card, framed color photo,
sponsorship booklet, regular progress reports–$6 to $40 per month;
T-shirts, sweatshirts, puppets, bandanas, posters, cookbooks,
books, tote bags, note cards, holiday cards, gift baskets

"If you love animals called pets...Why do you eat animals called dinner?"

Farm Sanctuary
P.O. Box 150
Watkins Glen NY 14891
607-583-2225

FELINES

⏤ PURPOSE ⏤
Prevention of cruelty to animals; assist animals through
fulfillment of needs for shelter, food and medical attention

⏤ ACTIVITIES ⏤
Operate a no-kill shelter, spay/neuter program, pet counseling,
placement, senior citizens foster parent program for homeless cats

⏤ GIFTS ⏤
Sweatshirts, T-shirts, nightshirts, note cards, cat toys

"Some day, every cat will have a home."

Felines, Inc.
P.O. Box 268020
Chicago IL 60626
312-465-4132 ♦ 312-465-6454 fax

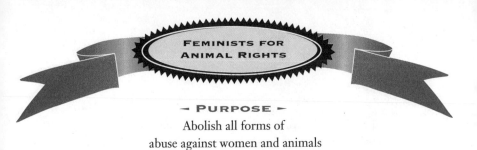

FEMINISTS FOR ANIMAL RIGHTS

⊸ **PURPOSE** ⊱

Abolish all forms of
abuse against women and animals

⊸ **ACTIVITIES** ⊱

Ecofeminism, education,
promotion of vegetarianism

⊸ **GIFTS** ⊱

Cookbooks, books, T-shirts

"Animal liberation is a feminist issue."

Feminists for Animal Rights
P.O. Box 694 Cathedral Station
New York NY 10025-0694
212-866-6422 phone/fax

Feminists for Animal Rights
P.O. Box 16425
Chapel Hill NC 27516
919-286-7333

FLORIDA AUDUBON SOCIETY CENTER FOR BIRDS OF PREY

⊸ PURPOSE ⊷
Conservation of birds of prey

⊸ ACTIVITIES ⊷
Treat, rehabilitate and release eagles, hawks and owls that come to the center from all over the state (The birds may be the victims of gunshot wounds, poisoning, power line collisions, etc.); maintain a permanent education center

⊸ GIFTS ⊷
Adopt-A-Bird: adoption certificate, color photo, biography of the bird and species information, newsletter subscription–$20 to $30

"Save these magnificent and majestic birds."

Center for Birds of Prey
Florida Audubon Society
460 HWY 436, Suite 200
Casselberry FL 32707
800-874-BIRD ✦ 407-260-8300
407-260-9652 fax

FLORIDA MARINE CONSERVATION CORP

◄ PURPOSE ►
Conservation of marine animals

◄ ACTIVITIES ►
Field research, habitat protection

◄ GIFTS ►
Adopt A Dolphin: stuffed dolphin toy, adoption
certificate, photo, research team updates, newsletter–$25

"Adopt a wild dolphin."

Florida Marine Conservation Corp
12295 Indian Mound Road
Lake Worth FL 33467
407-798-8201

⊸ PURPOSE ⊷

Education to promote the
adoption of a cruelty-free lifestyle

⊸ ACTIVITIES ⊷

Publications; public access programs;
demonstrations; assistance to speakers, students and projects

⊸ GIFTS ⊷

T-shirts, books

"Adopt a cruelty-free lifestyle."

Florida Voices for Animals, Inc.
P.O. Box 17523
Tampa FL 33682-7523
813-977-2585

FREE FLIGHT BIRD AND MARINE MAMMAL REHABILITATION

⊸ PURPOSE ⊱
Rehabilitate orphaned and injured wildlife,
specializing in birds of prey and marine mammals; education

⊸ ACTIVITIES ⊱
Daily care of the birds and marine mammals; education

⊸ GIFTS ⊱
T-shirts, sweatshirts

*"Whatever befalls the Earth befalls the sons of the Earth.
Man did not weave the web of life; he is merely a strand of it.
Whatever he does to the web, he does to himself." – Chief Seattle*

Free Flight Bird and Marine Mammal Rehabilitation
1185 Portland Avenue
Bandon OR 97411
503-347-3882

FREE WILLY FOUNDATION

⊸ PURPOSE ⊱
Relocate, rehabilitate and prepare to release the
orca whale named Keiko, star of Warner Brothers' hit film *Free Willy*

⊸ ACTIVITIES ⊱
Design and build a two million gallon deep water pool in
Oregon for Keiko's rehabilitation which will also serve as a release
center for other dolphins and whales

⊸ GIFTS ⊱
Keiko Adoption Kit: adoption certificate, full color poster,
Whale Watching booklet, updates on Keiko's progress–$24.95; T-shirts

*"Keiko's release will be the first time a
captive orca has ever been returned to the sea."*

The Free Willy Foundation
300 Broadway, Suite 28
San Francisco CA 94133
415-788-3666 ♦ 415-788-7324 fax

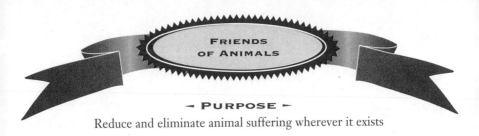

FRIENDS OF ANIMALS

⊰ PURPOSE ⊱

Reduce and eliminate animal suffering wherever it exists

⊰ ACTIVITIES ⊱

Low-cost nationwide spay/neuter programs; create
public and legislative support for wildlife and endangered species
protection; investigate and expose cruelty to animals

⊰ GIFTS ⊱

T-shirts, framable "Prayer for
Animals," pins

"Give animals a break."

T-shirt ◆ $14.00

Friends of Animals
777 Post Road, Suite 205
Darien CT 06820
203-656-1522 ◆ 203-656-0267 fax

FRIENDS OF BEAVERSPRITE

⭑ PURPOSE ⭑
Share the Earth with beavers
and other species for everyone's benefit

⭑ ACTIVITIES ⭑
Provide long term, nonlethal ways of resolving beaver/human
conflicts; continue Dorothy Richards' teachings that beavers and
other animals are sensitive beings who deserve humane treatment

⭑ GIFTS ⭑
T-shirts, sweatshirts, cookbooks,
stuffed toys, puppets, prints, books, videos

*"Beavers build beautiful ponds that create habitats for
many species of birds, waterfowl, amphibians, fish and other animals."*

Friends of Beaversprite
Box 591
Little Falls NY 13365
518-568-2077

FRIENDS OF CONSERVATION

⊸ PURPOSE ⊷
Conservation of wildlife and the environment

⊸ ACTIVITIES ⊷
Community conservation and education, school wildlife clubs, scientific wildlife and habitat studies, anti-poaching support, re-creation of habitats, rhino translocation and veterinarian program

⊸ GIFTS ⊷
Adopt A Rhino: adoption certificate, a copy of the Maro rhino family tree, signed rhino photo, newsletter–starting at $50; $75 includes rhino T-shirt; Whale Assist program: adopt a humpback whale and receive certificate, facsimile of your whale's unique tail I.D., photo, newsletter–starting at $50; $75 includes a whale T-shirt; German crystal, pendants, pins, posters

""There will not be a second chance..."

Friends of Conservation
1520 Kensington Road
Oak Brook IL 60521-2141
800-FOC-3060 ✦ 708-954-3388
708-954-1016 fax

FRIENDS OF THE AUSTRALIAN KOALA FOUNDATION

⊸ PURPOSE ⊱
Conservation of the Australian koala and its habitat

⊸ ACTIVITIES ⊱
Coordinate the "Koala Habitat Atlas," a satellite
mapping system that asesses koala habitat for its ability
to sustain wild koalas; research; education; dissemination
of scientific information

⊸ GIFTS ⊱
T-shirts, stuffed toys

"The conservation of the koala and its habitat is of global significance."

Friends of the Australian Koala Foundation
2027 "O" Street, N.W.
Washington DC 20036
800-MY-KOALA

FRIENDS OF THE SEA LION

⤙ PURPOSE ⤚

Conservation of sea lions and seals
of Orange County, California

⤙ ACTIVITIES ⤚

Rescue, rehabilitation, research, education

⤙ GIFTS ⤚

Adopt a seal or sea lion: adoption certificate,
choose the animal's name, visitation anytime, attendance
at the animal's release–$100; Holiday cards

"Every environment is a unique crucible of living species."

Friends of the Sea Lion
Marine Mammal Center
20612 Laguna Canyon Road
Laguna Beach CA 92651
714-494-3050

⊸ PURPOSE ⊷

Protect the southern sea otter, a rare and threatened species, as well as
sea otters throughout their north Pacific range and all sea otter habitats

⊸ ACTIVITIES ⊷

Reduce threats to the otters from oil spills, coastal pollution,
illegal gill netting and malicious killings; legislation and advocacy;
maintenance of the Sea Otter Retail and Education Center

⊸ GIFTS ⊷

Serving trays, dinnerware, mugs, platters, key rings, aprons,
coaster sets, canisters, glass art bowls, boxer shorts, greeting cards, stationery,
note cards, gift enclosure cards, calendars, pins, earrings, watches, tiles, holiday
cards, postcards, sweatshirts, T-shirts, sweaters, neckties, tree ornaments, gift bags
& wrap, tote bags, videos, prints, bookplates, books, figurines, switch plates,
pillows, magnets, wall hangings, boxes, picture frames, cross-stitch kits, clocks,
sticker sets, child's dish sets, rubber stamps, puzzles, baby bibs, stuffed toys, puppets

*"Only 2,400 southern sea otters are
left of a once thriving population."*

Pewter
otter key ring
♦ $4.50

Friends of the Sea Otter
2150 Garden Road B-4
Monterey CA 93940

Otter mini-notes
♦ 10/$5.25

408-625-3290 Retail Center ♦ 408-373-2747 Administration

FRIENDS OF WASHOE

⊸ PURPOSE ⊷

Save the wild chimpanzees and captive
chimpanzees from senseless exploitation and extinction;
enrich the lives of captive chimpanzees

⊸ ACTIVITIES ⊷

Support research at Central Washington University's Chimpanzee
and Human Communication Institute in chimpanzee language acquisition
and its application to human understanding; design entertaining and
challenging tasks for the enrichment of the chimpanzees

⊸ GIFTS ⊷

Sweatshirts, T-shirts, tote bags, posters, coffees

T-shirt
♦ $12.95

"Save our sibling species."

Friends of Washoe
The Chimpanzee and
Human Communication Institute
Central Washington University
400 East 8th Street
Ellensburg WA 98926-7573
509-963-2244 ♦ 509-963-2363
509-963-2234 fax

FUND FOR ANIMALS

⇥ Purpose ⇤
Foster humane conduct toward animals
and relieve animal suffering everywhere

⇥ Activities ⇤
Animal rescue and protection, humane
education, spaying programs, anti-hunting strategies

⇥ Gifts ⇤
T-shirts, sweatshirts, tote bags, cat bowls

"Support your right to arm bears."

The Fund for Animals
850 Sligo Avenue, Suite 300
Silver Spring MD 20910
301-585-2591

GORILLA FOUNDATION

⊸ PURPOSE ⊱
Aid the endangered gorilla

⊸ ACTIVITIES ⊱
Education, development of a gorilla preserve on Maui,
scientific research that includes communication with gorillas

⊸ GIFTS ⊱
Koko's Fan Club for a child: membership kit includes
a color photo of Koko and her famous cat Smoky, a poster,
a special letter directly from Koko, a personalized
membership card–$5; T-shirts, sweatshirts, posters,
pendant/charms, color prints, books, mugs

"There are other thinking beings in the universe."

Gorilla Foundation
P.O. Box 620-530
Woodside CA 94062
415-851-8505 ♦ 415-851-0291 fax

GREAT BEAR FOUNDATION

⇥ PURPOSE ⇤
Preservation of all eight species
of world bears and their ecosystems

⇥ ACTIVITIES ⇤
Development of curriculum on bears and ecosystems to distribute to teachers
worldwide, work with American and foreign naturalists and advocates to save bears,
reimbursement to ranchers of livestock lost to grizzlies, awarding of scholarships
and grants for educational work that benefits bears, monitor grizzly bear recovery
and the Endangered Species Act, support scientific research on bears, publications

⇥ GIFTS ⇤
T-shirts, sweatshirts, caps, earrings, necklaces, pins, bolo ties,
belt buckles, belts, key chains, figurines, videos, prints, books

*"Conserving wild bears
and their ecosystems worldwide"*

Great Bear Foundation
P.O. Box 1289
Bozeman MT 59771
406-586-5513 ♦ 406-586-6103

Bear pin
pewter ♦ $8.00
gold ♦ $16.00

GREYHOUND FRIENDS

⊸ PURPOSE ⊱
Save racetrack greyhounds and
place them in responsible homes

⊸ ACTIVITIES ⊱
Maintenance of a kennel for
20 greyhounds, adoption program

⊸ GIFTS ⊱
Dog sweaters, dog coats, dog collars, dog leashes,
note cards, postcards, key chains, books, hats, T-shirts,
sweatshirts, sweatshirt cardigans, calendars

"Greyhounds available for immediate adoption!"

Greyhound Friends, Inc.
167 Saddle Hill Road
Hopkinton MA 01748
508-435-5969

HAWK MOUNTAIN SANCTUARY

⊸ PURPOSE ⊸
Conservation of birds of prey and
the central Appalachian environment

⊸ ACTIVITIES ⊸
Carry out coordinated programs in education, research
and monitoring; operate a visitor center year round and maintain
the Sanctuary as a high quality natural area open to the public

⊸ GIFTS ⊸
Shirts, T-shirts, sweatshirts, caps, pins, books, prints,
tote bags, bandanas, stuffed toys, mugs, water bottles, compasses

Hawk Mountain Sanctuary
RR 2 Box 191
Kempton PA 19529-9449
610-756-6961 ♦ 610-756-4468 fax

⊸ PURPOSE ⊸

Monitor and promote the conservation
of hawks, eagles and other birds of prey

⊸ ACTIVITIES ⊸

Discovering new raptor flyways, conducting migration
counts and banding programs, sponsoring training of young
field biologists, environmental education programs

⊸ GIFTS ⊸

Adopt A Hawk: adoption certificate with color photo, your
bird's vital statistics (age, sex, weight, band number, location and
date your hawk was banded), fact sheet, membership with Hawkwatch
International, newsletter–starting at $35; T-shirts, sweatshirts, caps,
mugs, note cards, postcards, earrings, pins, bolo ties, posters, books

"Protecting raptors and our environment"

Hawkwatch International
P.O. Box 660
Salt Lake City UT 84110-0660
1-800-726-HAWK

HELEN WOODWARD ANIMAL CENTER

⏴ PURPOSE ⏵
Advancement of animal care, education and treatment

⏴ ACTIVITIES ⏵
Therapeutic horseback riding, pet encounter therapy for the mentally
and physically disabled, humane education, pet adoptions, Equine Hospital,
boarding, kennel, pet food delivery service for shut-in pet owners

⏴ GIFTS ⏵
T-shirts, sweatshirts, mugs

*"Life is much richer when love and understanding
exist as a bond between humans and animals."*

Helen Woodward Animal Center
P.O. Box 64
6525 Calle de Nido
Rancho Santa Fe CA 92067
619-756-4117 ♦ 619-452-9230
619-756-0613 fax

⚊ PURPOSE ⚊
Helping homeless cats

⚊ ACTIVITIES ⚊
Spay/neuter programs, education, adoption program

⚊ GIFTS ⚊
T-shirts, sweatshirts, note cards

*"Let's try to prevent the needless killings of our
helpless animals with an all-out spay/neuter wherever we live."*

Helping Homeless Cats, Inc.
P.O. Box 81
Tavernier FL 33070
305-852-3739 ♦ 305-852-3306
305-852-6323 fax

HEMLOCK HILL FARM SANCTUARY

⊸ PURPOSE ⊷
Provide shelter for abused
and unwanted farm animals

⊸ ACTIVITIES ⊷
Operation of the sanctuary,
placement of adoptable animals

⊸ GIFTS ⊷
Earrings, T-shirts

"Help us help the animals!"

Hemlock Hill Farm Sanctuary, Inc.
RFD #2 Box 474
North Lebanon ME 04027
207-457-1371

HOOVED ANIMAL HUMANE SOCIETY

⊸ PURPOSE ⊸

Promote humane treatment of hooved
animals whether they be used for show, work,
agriculture or pleasure

⊸ ACTIVITIES ⊸

Education, investigation, legal intervention when
necessary; maintenance of a 26 acre farm for
starved, neglected or abused horses, cattle, sheep, goats
and other large hooved animals

⊸ GIFTS ⊸

T-shirts, sweatshirts, caps, charms, posters

"Dedicated to the protection of hooved animals"

Hooved Animal Humane Society
P.O. Box 400
Woodstock IL 60098-0400
815-337-5563 ♦ 815-337-5569 fax

HORSE POWER PROJECTS

- PURPOSE -
Fight for the horse by
exposing cruelty to horses

- ACTIVITIES -
Education, legislation, networking

- GIFTS -
T-shirt dress/nightshirts, T-shirts, mugs, sculptures

*"Humane treatment for the greatest
possible number of horses"*

Horse Power Projects, Inc.
P.O. Box 1965
Monterey CA 93942
408-648-1965

HUMANE EDUCATION COMMITTEE

⊸ PURPOSE ⊷
Convert the rhetoric of humane education into action
via an animal welfare coalition effort with members of the
educational and animal rights communities, the media, students,
parents and the general public

⊸ ACTIVITIES ⊷
Publish articles pointing to the need for instructional growth,
sponsor humane and educational conferences and workshops, research
the problems and strategies involved in implementing humane education,
place videos and books in teacher resource centers, create awareness between
childhood cruelty to animals and adult violence, promote the right of students
to refuse to dissect, teacher training workshops, educators newsletter

⊸ GIFTS ⊷
T-shirts, sweatshirts, tote bags

"For a generation more humane than our own"

Humane Education Committee
P.O. Box 445
New York NY 10028
212-410-3095

HUMANE FARMING ASSOCIATION

⊸ PURPOSE ⊸
Protect consumers from the dangerous misuse
of chemicals in food production; eliminate the suffering
to which farm animals are subjected

⊸ ACTIVITIES ⊸
Public education, legislation, the National Veal Boycott
and the Campaign Against Factory Farming

⊸ GIFTS ⊸
T-shirts, coloring/activity books, note cards

"Farm animals need protection too."

Humane Farming Association
P.O. Box 3577
San Rafael CA 94912-8902
415-771-CALF

HUMANE SOCIETY OF THE UNITED STATES

⇥ PURPOSE ⇤

Protect animals through investigative,
legal, educational and legislative means

⇥ ACTIVITIES ⇤

Reducing the overbreeding of cats and dogs, eliminating
the suffering of animals used in research, stopping sport hunting,
improving conditions in zoos, shelters, pet stores, kennels and circuses

⇥ GIFTS ⇤

T-shirts, tote bags, posters, videos

"Animals...It's their world too."

Tote bag
♦ $16.95

Humane Society of the United States
2100 L Street, NW
Washington DC 20037-1598
202-452-1100 ♦ 202-778-6132 fax

IN DEFENSE OF ANIMALS

⤙ PURPOSE ⤚
End all animal suffering, exploitation
and abuse; fight for the protection of animals
including their rights, welfare and habitats

⤙ ACTIVITIES ⤚
Education, animal abuse telephone hotline, animal
rights lobbies, boycotts, investigations, civil disobedience
protests, legal action, activist support

⤙ GIFTS ⤚
T-shirts, sweatshirts, mugs, tote bags,
license plate frames, posters, note cards,
audio cassettes and CD's, videos, books

*"I am in favor of animal rights as well
as human rights. That is the way of a whole
human being."*—*Abraham Lincoln*

Benefit CD's & cassettes
featuring Pearl Jam,
REM, etc.
♦ $12.95 cassette

In Defense of Animals
816 West Francisco Boulevard
San Rafael CA 94901
415-453-9984 ♦ 415-453-0510 fax

INTERNATIONAL BIRD RESCUE RESEARCH CENTER

⊸ PURPOSE ⊷
Develop oiled wildlife cleaning
and rehabilitation techniques

⊸ ACTIVITIES ⊷
Training and consultation to the petroleum industry,
local, state, and federal fish and wildlife agencies, wildlife rehabilitators
and researchers; 24-hour-a-day oil spill response

⊸ GIFTS ⊷
T-shirts, sweatshirts

"Save oiled wildlife."

International Bird Rescue Research Center
699 Potter Street - Aquatic Park
Berkeley CA 94710
510-841-9086 ♦ 510-841-9089 fax

INTERNATIONAL CRANE FOUNDATION

⏤ PURPOSE ⏤
Protect cranes and their
wetland homes around the world

⏤ ACTIVITIES ⏤
Field research, captive propagation, public education

⏤ GIFTS ⏤
Books, T-shirts, pins

*"If the cranes are doing well, it means
the world's marshes are also doing well."*

International Crane Foundation
E-11376 Shady Lane Road
P.O. Box 447
Baraboo WI 53913-0447
608-356-9462

⊸ PURPOSE ⊱

Promote and ensure the just and
kind treatment of animals as sentient beings

⊸ ACTIVITIES ⊱

Campaign to ban the offshore commercial hunting of
Canadian baby whitecoat seals, support anti-poaching patrols
in Africa, campaign to ban fox and stag hunting in Britain,
petition to stop cosmetics testing on animals,
public education, publications

⊸ GIFTS ⊱

Books, videos, stuffed toys

Whale
stuffed toy
♦ $9.95

*"Animals feel fear and pain and they suffer
too much of both at the hand of man."* - Brian Davies

International Fund For Animal Welfare
P.O. Box 193
Yarmouth Port MA 02675-0193
508-362-4944 · 508-362-6268

INTERNATIONAL MARINE MAMMAL PROJECT

⊸ Purpose ⊱
Make oceans safe for marine mammals worldwide

⊸ Activities ⊱
Through education, legal intervention, lobbying and legislation strive to eliminate dolphin mortality caused by the international tuna fishing industry, end the use of driftnets, stop tuna purse seine vessels from encircling dolphins in their nets, stop the resumption of commercial whaling worldwide and promote sustainable fishing

⊸ Gifts ⊱
Dolphin Sponsorship: educational poster and sticker; return the registration card to become a dolphin sponsor and receive a color certificate of your dolphin and two updates throughout the year–$19.95; T-shirts, mugs, tote bags, posters, note cards, videos, calendars

"Where have all the dolphins gone?"

International Marine Mammal Project
Earth Island Institute
300 Broadway, Suite 28
San Francisco CA 94133
415-788-3666

INTERNATIONAL OSPREY FOUNDATION

⊸ PURPOSE ⊷

Protect and preserve the osprey worldwide

⊸ ACTIVITIES ⊷

Nest monitoring, research grants

⊸ GIFTS ⊷

T-shirts

"Healthy ospreys are an indicator of a healthy environment."

The International Osprey Foundation
P.O. Box 250
Sanibel FL 33957
813-472-5218

INTERNATIONAL PRIMATE PROTECTION LEAGUE

⊸ PURPOSE ⊶

Conserve and protect primates

⊸ ACTIVITIES ⊶

Create and control national parks and sanctuaries;
control of primate hunting, trapping and sale; education;
anti-poaching patrols

⊸ GIFTS ⊶

T-shirts, sweatshirts, note cards, gift wrap, stickers, videos, books

*"Working to protect gorillas
and all living primates"*

Baboon Orphan,
children's book
♦ $8.00

International Primate Protection League
P.O. Box 766
Summerville SC 29484
803-871-2280 ♦ 803-871-7988 fax

INTERNATIONAL SNOW LEOPARD TRUST

⊸ PURPOSE ⊸

Conservation of the endangered snow leopard and the biological diversity of its high mountain habitats while considering the needs of both the indigenous people and the environment

⊸ ACTIVITIES ⊸

Public education; teacher training in conservation education; field training; research and monitoring; establishment and management of protected areas

⊸ GIFTS ⊸

Note cards, sweatshirts, mugs

Snow leopard mug ◆ $7.00

"Time is running out for the snow leopards of the world."

International Snow Leopard Trust
4649 Sunnyside Avenue North
Seattle WA 98103
206-632-2421 ◆ 206-632-3967 fax

─ PURPOSE ─

Expose and seek to end the injustice of the
exploitation of animals and the suffering inflicted on them

─ ACTIVITIES ─

Through education and legal means work to abolish vivisection,
hunting and other animal abuses; sponsor animal rights conferences,
symposiums, seminars and Homeless Animals' Day observance

─ GIFTS ─

T-shirts, sweatshirts, nightshirts, umbrellas, mugs,
tote bags, pins, greeting cards, note cards, posters, books, key chains

*"America's dogs and cats are dying for you to be responsible.
Spay/Neuter. It stops the killing!"* ™

International Society for Animal Rights, Inc.
421 S. State Street
Clarks Summit PA 18411-1500
800-543-ISAR ♦ 717-586-2200
717-586-9580 fax

INTERNATIONAL
SOCIETY FOR COW
PROTECTION

⟿ PURPOSE ⟾

Lifetime cow protection by presenting alternatives to
present agricultural practices that support and depend upon
the meat industry and industrialized petroleum-powered machinery

⟿ ACTIVITIES ⟾

Train bull calves as working teams of oxen; teach alternative
agricultural practices as hands-on experience in living classroom
settings; encourage the production of methane bio-gas from cow
manure as a valuable alternative energy source; present the benefits
of a lacto-vegetarian diet; distribution of educational materials

⟿ GIFTS ⟾

T-shirts, coloring books, videos

"The ox is the backbone of the farm, not the soupbone."

International Society for Cow Protection
4607 Timberwood Trail
Efland NC 27243
919-563-3643

INTERNATIONAL SOCIETY FOR ENDANGERED CATS

⊷ PURPOSE ⊶
Save wild species from extinction

⊷ ACTIVITIES ⊶
Participate in worldwide education especially for children,
act as an information resource, fund research, participate in the
breeding of endangered species

⊷ GIFTS ⊶
T-shirts, sweatshirts, pens, figurines, postcards, note cards,
earrings, necklaces, pins, magnets, mugs, gourmet gift baskets

"Cats <u>don't</u> have nine lives!"

International Society for Endangered Cats
4638 Winterset Drive
Columbus OH 43220
614-451-4460

INTERNATIONAL WILDLIFE REHABILITATION COUNCIL

⊸ PURPOSE ⊶
Promote professional networking and
continuing education in wildlife rehabilitation as
well as a standardized approach to wildlife care

⊸ ACTIVITIES ⊶
Wildlife information hotline,
certified skills seminars, publications, annual
conference, quarterly journal

⊸ GIFTS ⊶
T-shirts, tote bags, greeting cards

"Better care through shared knowledge..."

International Wildlife Rehabilitation Council (IWRC)
4437 Central Place, Suite B-4
Suisun CA 94585
707-865-1761 ♦ 707-864-3106 fax

INTERNATIONAL WOLF CENTER

⇥ PURPOSE ⇤
To be a focal point for worldwide environmental education
about the wolf and its relationships with other species, including humans

⇥ ACTIVITIES ⇤
Field programs for the public, lectures and symposia with wolf experts,
national speaker's bureau to provide wolf programs to schools and adult groups,
publications, interactive Wolves AND Humans exhibit, library of research
materials, live animals in habitat, Internet accessibility

⇥ GIFTS ⇤
Wolf Watchers Program (wolf adoption): gift card, six issues of Wolf Watch
newsletter, photo and bio of your wolf, a selection of a children's Zoobook or
adult's eight page report on the status of wolf reintroduction in Yellowstone and
elsewhere–$25; Books, CD's, audio cassettes, videos, posters, T-shirts, shirts,
sweatshirts, jackets, caps, bandanas, note cards, postcards, calendars, mugs,
night-lights, magnets, tote bags, activity books, sticker activity books, coloring
books, rubber stamps, stuffed toys, animal replica toys, pins, earrings, necklaces

*"The greatest threat to the wolf is human misperception: the centuries-old
mythology that prevents a true understanding of this elusive and majestic animal."*

International Wolf Center
1396 Highway 169
Ely MN 55731
800-ELY-WOLF ♦ 218-365-4695
218-365-3318 fax

INTERSPECIES COMMUNICATION

◄ PURPOSE ►
Promote a better understanding of what is
communicated between human beings and other animals

◄ ACTIVITIES ►
Field research interfacing with wild animals
(especially dolphins and whales) through music, art and ceremony

◄ GIFTS ►
Books, audio cassettes

*"The environmental crisis we face is largely a
crisis in how we humans perceive our place within nature."*

Interspecies Communication, Inc.
273 Hidden Meadow Lane
Friday Harbor WA 98250

JANE GOODALL INSTITUTE

⊸ PURPOSE ⊸
Promote wildlife research, education, conservation
and the welfare of primates and chimpanzees in particular

⊸ ACTIVITIES ⊸
Research: Gombe Stream Research Center, ChimpanZoo Project;
Education: Roots & Shoots Environmental Education program,
lectures, newsletters, JGI literature and merchandise; Conservation:
Re-Forestation projects, Conservation Centers at African Chimp
Sanctuaries; Animal welfare activities: Chimpanzee Sanctuaries,
cooperative projects with other animal welfare organizations

⊸ GIFTS ⊸
Prints, posters, T-shirts, sweatshirts,
puzzles, mousepads, magnets, books, videos

*"Only when we understand, can we care; only if we care,
will we help; only if we help, shall they be saved." - Dr. Jane Goodall*

Jane Goodall Institute
P. O. Box 5216 (for merchandise)
Toms River NJ 08754

The Jane Goodall Institute
P.O. Box 599 (for other information)
Ridgefield CT 06877
203-431-2099 ♦ 203-431-4387 fax

JUST CATS

⊷ PURPOSE ⊶
Provide sanctuary for cats

⊷ ACTIVITIES ⊶
Operate a no-kill shelter for cats for life,
adoption programs for the adoptable, spay/neuter
programs, rabies clinics, humane education outreach

⊷ GIFTS ⊶
T-shirts, sweatshirts, pins

"A loving pet is a friend for LIFE."

Just Cats, Inc.
P.O. Box 531
Mansfield MA 02048
508-339-6717

JUSTICE FOR ANIMALS

⇥ PURPOSE ⇤
End animal abuse of ALL kinds

⇥ ACTIVITIES ⇤
Publishing and distributing newsletters and other educational
materials, tabling at national concerts, setting up information booths
at festivals and street fairs, JFA youth campaign for those under 18,
letter writing, boycotting, political activism, providing speakers
at schools and conferences

⇥ GIFTS ⇤
T-shirts, calendars, mugs, bookmarks,
memo pads, pens, pencils, name/address labels, books

"Dedicated to abolishing ALL animal abuse"

Justice for Animals
P.O. Box 4044
Flushing NY 11360
718-225-4103 ✦ 718-224-2531

LEND-A-PAW RELIEF ORGANIZATION

⌐ PURPOSE ¬
Reduce the number of
homeless animals in northern Virginia

⌐ ACTIVITIES ¬
Rescue cats and kittens, adoptions, spay/neuter
programs, humane education to school children,
Pet-Facilitated Therapy visits to nursing homes

⌐ GIFTS ¬
T-shirts, sweatshirts, tote bags, pins, watches,
books, videos, note cards, condolence cards,
cat care products

"Help a friend. Lend a paw."

Lend-A-Paw Relief Organization
P.O. Box 4864
Falls Church VA 22044
703-536-8809 ♦ 703-237-5467 fax

LOS ANGELES AUDUBON SOCIETY

⊸ PURPOSE ⊷
Wildlife and habitat conservation

⊸ ACTIVITIES ⊷
Education, research, field trips, writing
and calling elected officials, Audubon Adventures
for school children

⊸ GIFTS ⊷
T-shirts, sweatshirts, pins, aprons, birding equipment,
audio tapes, videos, video games, bird and seed feeders, books

"You can make a difference."

Los Angeles Audubon Society
7377 Santa Monica Boulevard
West Hollywood CA 90046-6694
213-876-0202 ♦ 213-876-7609 fax

LYNX EDUCATIONAL FUND FOR ANIMAL WELFARE

⤙ PURPOSE ⤚
Protect fur-bearing animals

⤙ ACTIVITIES ⤚
Advertising campaign showing the unpleasant
reality behind the glamorous image portrayed
by the fur industry

⤙ GIFTS ⤚
T-shirts

"Fur is a fashion statement that's been beat to death."

Lynx Educational Fund for Animal Welfare
10573 W. Pico Boulevard, Suite 155
Los Angeles CA 90064
818-883-3722

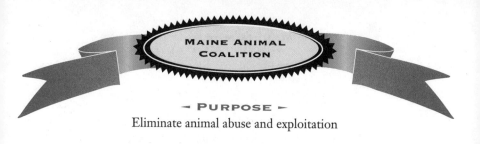

MAINE ANIMAL COALITION

⊸ PURPOSE ⊷

Eliminate animal abuse and exploitation

⊸ ACTIVITIES ⊷

Expose the suffering of farm animals, spay/neuter
education, promote the use of cruelty-free products, legislation,
demonstrating against rodeos and circuses

⊸ GIFTS ⊷

T-shirts, books, cookbooks

*"Using animals for human amusement, greed and
vanity will only serve to alienate us further from nature."*

Maine Animal Coalition
P.O. Box 6683
Portland ME 04101
207-781-7170

MARINE MAMMAL STRANDING CENTER

⚑ PURPOSE ⚐

Rescue and rehabilitate stranded or
otherwise stressed marine mammals and sea turtles

⚑ ACTIVITIES ⚐

Rescue, rehabilitate and release stranded marine
mammals in New Jersey (and neighboring states on request),
Sea Life Educational Center (open to the public)

⚑ GIFTS ⚐

T-shirts, sweatshirts, mugs, pins

*Every species deserves a chance. We strive to
provide that chance to these theatened species."*

Marine Mammal Stranding Center
3625 Brigantine Boulevard
P.O. Box 773
Brigantine NJ 08203
609-266-0538 ♦ 609-266-6300 fax

MEOW

⊶ PURPOSE ⊶

Improve the quality of life of abandoned cats,
educate people on responsible pet ownership, promote
the importance of the human-pet animal bond

⊶ ACTIVITIES ⊶

Maintenance of a cat shelter, adoption programs,
spay/neuter assistance, rabies clinics, humane education,
animal behavior consultations

⊶ GIFTS ⊶

Sponsor A Cat: picture and a history sheet
about your sponsored cat, visitation–$15 per month;
T-shirts, sweatshirts, tote bags, mugs

"Make Each Orphan Wanted."

MEOW, Inc.
P.O. Box 999
Litchfield CT 06759
203-567-3277

MEXICAN WOLF COALITION OF TEXAS

⊸ PURPOSE ⊢
Save the Mexican wolf from extinction

⊸ ACTIVITIES ⊢
Education on the plight of the Mexican wolf,
assist in the reintroduction of the Mexican wolf
into its native habitat in Texas and other parts of the
Southwest, support captive-breeding programs

⊸ GIFTS ⊢
T-shirts

"Return the Mexican wolf to the wild."

Mexican Wolf Coalition of Texas
P.O. Box 1526
Spring TX 77383-1526
713-443-0012 ♦ 713-461-2671 fax

MICHIGAN ANTI-CRUELTY SOCIETY

⊸ PURPOSE ⊱
Serve animals

⊸ ACTIVITIES ⊱
Operate an animal shelter, humane education, legislative action, animal rescues and adoptions, reunite lost pets with their families, cruelty investigations

⊸ GIFTS ⊱
Holiday cards, T-shirts, sweatshirts, mugs

"Make it a Be-Kind-To-Animals World."

Michigan Anti-Cruelty Society
13569 Joseph Campau
Detroit MI 48212
313-891-7188

MICHIGAN HUMANE SOCIETY

⊸ PURPOSE ⊷
Prevent and alleviate all animal suffering

⊸ ACTIVITIES ⊷
Shelter over 50,000 animals yearly, rescue operation
365 days per year, adoptions, cruelty investigations, three full-service
charitable animal hospitals, humane education and outreach,
pet-facilitated therapy, animal protection legislation

⊸ GIFTS ⊷
License plates, license plate frames, T-shirts,
sweatshirts, shorts, baseball hats, tote bags, mugs

"Dedicated to serving animals since 1877"

Michigan Humane Society
7401 Chrysler Drive
Detroit MI 48211-9986
810-852-7420 ◆ 810-852-0965 fax

MID-ATLANTIC GREAT DANE RESCUE LEAGUE

⊰ PURPOSE ⊱

Rescue and care for Great Danes who have been
given up or abandoned; provide service to Great Dane
owners; public information

⊰ ACTIVITIES ⊱

Rescue and care for Great Danes, screen prospective
adoptive families and place Great Danes in caring homes,
help owners with any Dane-related problems, act as a resource
referral service to people with Dane-related needs,
provide information to the public

⊰ GIFTS ⊱

T-shirts, mugs, notepaper, cookbooks, jewelry

"The doghouse of last resort"

Mid-Atlantic Great Dane Rescue League, Inc.
P.O. Box 1114
Vienna VA 22183-1114
703-938-9332

MISSION: WOLF

⊶ PURPOSE ⊷
Educate the general public about the nature of the wolf
in an effort to aid wild wolf recovery and discourage private
ownership of wild animals

⊶ ACTIVITIES ⊷
Operation of a wolf sanctuary, educational programs

⊶ GIFTS ⊷
Sponsor A Wolf: sponsorship certificate, 8x10 color photo,
one year membership, newsletter–starting at $25; T-shirts, sweatshirts,
tote bags, posters, bracelets, necklaces

"Sponsor a wolf. Give a living gift."

Mission: Wolf
P.O. Box 211
Silvercliff CO 81249
719-746-2919

MOUNTAIN LION FOUNDATION

⊸ PURPOSE ⊱
Ensure protection and survival for
American lions and their wilderness homes

⊸ ACTIVITIES ⊱
Monitor ongoing research and habitat studies, identify critical
habitat areas, public education, work to ban trophy hunting, publications,
defend Proposition 117 which bans the trophy hunting of mountain lions and
ensures protection of their habitats

⊸ GIFTS ⊱
Adopt-A-Lion: personalized adoption papers, photo, animal fact
sheet, newsletters–$25; T-shirts, calendars, books, note cards, greeting cards,
tote bags, posters

*"Since we humans have the better brain, isn't it our responsibility
to protect our fellow creatures from, oddly enough, ourselves?"–Joy Adamson*

Mountain Lion Foundation
P.O. Box 1896
Sacramento CA 95812
916-442-2666

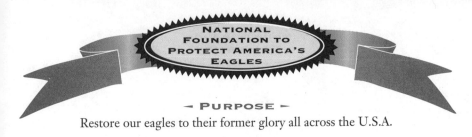

NATIONAL FOUNDATION TO PROTECT AMERICA'S EAGLES

◄ PURPOSE ►

Restore our eagles to their former glory all across the U.S.A.

◄ ACTIVITIES ►

Habitat protection, research,
education, rehabilitation, sanctuary management

◄ GIFTS ►

Adopt an Eagle or a Bird of Prey: adoption certificate, photo,
bird's biography–$500 for schools; $1000 for individuals; $5000 for
corporations. Adopt A Nest (of a family of bald eagles): adoption certificate,
a description of the nest location and related activity, invitation to name
the parent eagles and any young eagles hatched during the year of adoption
-a corporate contribution of $10,000; T-shirts, sweatshirts, caps

*"The Foundation is the caretaker for the largest
number of nonreleasable bald eagles in America."*

National Foundation to Protect America's Eagles
P.O. Box 120206
Nashville TN 37212
800-2-EAGLES

NATIONAL WILDLIFE REFUGE ASSOCIATION

⊸ PURPOSE ⊱
Protect and perpetuate the
National Wildlife Refuge System

⊸ ACTIVITIES ⊱
Education and advocacy especially regarding
funding, policy and management needs of the
Refuge System and its wildlife

⊸ GIFTS ⊱
Mugs, pins, prints

*"Be an advocate for the millions of
wild creatures that depend upon our nation's
unique refuge system."*

National Wildlife Refuge Association
10824 Fox Hunt Lane
Potomac MD 20854
301-983-9498 phone/fax

NATIONAL WOLF HYBRID ASSOCIATION

⊸ PURPOSE ⊷
Wolf and wolf hybrid conservation

⊸ ACTIVITIES ⊷
Wolf reintroduction efforts, research, breeding, public
education, registry and background research, yearly national
rendezvous, sanctioned shows and certified judges' workshops

⊸ GIFTS ⊷
T-shirts, caps

*"Domestic breeding with sensible
solutions to wolf and wolf hybrid survival"*

National Wolf Hybrid Association, Inc.
1059 Porter Morris Road
Chapmansboro TN 37035
615-746-3442

NATURE CONSERVANCY

⊸ PURPOSE ⊷
Preserve animals, plants and natural
communities by protecting the places they need to survive

⊸ ACTIVITIES ⊷
Internationally, indentify rare species;
protect habitats and establish and manage preserves

⊸ GIFTS ⊷
T-shirts, sweatshirts, caps, tote bags, duffel bags, potpourri,
candles-in-glasses, sculptures, pins, note cards, calendars, computer
screen savers, prints, posters, mugs, CD's, audio cassettes, books

"Conservation through private action"

Potpourri
fragrance
bag
♦ $12.50

The Nature Conservancy
P.O. Box 294
Wye Mills MD 21679
800-382-2386 ♦ 410-364-5215 fax

NETWORK FOR OHIO ANIMAL ACTION

⊸ PURPOSE ⊱

Halt all forms of animal
oppression and exploitation

⊸ ACTIVITIES ⊱

Education, activist workshops,
letter-writing campaigns, picketing

⊸ GIFTS ⊱

T-shirts, books

"Animals have rights!"

Network for Ohio Animal Action
P.O. Box 21004
Cleveland OH 44121
216-691-0662

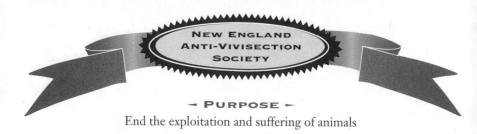

NEW ENGLAND ANTI-VIVISECTION SOCIETY

⌐ PURPOSE ⌐
End the exploitation and suffering of animals

⌐ ACTIVITIES ⌐
Public school education and community outreach;
cruelty-free guides; sanctuary support for animals rescued
from labs; conferences; legislative campaigns

⌐ GIFTS ⌐
T-shirts, note cards, books

*"The greatness of a nation and its
moral progress can be judged by the way
its animals are treated."–Gandhi*

*Kids Can Save
the Animals,*
children's book
♦ $6.99

New England Anti-Vivisection Society
333 Washington Street, Suite 850
Boston MA 02108-5100
617-523-6020 ♦ 617-523-7925 fax
617-523-0181 TTD/TTY

NEW YORK TURTLE AND TORTOISE SOCIETY

⇥ PURPOSE ⇤
Conservation and preservation of
turtles and tortoises and their habitats

⇥ ACTIVITIES ⇤
Care and rehabilitation of injured wild turtles,
promote captive propagation and proper husbandry techniques,
education, publications, seminars, field trips, Annual Turtle Show,
Photography and Poster Contest

⇥ GIFTS ⇤
T-shirts, magnets, games, books

"Leave wild turtles in the wild."

The New York Turtle and Tortoise Society
P.O. Box 878
Orange NJ 07051-0878
212-459-4803

NOAH'S FRIENDS

– PURPOSE –
Expose the suffering of animals
caused by the fur industry

– ACTIVITIES –
Graphic truth campaigns

– GIFTS –
T-shirts

"Animals can't fight back. But people can."

Noah's Friends
P.O. Box 36197
Richmond VA 23235
804-320-7090

⊸ PURPOSE ⊱
Support management and conservation of bear and
other North American wildlife populations for the benefit
of the general public and future generations

⊸ ACTIVITIES ⊱
Education, habitat enhancement, legislation

⊸ GIFTS ⊱
Prints, T-shirts, stuffed toys, hats, suspenders, books

*"By enhancing the environment of the bear,
we enhance life for all species, including our own."*

North American Bear Society
P.O. Box 9281
Scottsdale AZ 85252
602-451-7439

NORTH AMERICAN LOON FUND

⊸ PURPOSE ⊹
Promote the preservation
of loons and their lake habitats

⊸ ACTIVITIES ⊹
Research, public education,
publications, conferences

⊸ GIFTS ⊹
Calendars, audio cassettes,
CD's, videos, books

"Loons – Spirits of the Wilderness"

North American Loon Fund
6 Lily Pond Road
Gilford NH 03246
603-528-4711

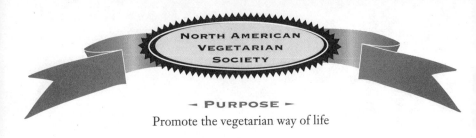

NORTH AMERICAN VEGETARIAN SOCIETY

⊸ PURPOSE ⊷
Promote the vegetarian way of life

⊸ ACTIVITIES ⊷
Educational programs including
conferences, distribution of publications

⊸ GIFTS ⊷
T-shirts, sweatshirts,
tote bags, cookbooks, books

"Vegetarianism is serious environmental action."

North American Vegetarian Society
Box 72
Dolgeville NY 13329
518-568-7970

NORTH AMERICAN WOLF SOCIETY

⌐ PURPOSE ¬

Assure the continued existence of
native wild canids in North America

⌐ ACTIVITIES ¬

Education, review wolf recovery plans
and other legislation, survey state wildlife agencies
regarding wolf reintroduction

⌐ GIFTS ¬

Prints, pins

*"Everytime you make a decision about
energy use or resource consumption you have
done something which affects wildlife."*

North American Wolf Society
P.O. Box 82950
Fairbanks AK 99708

OCEANIC PROJECT DOLPHIN

→ PURPOSE ←
Protect wild dolphins

→ ACTIVITIES ←
Research, education

→ GIFTS ←
Adopt A Wild Dolphin: adoption certificate with color photo,
biographical information on your dolphin, newsletters–$35; Books,
Whale Watch gift certificates, Farallon Islands cruise gift certificates

"Dolphins are in peril worldwide."

Oceanic Project Dolphin
Oceanic Society Expeditions
Fort Mason Center, Building E
San Francisco CA 94123
800-326-7491 ♦ 415-441-1106
415-474-3395 fax

OLYMPIC WILDLIFE RESCUE

⌐ PURPOSE ¬

Save injured and orphaned wildlife;
educate the public about wildlife and its habitats

⌐ ACTIVITIES ¬

Operation of a wildlife
rehabilitation center, education, internships

⌐ GIFTS ¬

Adopt An Animal: choose an eagle, elk,
raccoon, owl, hawk or opossum; adoption certificate–$30

"Rescue – Rehabilitate – Release"

Olympic Wildlife Rescue
1393 Mox-Chehalis Road
McCleary WA 98557
360-495-DEER

OPOSSUM SOCIETY OF CALIFORNIA

⊸ PURPOSE ⊷
Protect and preserve the Virginia opossum

⊸ ACTIVITIES ⊷
Arrange veterinary care for injured
opossums, raise orphaned opossums, education

⊸ GIFTS ⊷

T-shirts, sweatshirts, tank tops, note cards, holiday cards,
coloring books, stickers, puzzles, rubber stamps, hand puppets,
earrings, pins, tie tacks, wreaths, sculptures, magnets,
license plate frames, decorative boxes, prints

*"Opossums are North America's only
marsupial – the same species as kangaroos
and koala bears."*

Opossum family wood puzzle
♦ $9.00

Opossum Society of California
P.O. Box 16724
Irvine CA 92713
714-536-3538

ORANGE COUNTY PEOPLE FOR ANIMALS

⊸ PURPOSE ⊱

Inform Orange Countians of the many forms of
animal abuse that are accepted and institutionalized
in our society i.e. vivisection, factory farming,
animals in entertainment, hunting, whaling

⊸ ACTIVITIES ⊱

Education through radio and bus stop shelter advertising,
public demonstrations, speaking engagements, letter writing,
political action, boycotts, telemarketing

⊸ GIFTS ⊱

T-shirts

*"I am in favor of animal rights as well as human rights.
That is the way of a whole human being." – Abraham Lincoln*

Orange County People for Animals
Box 14187
Irvine CA 92713-4187
714-751-OCPA

⊸ PURPOSE ⊸
Conservation of the wild orangutan
and endangered orangutans everywhere

⊸ ACTIVITIES ⊸
Research, worldwide conservation education, repatriate
smuggled orangutans, conferences, forest restoration, orangutan
sanctuary, chapters in Taiwan, U.K., Australia, Canada and Indonesia

⊸ GIFTS ⊸
Orangutan Foster Parent Program: certificate, photo/description of
foster orangutan, foster parent T-shirt–$50; Forest Restoration Program:
certificate of appreciation for planting 10 trees in Borneo–$10;
T-shirts, posters, prints, note cards, videos, books, figurines

"Orangutan means 'Person of the Forest' in Malay."

President Birute Galdikas
Orangutan Foundation International
822 S. Wellesley Avenue
Los Angeles CA 90049
800-ORANGUTAN

ORPHAN ALLEY

⤙ PURPOSE ⤚
Provide lifelong care of previously abused or
severely injured cats and dogs; educate the public on the need
for pet population control, vaccinations and proper pet care

⤙ ACTIVITIES ⤚
Maintain a homeless animal
shelter, educational materials

⤙ GIFTS ⤚
Adopt A Foster Kitty: photo and
personal letter about your foster kitty–$10

*"The animals at Orphan Alley are very
grateful to be safe, warm, well-fed and loved!"*

Orphan Alley
N 7458 County Road A
Gresham WI 54128
715-787-4265

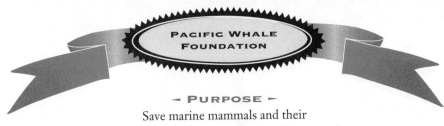

PACIFIC WHALE FOUNDATION

― PURPOSE ―

Save marine mammals and their
ocean environment through scientific research,
public education and conservation

― ACTIVITIES ―

Marine conservation, research, experiential learning programs,
whalewatches, publications, internships in Hawaii and Australia

― GIFTS ―

Adopt-A-Whale: adoption certificate, photo, letter of whale's latest
activities, map of the whale's location when last sighted, newsletter– $25;
a humpback whale will be named by you in an exclusive adoption– $75;
Sweatshirts, pendants, books

"Help the humpbacks make a comeback – Become an adoptive parent."

Pacific Whale Foundation
Kealia Beach Plaza, Suite 21
101 North Kihei Road
Kihei, Maui HI 96753-8833
808-879-8860 ♦ 808-879-2615 fax

PACIFIC WILDLIFE PROJECT

⊸ PURPOSE ⊢
Protect native wildlife through conservation education,
data studies of wildlife injuries and diseases and the practice
and promotion of the art of medical care for injured wildlife

⊸ ACTIVITIES ⊢
Provide medical care in a wildlife trauma clinic, rehabilitate injured
and orphaned wildlife and return them to the wild, education programs,
distribution of wildlife publications, scientific study and publication
of wildlife medical treatment and aftercare techniques

⊸ GIFTS ⊢
Adopt A Pelican (hospitalized): adoption certificate,
a year of newsletters and mailings, limited edition 20x26
lithograph–$100; T-shirts, sweatshirts, prints

"Help us keep our wildlife healthy."

Pacific Wildlife Project
P.O. Box 7673
Laguna Niguel CA 92607
714-831-1178

⊸ PURPOSE ⊷
Identify and develop ways to establish
mutually beneficial working relationships between
people with disabilities and dogs

⊸ ACTIVITIES ⊷
Train and place hearing and service dogs, education

⊸ GIFTS ⊷
Stuffed toys, T-shirts, sweatshirts, jackets, caps,
mugs, tote bags, golf hats, license plates, pins, magnets,
coloring books, cookbooks, note cards

*"These special animals provide
the miracle of independence."*

Paws With A Cause
1235 100th Street SE
Byron Center MI 49315
800-253-PAWS ✦ 616-698-0688
616-698-2988 fax

Voyager jacket
✦ $85.05

PELICAN MAN'S BIRD SANCTUARY

⊸ PURPOSE ⊶
Rescue, rehabilitate and release back into the wild injured birds
and other wildlife; educate the public about wildlife and our environment

⊸ ACTIVITIES ⊶
Treat 5,000 injured birds and other animals in our wildlife
hospital yearly; permanently house and care for over 200 unreleaseable birds
at the Sanctuary; provide rescue trucks 365 days a year

⊸ GIFTS ⊶
Adopt-A-Pelican: choose a pelican or any other
permanent resident bird and receive a color photo and history
of your bird–$25; Holiday cards

"To help wildlife in distress, to get them well and back into the wild"

Pelican Man's Bird Sanctuary
1708 Ken Thompson Parkway
Sarasota FL 34236-1000
813-388-4444 ♦ 813-388-3258 fax

PEOPLE FOR ABANDONED PETS

◄ PURPOSE ►
Stop pet overpopulation

◄ ACTIVITIES ►
Spay/neuter programs, education

◄ GIFTS ►
T-shirts

T-shirt
♦ $14.00

*"A pet can improve our health,
lower stress and give emotional support."*

People for Abandoned Pets
P.O. Box 70025
Bellevue WA 98007
206-453-9222

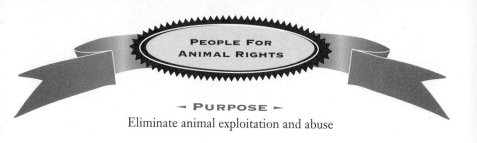

PEOPLE FOR ANIMAL RIGHTS

⊸ PURPOSE ⊷
Eliminate animal exploitation and abuse

⊸ ACTIVITIES ⊷
Public education and outreach programs; peaceful
demonstrations, protests and marches against such animal
abuses as research, the fur industry, puppy mills, animals
in entertainment, pet theft, farm animals and overpopulation;
legislation; letter writing; conferences

⊸ GIFTS ⊷
T-shirts, sweatshirts, caps, pens, books

"Spay or neuter your pet!"

People For Animal Rights
P.O. Box 2928
Olathe KS 66062-0928
816-767-1199

PEOPLE FOR THE ETHICAL TREATMENT OF ANIMALS

⊸ PURPOSE ⊶
End animal oppression and exploitation

⊸ ACTIVITIES ⊶
Animal rights education, investigations of
animal abuse, publications, workshops, demonstrations

⊸ GIFTS ⊶
T-shirts, cookbooks, razors,
cat grooming tools, humane mousetraps

*"Animals are not ours to eat, wear,
experiment on, or use for entertainment."*

People for the Ethical Treatment of Animals
P.O. Box 42516
Washington DC 20015-0516
301-770-PETA ♦ 301-770-8969 fax

PEREGRINE FUND

⚊ PURPOSE ⚊
Focus on birds for conservation of nature

⚊ ACTIVITIES ⚊
Captive breeding, research, public education

⚊ GIFTS ⚊
Scarves, neckties, crystal sculptures, educational toys,
Russian stacking owls, note cards, hummingbird feeders, stuffed toys,
Make-A-Plates, Make-A-Mugs, caps, kites, collector plates,
coloring books, activity books, books

"Your purchases help keep the birds flying!"

Flying
falcons tie
♦ $25.00

The Peregrine Fund, Inc.
World Center For Birds Of Prey
5666 West Flying Hawk Lane
Boise ID 83709
208-362-3716 ♦ 208-362-2376 fax

PET PRIDE OF NEW YORK

⊶ PURPOSE ⊷
Provide shelter and veterinarian
care for homeless and unwanted cats

⊶ ACTIVITIES ⊷
Operation of a shelter, adoption
programs, spay/neuter programs, education

⊶ GIFTS ⊷
Calendars, books, cat care
products and toys, posters, note cards

"The no-kill humane society for cats only"

Pet Pride of New York, Inc.
3 Mendon-Ionia Road
P.O. Box 338
Mendon NY 14506
716-582-1088

PIGS, A SANCTUARY

⊸ PURPOSE ⊸
Provide a safe haven for abused, abandoned
and neglected miniature and pot-bellied pigs

⊸ ACTIVITIES ⊸
Operation of the sanctuary, educational tours of the
sanctuary, educational seminars in schools and colleges, legislation

⊸ GIFTS ⊸
PIGS Provider: Pigs Provider certificate, photo
and story of the pig sponsored, periodic newsletters-
$25 per month; T-shirts

*"Support the sanctuary that is providing for
America's latest throwaway animal – the pot-bellied pig."*

PIGS, a sanctuary
P.O. Box 629
Charles Town WV 25414
304-725-PIGS phone/fax

PIONEERS FOR ANIMAL WELFARE SOCIETY

⊸ PURPOSE ⊱
Provide humane
services to needy animals

⊸ ACTIVITIES ⊱
Humane education programs, low cost spay/neuter
programs, adoptions, Meals On Wheels For Pets (supply food
for pets of the frail, elderly, homebound, or physically
challenged), assist needy families with large veterinary bills

⊸ GIFTS ⊱
T-shirts, sweatshirts, gift wrap

"Pets are worth saving."

Pioneers for Animal Welfare Society
P.O. Box 861
Hicksville NY 11802
516-364-PAWS

PREDATOR PROJECT

⊸ PURPOSE ⊱
Protect imperiled and other predatory species
as an ecological rallying point for ecosystem protection

⊸ ACTIVITIES ⊱
Monitor wildlife and land management agencies; develop
administrative, legal and public pressure strategies to correct
agency wrongdoing; inform the public on how it may be involved

⊸ GIFTS ⊱
Limited edition prints

"North America needs predators for intact ecosystems."

Predator Project
P.O. Box 6733
Bozeman MT 59771
406-587-3389 phone/fax

⊸ PURPOSE ⊱
Save the Amazon River pink dolphin

⊸ ACTIVITIES ⊱
Rescue and relocate imperiled pink dolphins, demonstrate to
the Amazon River natives that money can be made from the dolphins
without killing them for body parts sold in the marketplace

⊸ GIFTS ⊱
Adopt A Dolphin: you may select a name for your dolphin, and receive an 11x17
color print of the dolphin which your contribution saved, a video tape of the PARD
project, a handcrafted pink dolphin pin, and project updates–$1000; Save an Acre
of the Rainforest (pays for anti-poaching teams of local people): color
certificate–$35; Baskets, necklaces, bracelets, fans, belts, videos

"Save the pink dolphins."

Preservation of the Amazon River Dolphin
International Society for the Preservation of the Tropical Rainforest
3302 North Burton Avenue
Rosemead CA 91770
818-572-0233 ♦ 818-572-9521 fax

PROGRESSIVE ANIMAL WELFARE SOCIETY

⚊ PURPOSE ⚊

Promote and protect the rights,
interests and well-being of all animals

⚊ ACTIVITIES ⚊

Provide shelter, adoption and lost and found
services for companion animals, care for injured
and orphaned wildlife, education, legislation

⚊ GIFTS ⚊

T-shirts, sweatshirts, tote bags, holiday cards,
calendars, key chains, books, cookbooks, soaps, vitamins

"Reaching out to help animals"

Progressive Animal Welfare Society
15305 44th Avenue
P.O. Box 1037
Lynwood WA 98046
206-787-2500 ♦ 206-742-5711 fax

PURPLE MARTIN CONSERVATION ASSOCIATION

‹ PURPOSE ›
Conservation of the purple martin

‹ ACTIVITIES ›
Scientific research, modern wildlife
management techniques, public education

‹ GIFTS ›
Stationery, note cards, mugs, tote bags, T-shirts,
sweatshirts, books, coloring books, audio cassettes, bird houses,
bird feeders, gourds, photographs, earrings, tie tacks

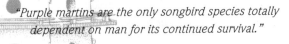

*"Purple martins are the only songbird species totally
dependent on man for its continued survival."*

Martin house
♦ $99.95

Purple Martin Conservation Association
Edinboro University of Pennsylvania
Edinboro PA 16444
814-734-4420 ♦ 814-734-5803 fax

**RAPTOR CENTER
AT THE UNIVERSITY
OF MINNESOTA**

‑ PURPOSE ‑
Conservation of birds of prey

‑ ACTIVITIES ‑
Treat, rehabilitate and release injured birds of prey; educate
the general population about the need to preserve raptor species and
their habitats; facilitate reintroduction of endangered/threatened species
to their natural habitats; scientific investigation to improve survival rates

‑ GIFTS ‑
T-shirts, earrings, mugs, calendars, coloring books, mobiles, books

*"To help birds fly free; to enable their human counterparts
to understand our need for biodiversity"*

The Raptor Center, University of Minnesota
100 Gabbert Raptor Center
1920 Fitch Avenue
St. Paul MN 55108
612-624-4745 ◆ 612-624-8740 fax

RAPTOR EDUCATION FOUNDATION

← PURPOSE ►

Utilize non-releasable raptors to focus
awareness towards ecological principles and issues

← ACTIVITIES ►

Special programs featuring live raptors for schools, sportsmen's
expositions, state fairs, festivals, museums and zoos; membership
publications; environmental study/action packages
for students and teachers

← GIFTS ►

T-shirts, sweatshirts, neck ties, pins, coloring books

"Bringing knowledge for the preservation of ecological diversity"

Raptor Education Foundation
21901 East Hampden Avenue
Aurora CO 80013
303-680-8500 ♦ 303-680-8502 fax

REDWINGS HORSE SANCTUARY

⊸ PURPOSE ⊸
Educate about the plight of horses, ponies and
donkeys and protect them from abuse and slaughter

⊸ ACTIVITIES ⊸
Operation of the Sanctuary, education, publications distribution

⊸ GIFTS ⊸
Adopt A Horse: adoption certificate, twice yearly report on
your horse with his photo–starting at $10; Calendars, holiday
cards, note cards, T-shirts, sweatshirts, caps, posters

*"Whenever an animal is forced into service of men,
every one of us must be concerned for any suffering it
bears on that account..."–Dr. Albert Schweitzer*

Horse note
cards
♦ 5/$7.95

Redwings Horse Sanctuary
P.O. Box 222705
Carmel CA 93922
408-624-8464 ♦ 408-622-9451 fax

ROAR FOUNDATION

➤ PURPOSE ➤

Provide protection, shelter, care and maintenance for the
wild animals of the Shambala Preserve northeast of Los Angeles;
conduct wildlife conservation educational programs for the public

➤ ACTIVITIES ➤

Operation of the Shambala Preserve which is a home for great cats
and African elephants who have been abused or abandoned; educational
presentations at the Preserve, at schools and for private groups

➤ GIFTS ➤

Adopt A Wild One: adoption certificate, an 8x10 color
photo and a wallet-size photo of your animal at the Preserve,
special visiting rights–starting at $50; Books, videos

*"Shambala...A meeting place of peace
and harmony for all beings, animal and human"*

Roar Foundation
P.O. Box 189
Acton CA 93510
805-268-0380

ROCKY MOUNTAIN RAPTOR PROGRAM

⊸ PURPOSE ⊱
Provide medical care and rehabilitation to injured
birds of prey and environmental education to the public

⊸ ACTIVITIES ⊱
Feed, medicate and rehabilitate injured eagles, hawks,
falcons, and owls for release back to the wild; educational
presentations to schools, service clubs and other groups

⊸ GIFTS ⊱
Adopt A Raptor: adoption certificate, matted and
framed photo of the bird, a Christmas card, newsletter, updates
on the bird's activities–starting at $15; T-shirts, sweatshirts,
note cards, books, prints, pins, earrings

*"Help support the Rocky Mountain Raptor Program
and give a bird of prey a second chance at freedom."*

Rocky Mountain Raptor Program
Colorado State University
Veterinary Teaching Hospital
300 West Drake
Fort Collins CO 80523
303-491-0398

⊸ PURPOSE ⊷

Protect and provide for our community's animals in need,
while fostering an awareness of their importance in our lives

⊸ ACTIVITIES ⊷

Operate the Animal Shelter; find homes for difficult-to-place sick, injured
or older animals; provide extensive medical care to make the animals healthy and
adoptable; low cost spay/neuter clinic; animal behavior counseling; hearing dog
training program; animal-assisted therapy with patients in hospitals and rehabilitation centers; foster care programs; grooming college; police horse retirement farm;
humane education programs; animal welfare advocacy

⊸ GIFTS ⊷

Pet adoption and grooming gift certificates, posters

*"The model shelter of tomorrow that's here today, guaranteeing
a second chance of life for every adoptable dog and cat in San Francisco"*

San Francisco Society For The Prevention Of Cruelty To Animals
2500 16th Street
San Francisco CA 94103-6589
415-554-3000

SANGRE DE CRISTO ANIMAL PROTECTION

⊸ PURPOSE ⊹
Promote the humane treatment of
animals and further the cause of animal rights

⊸ ACTIVITIES ⊹
Provide subsidized spay/neuter programs, provide veterinary care to
companion animals of the low-income elderly, hotline for students not wishing
to dissect in the classroom, provide dog houses to low-income people for their pets,
humane education, work to reform or eliminate the Animal Damage Control
Program in New Mexico, work to end the practice of selling shelter animals for live
animal experiments, publications, pass animal protection legislation

⊸ GIFTS ⊹
T-shirts, pendants, pins, key chains,
audio cassettes, compact discs, posters, cookbooks, books

"Animal liberation is human liberation."

Sangre de Cristo Animal Protection, Inc.
P.O. Box 11395
Albuquerque NM 87192-0395
505-281-0032 ♦ 505-281-0083 fax
505-983-2200 Santa Fe ♦ 505-382-7140 Las Cruces

SAVE OUR STRAYS

⊸ PURPOSE ⊱

Arrange for treatment, care and placement
of homeless animals, as well as family pets, living in
New York City and the close surrounding areas

⊸ ACTIVITIES ⊱

Phone lines to assist with referral information, adoption
and placement programs, spay/neuter programs, discounted veterinary services
card, national pet registration tags, reporting of lost or found animals

⊸ GIFTS ⊱

Stationery, pens, pill boxes,
mirrors, lipstick caddies, tote bags

Pill Box
♦ $2.50

"Prevent strays....spay and neuter!"

Save Our Strays
P.O. Box 021286
Brooklyn NY 11202-0028
718-332-3956

SAVE THE DOLPHINS PROJECT

⤙ PURPOSE ⤚
Eliminate the injury and death of dolphins caused by the international
tuna fishing industry and driftnets; stop the capture of live dolphins for display

⤙ ACTIVITIES ⤚
Education of Congressional lawmakers to close the loopholes
that allow the killing of dolphins, suing the National Marine Fisheries Service
for better enforcement of laws protecting dolphins, monitor domestic
and international tuna companies at all stages to ensure they use only
tuna caught with methods safe to dolphins

⤙ GIFTS ⤚
Sponsor a Dolphin: adoption certificate, information on the species
adopted, large wall poster of a dolphin, updates about the chosen species
throughout the year–$22; T-shirts, calendars, posters, videos

*"The slaughter of dolphins by the tuna industry is the
largest killing of dolphins in the world. Buy only dolphin-safe tuna."*

Save The Dolphins Project
Earth Island Institute
300 Broadway #28
San Francisco CA 94133
800-DOLPHIN ✦ 415-788-3666
415-788-7324 fax

⤙ PURPOSE ⤚
Conservation of Florida's state
marine mammal, the endangered manatee

⤙ ACTIVITIES ⤚
Lobbying for legislation, public
awareness, education, research

⤙ GIFTS ⤚
Adopt-A-Manatee: adoption certificate, biography of an
individual manatee, an underwater photo, manatee fact sheet, four
newsletters–starting at $20 for individuals; $10 for school classes;
Stuffed toys, postcards, books, videos

*"About 80% of all human-related manatee
deaths are from collisions with watercraft."*

Save The Manatee Club
500 N. Maitland Avenue, Suite 210
Maitland FL 32751
800-432-JOIN ✦ 407-539-0990
407-539-0871 fax

SAVE THE WHALES

⊸ PURPOSE ⊷
Marine mammal conservation education

⊸ ACTIVITIES ⊷
Classroom and public education presentations, letter
writing, media appearances, legislation, financing research

⊸ GIFTS ⊷
Adopt A Whale: adoption certificate; 8x10 glossy color photo
of an orca in the wild; an orca box to color, cut out and
assemble; newsletter; Save The Whales window decal–$15;
T-shirts, shoes, greeting cards, note cards, earrings,
stuffed toys, stencils, pencils, stickers, key chains, books, puzzles,
coloring books, posters, videos, audio tapes & CD's

*"Education is the best tool we have to save
the whales, the oceans and the planet."*

Save The Whales
P.O. Box 2397
Venice CA 90291
310-230-9995 ♦ 310-230-9995 fax

Silver Whale Earrings
♦ $17.95

SEA SHEPHERD CONSERVATION SOCIETY

⊸ PURPOSE ⊱
Investigate violations of international marine
wildlife laws and enforce these laws where there is no
enforcement by governments or regulatory organizations

⊸ ACTIVITIES ⊱
Operate ships armed with volunteers, cameras
and video tape to document illegal marine wildlife
exploitation to publicize these violations

⊸ GIFTS ⊱
T-shirts

"Support your oceanic police force."

Sea Shepherd Conservation Society
3107-A Washington Boulevard
Marina del Rey CA 90292
310-301-7325 ♦ 310-574-3161 fax

SEA TURTLE RESTORATION PROJECT

→ PURPOSE ←
Save the sea turtle from extinction

→ ACTIVITIES ←
Media campaigns and boycotts to pressure the shrimping industry
to use lifesaving Turtle Exclusion Devices, education to other nations
about TED's, sue the U.S. government to enforce its own laws protecting
giant sea turtles, conservation expeditions to Costa Rica, Nicaragua and
Mexico to help local environmentalists protect the giant turtle

→ GIFTS ←
Adopt-A-Nest (of sea turtle hatchlings): adoption certificate, photo
of the hatchlings pushing their heads out of the nest, turtle fact sheet,
one year subscription to the Earth Island Journal–$35;
T-shirts, greeting cards, prints, books

*"Sea turtles outlasted the dinosaurs.
Help us save the world's oldest vertebrates
from extinction by the shrimp industry."*

Sea Turtle greeting cards
♦ 6/$12.00

Sea Turtle Restoration Project
Earth Island Institute
300 Broadway, Suite 28
San Francisco CA 94133
415-788-3666 ♦ 415-788-7324 fax

SINAPU

⊸ PURPOSE ⊷

Recovery of the gray wolf in Colorado and
restoration of the wild habitat in which all species
flourish (Sinapu is the Ute Indian word for wolves.)

⊸ ACTIVITIES ⊷

Public education, grass roots political
action, habitat protection and restoration

⊸ GIFTS ⊷

T-shirts, postcards

"Restore the wolf; restore the balance."

Sinapu
Box 3243
Boulder CO 80307
303-447-8655 ♦ 303-447-8612 fax

SUNCOAST SEABIRD SANCTUARY

⊸ PURPOSE ⊷
Rescue, repair, recuperate and release
sick and injured wild birds back into their
natural environments

⊸ ACTIVITIES ⊷
Operation of the wild bird hospital,
public education, free avian zoological park

⊸ GIFTS ⊷
Adopt A Bird: adoption certificate, color photo
of your adopted bird, bird fact sheet, Sanctuary sticker,
thank you letter, quarterly newsletter subscription, unlimited
visitation privileges–starting at $15; T-shirts, sweatshirts, books

"The Suncoast Seabird Sanctuary is the
largest nonprofit wild bird hospital in the U.S."

Suncoast Seabird Sanctuary, Inc.
18328 Gulf Boulevard
Indian Shores FL 34635-2097
813-391-6211 ♦ 813-399-2923 fax

SUPRESS

⊸ PURPOSE ⊱
Educate the public about the medical and
scientific invalidity and counter-productiveness
of animal experimentation and testing

⊸ ACTIVITIES ⊱
Produce and distribute educational materials; reach
the public via documentaries, television and radio spots;
provide knowledgeable speakers and spokespersons for appearance
on TV and radio programs, debates, training sessions,
school presentations, etc.

⊸ GIFTS ⊱
T-shirts, books, videos

"Human medicine cannot be based on veterinary medicine."

SUPRESS, Inc.
P.O. Box 10400
Glendale CA 91209-3400
800-545-5848 ✦ 818-790-6383
818-790-9660 fax

SUTTON AVIAN RESEARCH CENTER

⌐ PURPOSE ⌐
Seek solutions to environmental problems through
scientific research, education and cooperative projects that focus on birds

⌐ ACTIVITIES ⌐
Bald Eagle Restoration Project which releases and monitors bald eagles
in the southeastern U.S., long-term study of declining prairie bird species,
captive breeding, educational presentations of endangered birds, field studies
of various raptor studies, worldwide habitat preservation

⌐ GIFTS ⌐
T-shirts, note cards, prints, calendars,
bookmarks, books, coloring books, videos

*"The weight of saving our wildlife and environment falls
on the shoulders of those who will accept it. We do."*

Sutton Avian Research Center
P.O. Box 2007
Bartlesville OK 74005-2007
918-336-7778 ♦ 918-336-7783 fax

TIMBER WOLF ALLIANCE

⊸ PURPOSE ⊸

Increase public awareness and acceptance of the
timber wolf in its natural habitat in the Great Lakes region,
with special emphasis in the Lake Superior Basin

⊸ ACTIVITIES ⊸

Publish and distribute educational
materials, teacher in-service programs

⊸ GIFTS ⊸

Adopt-A-Wolf-Pack: certificate, pack history,
wolf photo, newsletter, video on wolf biology–$100;
T-shirts, sweatshirts, prints, activity books

*"Through education, negative attitudes are being replaced
with understanding and appreciation of wolves."*

Timber Wolf Alliance
Sigurd Olson Environmental Institute
Northland College
Ashland WI 54806-3999
715-682-1490 ♦ 715-682-1218 fax

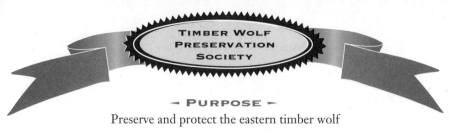

⌐ PURPOSE ⌐
Preserve and protect the eastern timber wolf

⌐ ACTIVITIES ⌐
Public education, reintroduction of wolves into
suitable habitats, maintenance of a farm with 15
full-blooded eastern timber wolves

⌐ GIFTS ⌐
Adopt A Wolf: 5x7 color portrait of your wolf, visitation
anytime–$15; T-shirts, sweatshirts, summer jackets, winter jackets,
belt buckles, pins, bolos, brooches, audio cassettes, prints,
note cards, books

*"Only the mountain has lived long enough to listen objectively to the howl
of the wolf." (The wolf has been around for 50 million years.) –Aldo Leopold*

Timber Wolf Preservation Society
6669 South 76th Street
Greendale WI 53129
414-425-6107 ♦ 414-425-8264

TREE HOUSE ANIMAL FOUNDATION

⊸ PURPOSE ⊸
Animal welfare; operate a humane
non-euthanizing shelter for homeless animals

⊸ ACTIVITIES ⊸
Rescue and treat ill and injured strays, provide pet food to needy
pet owners, supplement emergency veterinary costs for needy pet owners,
adoption programs, humane education, low-cost and no-cost spay/neuter/
vaccination program, publications, pet behavior counseling, provide pet therapy
for elderly, handicapped, psychiatric and emotionally troubled patients

⊸ GIFTS ⊸
Adopt A Pet (Foster Parent Program): personal letters, photos of
the foster pet and updates from a Tree House correspondent–$15 per month;
T-shirts, sweatshirts, polo shirts, tote bags, notepads,
letter openers, stickers, magnets, mugs, sports bottles

"Have a heart for animals."

Tree House Animal Foundation, Inc.
1212 West Carmen Avenue
Chicago IL 60640
312-784-5605 ◆ 312-784-5488
312-784-2332 fax

T-shirt
◆ $12.95

TRUMPETER SWAN SOCIETY

⊸ PURPOSE ⊹
Conservation and
restoration of the trumpeter swan

⊸ ACTIVITIES ⊹
Develop and distribute educational
information, conferences, research, field studies

⊸ GIFTS ⊹
T-shirts, sweatshirts, note cards,
posters, videos, books, prints

"...helping the magnificent trumpeter survive and flourish..."

Trumpeter Swan Society
3800 County Road 24
Maple Plain MN 55359
612-476-4663 ◆ 612-476-1514

UNITED POULTRY CONCERNS

⊸ PURPOSE ⊷
Promote the compassionate and
respectful treatment of domestic fowl

⊸ ACTIVITIES ⊷
Demonstrations, education, publications

⊸ GIFTS ⊷
Shirts, leggings, postcards, cookbooks, books

"We can be thankful at Thanksgiving without a turkey."

United Poultry Concerns
P.O. Box 59367
Potomac MD 20859
301-948-2406

VEGETARIAN RESOURCE GROUP

⭤ PURPOSE ⭢
Educate the public about vegetarianism

⭤ ACTIVITIES ⭢
Produce and distribute
educational materials, conferences

⭤ GIFTS ⭢
Books, cookbooks, activity books,
coloring books, postcards

"Be kind to animals. Don't eat them."

The Vegetarian Resource Group
P.O. Box 1463
Baltimore MD 21203
410-366-VEGE

WHALE ADOPTION PROJECT

⊣ PURPOSE ⊢
Rescue, nurture and protect marine mammals

⊣ ACTIVITIES ⊢
Move stranded whales and dolphins back into the water, study whales at sea,
give emergency care to marine mammals, work to protect the ocean environment

⊣ GIFTS ⊢
Whale adoption: personalized adoption certificate, photo, biographical
sketch, decal, First Mate membership card, four Whalewatch newsletters
(child or adult edition), 11x7 whale poster/migration map–$17; Sweatshirts, T-shirts,
wind chimes, mobiles, tote bags, duffel bags, wind socks, stuffed toys, audio tapes,
videos, stickers, neckties, watches, pins, tie tacks, games, mugs, prints, caps, books

"I love my humpback whale."

Whale Adoption Project
International Wildlife Coalition
70 East Falmouth Highway
P.O. Box 388
East Falmouth MA 02536-5954
508-548-8328 ♦ 508-548-8542 fax

WHALE CONSERVATION INSTITUTE

⊷ PURPOSE ⊷
Protect and conserve whales

⊷ ACTIVITIES ⊷
Field studies and ground-breaking research, promote
conservation and education measures to protect endangered
whales internationally

⊷ GIFTS ⊷
Adopt A Whale: adoption certificate, photo of your whale,
a sighting history, whale fact sheet, choose a humpback or southern right
whale–$25; Caps, tree ornaments, bookmarks, books, videos, software,
audio cassettes, compact discs

*"The Institute was founded in 1971 by Dr. Roger Payne
who co-discovered tthat humpback whales sing songs."*

Whale Conservation Institute
191 Weston Road
Lincoln MA 01773
617-259-0423 ♦ 617-259-0288 fax

⊸ PURPOSE ⊷
Increase public understanding of the marine
environment with a focus on whales

⊸ ACTIVITIES ⊷
Exhibit management, research, educational programs,
participate in mammal stranding network, phone line for reporting
whale sightings and strandings

⊸ GIFTS ⊷
Adopt An Orca: parchment adoption certificate with adopted orca's ID
photo attached, the whale's biography, *National Geographic Killer Whales:
Wolves of the Sea* video, four issues of the newsletter–$35; T-shirts, pins,
stuffed toys, games, card games, puzzles, wooden models, coloring books,
activity books, books, videos, audio cassettes, CD's, mugs

*"Protect your watersheds! The Southern resident orcas live here
year round and eat primarily salmon. The salmon need healthy watersheds
in which to spawn. You can make a difference!"*

The Whale Game
♦ $19.95

The Whale Museum
62 First Street North
P.O. Box 945
Friday Harbor WA 98250
360-378-4710 ♦ 360-378-5790 fax

WHERE WOLVES RESCUE

⌐ PURPOSE ⌐
Rescue and house wolf hybrids,
coyotes and coyote-dog mixes in foster homes

⌐ ACTIVITIES ⌐
Placement of adoptable animals, permanently care
for unplaceable animals, lost and found assistance, education
on wolf hybrids, individual assistance on behavioral
problems with these and other dogs

⌐ GIFTS ⌐
Adopt A Hybrid: adoption certificate, photo of your
adopted animal, one year membership in WWR–starting at $30;
T-shirts, earrings, pendants, pins, posters

*"Where Wolves Rescue works to educate the public
and the dog community to view wolf hybrids as dogs."*

Where Wolves Rescue
30040 N. 167th Avenue
Sun City AZ 85375
602-546-WOLF

WILD BURRO RESCUE

⤚ PURPOSE ⤛
Rescue, rehabilitate and preserve
otherwise doomed wild burros

⤚ ACTIVITIES ⤛
Participate in rescues, provide permanent sanctuary
and medical care, arrange for adoptions to qualified homes

⤚ GIFTS ⤛
T-shirts, greeting cards

*"Wild burros are living symbols
of the historic and pioneer West."*

Wild Burro Rescue, Inc.
665 Burnt Ridge Road
Onalaska WA 98570
306-985-7282

⌐ PURPOSE ⌐
Ensure the survival of wolves through
captive breeding, public education and research

⌐ ACTIVITIES ⌐
Captive breeding of endangered wolves, research,
educational programs, clearinghouse for wolf scientific data

⌐ GIFTS ⌐
Adopt-A-Wolf: adoption certificate, a photo of a representative of your pack,
updates, newsletters–$100 to adopt a pack for one year; T-shirts, sweatshirts, caps,
nightshirts, ponchos, tie tacks, earrings, pendants, pins, bow ties, wallets, belt
buckles, socks, shoestrings, stuffed toys, masks, puppets, card games, puzzles, mugs,
desk sets, statues, decorative boxes, clocks, tote bags, tree ornaments,
note cards, birthday cards, pencils, pens, stationery, blank books, letter openers,
rubber stamps, rulers, postcards, gift bags, mobiles, magnets, posters, books, bookmarks, cross-stitch designs, audio cassettes, CD's, videos

*"The wolf has a highly evolved family structure and an advanced
system of communication. It is among the most intelligent of all living creatures."*

Wild Canid Survival And Research Center
Washington University's Tyson Research Center
P.O. Box 760
Eureka MO 63025
314-938-5900 ♦ 314-938-6490 fax

WILDCARE

⊸ PURPOSE ⊶
Preserve the natural abundance and diversity
of wildlife through rehabilitation and education

⊸ ACTIVITIES ⊶
Rehabilitate injured, orphaned and ill birds
and mammals; public education; development of
wildlife care techniques

⊸ GIFTS ⊶
"Adopt" an animal: adoption certificate in calligraphy,
subscripton to the quarterly newsletter–starting at $10;
T-shirts, sweatshirts

"Living with wildlife"

WildCare
76 Albert Park Lane
San Rafael CA 94915-0957
415-456-SAVE

⊰ PURPOSE ⊱
Provide a permanent home for wild horses
and burros that would otherwise be destroyed

⊰ ACTIVITIES ⊱
Operate the Sanctuary, weekend pack
trips for the public in the summer as fund
raising for the Sanctuary

⊰ GIFTS ⊱
Sponsor A Horse Or Burro: certificate describing
your horse or burro, color photo–$38 per month;
Weekend pack trips, T-shirts, prints, posters

*"Enjoy supporting the Wild Horse Sanctuary with
an educational and exciting weekend trail trip in the
scenic wilderness of the Old West."*

Wild Horse Sanctuary
P.O. Box 30
Shingletown CA 96088
916-474-5770

WILDLIFE CENTER OF VIRGINIA

⊣ PURPOSE ⊢
Provide veterinary care to injured wild animals
in the Mid-Atlantic states and return them to the wild;
promote wildlife conservation

⊣ ACTIVITIES ⊢
Operation of a professional teaching and research
hospital for native wildlife, environmental education

⊣ GIFTS ⊢
Adopt An Animal (Kids For Critters): sponsorship
certificate, animal's case history and species information,
photo of your animal–starting at $20

"We see environmental problems through the eyes of wildlife."

The Wildlife Center of Virginia
P.O. Box 1557
Waynesboro VA 22980
703-942-WILD ♦ 703-943-WILD fax

WILDLIFE CONSERVATION SOCIETY

⊸ PURPOSE ⊷
Wildlife conservation

⊸ ACTIVITIES ⊷
Captive breeding programs, field research, assist
with establishing wildlife preserves around the world

⊸ GIFTS ⊷
Sponsor-A-Species: personalized certificate,
photo of your chosen animal, animal species
information–starting at $50

*"When the last individual of a race of living beings breathes
no more, another heaven and another earth must pass before
such a one can be again." –Dr. William Beebe*

Wildlife Conservation Society
185th Street & Southern Boulevard
Bronx NY 10460
718-220-5111

WILDLIFE HABITAT ENHANCEMENT COUNCIL

⌐ PURPOSE ⌐
Enhance and preserve wildlife habitats

⌐ ACTIVITIES ⌐
Conduct habitat enhancement projects cooperatively
with corporations, community members, conservation groups
and government agencies; provide environmental education
opportunities in the workplace and increase environmental awareness
of the work force; conferences; develop databases and educational
materials to aid in wildlife land management

⌐ GIFTS ⌐
Calendars, nest boxes, hopper feeders, field guides

"A new generation of conservation"

Wildlife Habitat Enhancement Council
1010 Wayne Avenue, Suite 920
Silver Spring MD 20910
301-588-8994 ◆ 301-588-4629 fax

WILDLIFE PRESERVATION TRUST INTERNATIONAL

⊸ PURPOSE ⊷
Protect endangered species threatened with extinction

⊸ ACTIVITIES ⊷
Public education programs, field research, propagation and reintroduction
of endangered species to native habitats, training of conservation professionals

⊸ GIFTS ⊷
Dodo Club Gift Membership (for children aged 7-16): coloring book,
lapel pin, cloth patch, Dodo Dispatch newsletter three times a year, 15x22 color
poster of an endangered species, Dodo Club Book Of Threatened Species–$8;
T-shirts, sweatshirts, mugs, tote bags, pins, bracelets, stuffed toys,
note cards, holiday cards, posters, prints, books

*"The best way to save endangered species is through local
action by local scientists and educators and WPTI makes this possible."*

Wildlife Preservation Trust International (WPTI)
3400 West Girard Avenue
Philadelphia PA 19104-1196
203-488-6836 (merchandise order)
203-481-7100 fax (merchandise order)
215-222-3636 ♦ 215-222-2191 fax

WILLIAM HOLDEN WILDLIFE FOUNDATION

⊷ PURPOSE ⊷

Wildlife conservation

⊷ ACTIVITIES ⊷

Operation of the William Holden Wildlife Education
Center in Kenya to educate the public and conservationists,
outreach programs into rural communities of Kenya

⊷ GIFTS ⊷

T-shirts, posters

"Wildlife is an echo of our own beginnings..."

William Holden Wildlife Foundation
P.O. Box 67981
Los Angeles CA 90067
310-274-3169

WOLF HAVEN INTERNATIONAL

⌐ PURPOSE ¬
Wolf conservation

⌐ ACTIVITIES ¬
Provide homes for wolves that cannot live in the wild; protect the remaining wild wolves and their habitats; promote wolf re-establishment in historic ranges; public education on the value of all wildlife, including predators; provide information to federal and state agencies to assist wolf recovery efforts in Washington

⌐ GIFTS ¬

Adopt A Wolf: adoption certificate, photo and biography of your wolf, silk bookmark–$20; T-shirts, pins, audio tapes, books, posters

"Contrary to their savage image, wolves are loving, social animals, living together in families that care for each other."

Long sleeve T-shirt; purple or jade
♦ $14.00-$15.00

Wolf Haven International
3111 Offut Lake Road
Tenino WA 98589
800-GIV-WOLF ♦ 360-264-4695
360-264-4639 fax

WOLF HOLLOW WILDLIFE REHABILITATION CENTRE

◄ PURPOSE ►
Wildlife rehabilitation

◄ ACTIVITIES ►
Rescue, care for and release injured and orphaned
wild animals, public education, non-invasive research, internships

◄ GIFTS ►
T-shirts, mugs

"Wolf Hollow gives wildlife a second chance."

Wolf Hollow Wildlife Rehabilitation Centre
P.O. Box 391
Friday Harbor WA 98250
360-378-5000

WOLF SONG OF ALASKA

⊸ PURPOSE ⊱
Promote an understanding of the wolf

⊸ ACTIVITIES ⊱
Public education programs, exhibits, research,
development of a wolf observation facility in the Anchorage area

⊸ GIFTS ⊱
Adopt an Alaska Wolf: adoption certificate, fact sheet–$15;
Clocks, banners, books, activity books, T-shirts, mugs, prints,
posters, pins, caps, audio cassettes

*"We must learn about the wolf, understand what we have learned,
and then respect the role of the wolf in our ecosystem."–Tom Talasz*

Wolf Song of Alaska
P.O. Box 110309
Anchorage AK 99511-0309
800-243-WOLF ♦ 907-346-3073
907-346-1221 fax

Wolf Song
mug
♦ $8.00

WOODSTOCK ANIMAL RIGHTS MOVEMENT

⊸ PURPOSE ⊷
Promote the rights of animals

⊸ ACTIVITIES ⊷
Public education, consumer activism,
demonstrations, letter writing, legislation

⊸ GIFTS ⊷
Soaps, shampoos, hair conditioners, makeup, face creams, hand and body
lotions, massage oils, perfumes and colognes, body powders, hennas, window
gardens, kids' gardens, flower and leaf press sets, T-shirts, sweatshirts, lunch bags,
juggling toys, stuffed toys, hand puppets, rubber animals, rubber stamps, rubber
stamp sets, ink pads, cookbooks, books, medicine cards, audio cassettes, compact
discs, videos, bat house kits, bird house kits, cedar feeder kits, wood birdfeeder kits,
pet foods, animal care products, shower curtains, umbrellas, mugs, tote bags,
duffel bags, candles, flags, wall plaques, backpacks, briefcases, shoulder bags,
key rings, pendants, bracelets, pins, earrings

*"Never doubt that a small group of citizens
can change the world; indeed it's the only thing that ever has."*

The Warm Store
Woodstock Animal Rights Movement
31 Mill Road
Woodstock NY 12498
800-889-WARM ◆ 914-679-4242

WORLD BIRD SANCTUARY

⏤ PURPOSE ⏤
Preserve all wildlife,
particularly birds of prey and parrots

⏤ ACTIVITIES ⏤
Breeding and releasing endangered species,
treating and returning injured birds to the wild, education

⏤ GIFTS ⏤
Adopt-A-Bird: adoption certificate, photo, newsletter,
species information, biography of your bird–starting at $50;
T-shirts, sweatshirts, shirts, jackets, caps, magnets, mugs, tote bags,
key chains, pencils, erasers, wood sculptures, activity books,
pins, note cards, bird feeders

"Preserve habitat to preserve diversity."

World Bird Sanctuary
P.O. Box 270270
St. Louis MO 63127
314-938-6193 ♦ 314-225-4390

WORLD WILDLIFE FUND

⊸ PURPOSE ⊷

Wildlife conservation

⊸ ACTIVITIES ⊷

Protect tropical forests, create and defend national
parks and reserves, help people in developing countries
improve their lives without sacrificing their surroundings,
train park guards, equip anti-poaching teams

⊸ GIFTS ⊷

T-shirts, sweatshirts, nightshirts, slippers, vests, mirrors,
cotton throws, bookends, clocks, telephones, duffel bags, calendars

Jungle print
duffel bag
♦ $25.00

"Saving life on Earth"

World Wildlife Fund
P.O. Box 224
Peru IN 46970
800-833-1600 ♦ 317-472-5901 fax

Alphabet
elephant puzzle
♦ $22.50

XERCES SOCIETY

⊸ PURPOSE ⊱
Conservation of invertebrates and preservation of critical
ecosystems worldwide (Invertebrates are creatures without backbones,
including butterflies, beetles, ants, worms, and myriad creatures of the sea.)

⊸ ACTIVITIES ⊱
Monarch butterfly winter habitats preserved in California; add critical nesting habitats
for bees in Costa Rica; developed a sustainable resource management program
in Madagascar; establishing a butterfly farm (with the San Diego Zoo) in Costa Rica
to teach local people how to raise and market native butterflies to generate
income for the village, thereby teaching responsible, sustainable resource use

⊸ GIFTS ⊱
T-shirts, note cards, coloring books, journals, books

"Preserving the little things that run the world"

The Xerces Society
10 S.W. Ash Street
Portland OR 97204
503-222-2788 ♦ 503-222-2763 fax

CENTER FOR MARINE
CONSERVATION
Dolphin hoop earrings
with azurite &
malachi beads
♦ $14.50

CENTER FOR
MARINE CONSERVATION
Umbrella with penguins
♦ $22.00

WOODSTOCK ANIMAL
RIGHTS MOVEMENT
Beauty Without Cruelty
skincare ♦ $4.95–$12.95

Zoos And Aquariums

The following is a sampling of zoos and aquariums accredited by the American Zoo and Aquarium Association that also have animal adoption programs and/or other gifts available by mail.

AKRON ZOOLOGICAL PARK

500 Edgewood Avenue   216-375-2550
Akron OH 44307   216-375-2575 fax

Care for a Critter: adoption certificate, animal fact sheet, photo of your animal, your name along with the name of your adopted animal in an issue of ZooTales –starting at $15

ALEXANDRIA ZOO

P.O. Box 6015   318-473-1385
Alexandria LA 71307   318-473-1392

Zoo Parent Program: adoption certificate, invitation to a Zoo Parents Party at the Zoo, your name on the Zoo Parents recognition sign–starting at $15

BALTIMORE ZOO

Druid Hill Park   410-396-7102
Baltimore MD 21217-9973   410-396-6464

Adopt an Animal: adoption certificate, photo, VIP decal, WILD WORDS newsletter, a Mother's Day or Father's Day card from the adopted animal, a listing on the Adoption Recognition Display near the Zoo entrance, free admission to the Zoo for the annual Adopters' Party–starting at $15

BALTIMORE ZOO (CONT.)

Also available by mail: T-shirts, sweatshirts, aprons, pins, necklaces, earrings, balls, stickers, puppets, watercolor sets, puzzles, rubber stamps, card games, art sets, rugs, picture frames, soaps, duffel bags, tote bags, school bags, drawstring bags, journals, note cubes, holiday cards, tree ornaments, books

BATON ROUGE ZOO

P.O. Box 60   504-775-3877
Baker LA 70704   504-775-3931 fax

Adopt-An-Animal: adoption certificate, animal fact sheet, photo of your "wild child," three passes to the Zoo, your name on the Zoo Parents' Honor Roll along with the name of the animal you have adopted–starting at $25

BEARDSLEY ZOO

1875 Noble Avenue   203-576-8126
Bridgeport CT 06610   203-576-7534 fax

Share the Care Animal Sponsorship Program: certificate, bumper sticker, information about the animal sponsored –starting at $15

BERGEN COUNTY ZOO

216 Forest Avenue   201-262-3771
Paramus NJ 07652   201-986-1788 fax

Animal Sponsorship: sponsor's certificate, special privileges with visitation–starting at $15

BINDER PARK ZOO
7400 Division Drive   616-979-1351
Battle Creek MI 49017-9500   616-979-8834 fax
A.D.O.P.T. an Animal (Animals Depend On People Too):
adoption certificate, photo of your animal, invitation to our
annual Zooper Parent Party, your name on our A.D.O.P.T.
Honor Roll, your name listed in the Zoo's membership
publication–starting at $30

BLANK PARK ZOO
7401 SW 9th Street   515-285-4722
Des Moines IA 50315
Adopt an Animal: adoption certificate, photo, your name on
our recognition board at the Zoo, invitation to Parents
Weekend, ZooTracks newsletter–starting at $30

BRANDYWINE ZOO
1001 North Park Drive   302-571-7788
Wilmington DE 19802   302-571-7787 fax
A.D.O.P.T. Program: adoption certificate, stickers, a copy of
Zoo News, your name displayed on the Honor Roll of Zoo
Parents–starting at $15

BROOKFIELD ZOO
3300 Golf Road
Brookfield IL 60513
708-485-3532 fax

708-485-0263
ext. 341 (animal adoptions)
ext. 638 (gift shop)

Animal adoption: adoption certificate, animal fact sheet, color photo, window decal, an update on your animal during the year, invitation to the annual Parents' Evening picnic –starting at $25. Also available by mail: puppets, art sets, jumbo crayons, stuffed toys, hand carved wooden African animals, lunch bags, audio tapes, CD's

BUFFALO ZOO
300 Parkside Avenue
Buffalo NY 14214-1999

716-837-3900
716-837-0738 fax

Adopt-An-Animal: adoption certificate, animal fact sheet, window decal, your name prominently displayed on our Adopt-An-Animal plaque–starting at $25

BURNET PARK ZOO, FRIENDS OF
1 Conservation Place
Syracuse NY 13204

315-422-1223
315-422-1224 fax

Adopt an Animal: adoption certificate, animal fact sheet, invitation to the annual party honoring our Zoo Parents, your name on our Zoo Parents Honor Roll, bumper sticker –starting at $25

CENTRAL FLORIDA ZOOLOGICAL PARK
P.O. Box 470309   407-323-4450
Lake Monroe FL 32747-0309   407-321-0900 fax
Adopt an Animal: adoption certificate, fact sheet, photo
–starting at $25

CHARLES PADDOCK ZOO
P.O. Box 8
Atascadero CA 93423   805-461-5083
Adopt An Animal: adoption certificate, Zoo decal, educational
information about your animal, your name on the adoption
board at the Zoo–starting at $15

CHEYENNE MOUNTAIN ZOO
4250 Cheyenne Mountain Zoo Road   719-633-9925
Colorado Springs CO 80906   719-633-2254
Adopt A Wild Child: adoption certificate, animal fact sheet,
your name on the Zoo Display Board, a subscription to the
Zoo newsletter, invitations to Zoopendous events, two invi-
tations to the annual Adopt-An-Animal Day at the
Zoo–starting at $25; $50 includes a coffee mug; $100 includes a
T-shirt; $251 includes a color photo of the Wild Child
adopted; $500 includes a behind-the-scenes tour of the Wild
Child's habitat

CINCINNATI ZOO AND BOTANICAL GARDEN

3400 Vine Street   513-559-7716
Cincinnati OH 45220   513-559-7790 fax
ADOPT an animal: color photo, fact sheet, certificate, invitations to special events, recognition on Sponsor Board–$30

CLEVELAND ZOOLOGICAL SOCIETY

P.O. Box 609281   216-661-6500, ext. 220
Cleveland OH 44109
Adopt An Animal: adoption certificate, animal fact sheet, photo, recognition on our Adopt An Animal Honor Roll plaque at the Zoo, invitation to the annual Parents' Night at the Zoo; donors of $50 or more also receive a Zoo Parents T-shirt with the Adopt An Animal logo

COLUMBUS ZOO

Box 400   614-645-3550
Powell OH 43065-0400   614-645-3465 fax
Adopt-an-Animal: adoption certificate, animal fact sheet, bumper sticker, window decal, T-shirt transfer, an invitation to ADOPT-AN-ANIMAL Day, a personalized engraved plaque at the Zoo for your year of adoption–starting at $20

COMO ZOOLOGICAL SOCIETY

P.O. Box 131192   612-487-1485
St. Paul MN 55113   612-487-0388 fax
Adopt An Animal: sponsorship certificate, information on your chosen animal, invitations to exclusive functions, recognition

on the Sponsor Board, a 10% coupon at Zoodale gift shop, two issues of the Zoo newsletter-starting at $25; $75 includes two more issues of the newsletter, a 15% discount coupon at Zoodale gift shop, a Zoo sticker; $150 includes all issues of the Zoo newsletter, a 20% discount coupon at Zoodale gift shop, a special meeting with your sponsored animal and its keeper

DAKOTA ZOO
P.O. Box 711   701-223-7543
Bismarck ND 58502
Adopt An Animal: adoption certificate with a picture of your animal, your name displayed on the Zoo's Adoption Center sign, an "I Adopted An Animal" bumper sticker, Adopt-An-Animal iron-on decal–starting at $20

DALLAS ZOO
621 East Clarendon Drive   214-670-6825
Dallas TX 75203-2996   214-9-4-ADOPT
                                      214-670-6717 fax
Adopt-an-Animal: adoption certificate with a color photo of your adopted animal, a "Zookeeper's Report" on your animal, subscription to the Dallas Zoo Parents' Newsletter, an invitation to the annual Parents' Party, a listing on the Parents' Honor Roll at the Zoo's main entrance–starting at $15
Also available by mail: lithographs

DENVER ZOO
City Park   303-331-4100
Denver CO 80205-4899   303-331-4125
Adopt-an-Animal: adoption certificate, animal information
sheet, your name on the Zoo Parents' recognition board, an
invitation to the annual Zoo Parents' Picnic, Zoo Parents'
logo pin–starting at $15

DETROIT ZOOLOGICAL INSTITUTE
8450 West Ten Mile Road
P.O. Box 39   810-398-0900
Royal Oak MI 48068-0039   810-398-0504 fax
Adopt An Animal Club Membership: adoption certificate,
animal fact sheet, membership card, T-shirt–starting at $25

DICKERSON PARK ZOO
3043 N. Fort
Springfield MO 65803   417-833-1570
Adopt An Animal: adoption certificate, animal fact sheet, 3x5
photo of your animal, Adopt An Animal magnet, your name
on the Zoo Parents Board for one year, two Zoo passes–$30;
$50 includes a 5x7 photo and four Zoo passes; $100 includes a
framed 8x10 color photo and a subscription to Wildlife
Conservation magazine

DREHER PARK ZOO
1301 Summit Boulevard   407-533-0887
West Palm Beach FL 33405-3098   407-585-6085 fax
Adopt-An-Animal: adoption certificate, photo of animal,

animal fact sheet, your name on the Adoption Board at the
Zoo, invitation to the annual parent party, subscription to the
Zoo's magazine–starting at $15

EL PASO ZOO
P.O. Box 10179
El Paso TX 79992-0179   915-532-8156
Adopt An Animal: adoption certificate, animal fact sheet, a
bumper sticker, an invitation to a party for Zoo Parents, your
name posted on the Zoo grounds–starting at $20

FOLSOM CHILDREN'S ZOO
AND BOTANICAL GARDENS
1222 S. 27th Street   402-475-6741
Lincoln NE 68502   402-475-6742 fax
Adopt An Animal: adoption notification to the "Zoo Parent,"
a 15-word message on a sign near the chosen animal's exhibit–
starting at $25; Animal Stock Certificate: framable stock
certificate showing donor's name and the name of the animal
selected–$5 per share

FORT WAYNE CHILDREN'S ZOO
3411 Sherman Boulevard   219-482-4610
Fort Wayne IN 46808
Adopt an Animal; adoption certificate, animal fact sheet, decal,
your name and adopted animal's name listed in an issue of
Wildlife Conservation magazine, an invitation to the VIP
(Very Important Parent) event at the Zoo–starting at $15

FORT WORTH ZOO

1989 Colonial Parkway   817-871-7000
Fort Worth TX 76110   817-871-7050
Zoo Parents Animal Adoption Program: adoption certificate,
T-shirt transfer, bumper sticker, subscription to the Zoo's
quarterly publication–starting at $35

GREATER LOS ANGELES ZOO ASSOCIATION

5333 Zoo Drive   213-664-1100
Los Angeles CA 90027-1498   213-662-6879 fax
Animal Adoption Program: (you may name your "wild child),
an invitation to a ceremony at the adopted animal's enclosure,
a bronze engraved recognition plaque, one year's free
admission to the Zoo, subscription to the Zoo's quarterly
magazine Zooview and the bi-monthly membership newsletter
Zooscape–starting at $1100; Wildlife Savers: Wildlife Savers
certificate–starting at $25; donors of $75 or more also are
recognized in the Zoo's Donor Showcase for one year

HAPPY HOLLOW PARK & ZOO

1300 Senter Road   408-295-8383
San Jose CA 95112   408-277-4470 fax
Adopt an Animal: adoption certificate, animal fact sheet,
picture of the animal, recognition on the V.I.P. (Very
Important Parent) showcase at the Zoo, invitation to the
annual Zoo Parent Reunion, Adventure Club discount
card–starting at $25

HONOLULU ZOO
151 Kapahulu Avenue   808-926-3191
Honolulu HI 96815
Adopt A Wild Child: adoption certificate, animal fact sheet,
letter acknowledging your adoption, newsletter subscription,
your name on the Recognition Posts in the center of the Zoo,
bumper sticker, current brochures and literature–starting at $20

INDIANAPOLIS ZOO
1200 W. Washington Street   317-630-2025
Indianapolis IN 46222-4500   317-630-2015
      317-630-5153
Animal Amigo: Animal Amigo Club certificate, bi-annual
newsletter, your name listed on the Animal Amigo Board, invitation to the Animal Amigo Party–starting at $25;
$50 includes a photo of your animal

JOHN BALL ZOO
1300 W. Fulton Street NW   616-336-4300
P.O. Box 1133
Grand Rapids MI 49501-1133
Adopt An Animal: adoption certificate, Zoo Parent button,
animal fact brochure–$25

KNOXVILLE ZOO
P.O. Box 6040   615-637-5331 ext. 305
Knoxville TN 37914
Zoo Parents: adoption certificate, animal fact sheet, newsletter,
invitation to Zoo Parents party, name displayed on recognition
boards–starting at $20

LAKE SUPERIOR ZOO

7210 Fremont Street   218-723-3748
Duluth MN 55807
A.D.O.P.T. an Animal: sponsorship certificate, your name
listed on the A.D.O.P.T. Board at the Zoo, one year
subscription to the Zoo's newsletter, two passes to the annual
Zoo Family Day–$25

LINCOLN PARK ZOO

2200 North Cannon Drive   312-742-2000
Chicago Il 60614   312-742-2137 fax
A.D.O.P.T. an Animal: adoption certificate, plush animal,
animal photo and fact sheet, invitation to the Zoo's annual
SuperZooPicnic–starting at $30

LOUISVILLE ZOO

1100 Trevilian Way   502-459-2181
P.O. Box 37250   502-459-CATS
Louisville KY 40233   502-459-2196 fax
Adopt A Zooper Child: adoption certificate, photo, your name
on the Zooper Parent Recognition Board, two VIP passes to
visit the animal–starting at $25

MEMPHIS ZOO

2000 Galloway   901-725-3451
Memphis TN 38112   (animal adoption)
901-276-9305 fax   901-276-9453
Adopt-An-Animal: adoption certificate, animal fact sheet,
recognition on the Zoo Parents Board, special "Zoo-Prize,"

invitation to an annual Zoo-Parents picnic, one year
subscription to the newsletter–starting at $15

MESKER PARK ZOO

2421 Bement Avenue   812-428-0715, ext. 410
Evansville IN 47720   812-428-2529 fax

P.E.A.C.E.(Protection of Earth's Animals and Conservation of
the Environment): certificate, bumper sticker, recognition on
the P.E.A.C.E. Wall of fame, coupon for Ritzy's Restaurant,
subscription to the Zoo's quarterly newsletter, fact sheet on
sponsored animal, animal photo–starts at $100; other packages
available for less

MIAMI METROZOO

12400 SW 152 Street   305-255-5551
Miami FL 33177-1499   305-255-7126

Adopt-An-Animal: adoption certificate, animal fact sheet,
Adopt-An-Animal decal–starting at $25; $50 includes a
Zoobook; $75 includes an invitation to a Family Reunion at
the Zoo; $100 includes a color photo of the animal adopted;
$150 includes an African wildlife mug; $250 includes a Zoo
Brick personally engraved with a special message to be permanently displayed on the MetroZoo's Walls of the Wild, a
behind-the-scenes cart tour for five people, a Zoo Society
family membership; $500 includes a limited edition poster;
$1000 includes a gift-boxed animal tile personally engraved

MICKE GROVE ZOO

11793 North Micke Grove Road   209-953-8840
Lodi CA 95240   209-331-7270
Adopt An Animal: adoption certificate, Zoo Parent bumper
sticker, your name on the Adopt An Animal Honor Roll at the
Zoo, an invitation to a special party at the Zoo–starting at $15

MILLER PARK ZOO

1020 S. Morris Avenue   309-823-4250
Bloomington IL 61701
Adopt an Animal: adoption certificate, fact sheet–starting
at $25

MILWAUKEE COUNTY ZOO

10005 W. Bluemound   414-258-2333
Milwaukee WI 53226   414-258-6311 fax
Sponsor an Animal: certificate of sponsorship, information
about your animal, your name and the animal's name listed on
the donor recognition board, sponsor key chain, invitation to
Twilight Safari for sponsors only–starting at $15

MINNESOTA ZOO

13000 Zoo Boulevard   612-431-9216
Apple Valley MN 55124-8199   612-431-9300 fax
Adopt an Animal: certificate, gift card, animal fact sheet,
bumper sticker, invitation to the annual Adopt an Animal
party, name listed on the Adopt an Animal sponsor wall at the
Zoo–starting at $25

MONTGOMERY AREA ZOOLOGICAL SOCIETY
P.O. Box 3242   334-240-4588
Montgomery AL 36109
Animal Adoption Program: adoption certificate, fact sheet on
your chosen animal, special decal, your name on the Wild
Parent Wall at the Zoo, an invitation to the annual party for
adoptive parents-fees vary with chosen animal

MYSTIC MARINELIFE AQUARIUM
55 Coogan Boulevard   203-572-5955
Mystic CT 06355
Animal Parents (adopt your favorite species): personalized
certificate, wallet ID card, invitation to PARENT'S Day at the
Aquarium where you can participate in "Parents Only"
meetings with the animal care providers–starting at $25

NATIONAL AVIARY
Allegheny Commons West   412-323-7235
Pittsburgh PA 15212
Adopt-A-Bird: adoption certificate, bird photo, bird fact sheet,
your name inscribed on a gold plaque in the Aviary lobby, invitation to the annual Adopt-a-Bird Appreciation Party
–starting at $25

NORTHWEST TREK WILDLIFE PARK

11610 Trek Drive East	360-832-6117
Eatonville WA 98328	360-832-6118 fax

Adopt An Animal: adoption certificate, TREKparent button, thank you letter, annual subscription to the bi-monthly newsletter, recognition on the breezeway signage for 12 months, permanent recognition in the TREKparent family album–$35; $100 includes an animal fact sheet, invitation to a parent appreciation event, TREKparent T-shirt; $250 includes four guest passes to the park, an 8x10 color photo of the species adopted; $500 includes an annual family pass and a behind-the-scenes private tour of Trek; $1000 includes a plaque and an invitation to the annual reception for "Grand" parents

OAKLAND ZOO

P.O. Box 5238

9777 Golf Links Road	510-632-9525
Oakland CA 94605	510-635-5719 fax

Adopt-An-Animal: adoption certificate, animal fact sheet, photo, your name in the newsletter–starting at $50

OKLAHOMA CITY ZOOLOGICAL PARK

2101 N.E. 50th Street	405-424-3344
Oklahoma City OK 73111	405-425-0207 fax

Adopt An Animal: adoption certificate, animal fact sheet, invitation to the annual "Meet Your Keeper" party at the Zoo –starting at $20

PHILADELPHIA ZOO

P.O. Box 41877-422   215-243-1100
Philadelphia PA 19101-9843   215-387-6400

Adopt An Animal: adoption certificate, animal fact sheet, newsletter, invitation to ADOPT Parents' Recognition Day–starting at $25; $100 includes an 8x10 photo of your adopted animal

PHOENIX ZOO

455 North Galvin Parkway   602-273-1341, ext. 7414
Phoenix AZ 85008-3431

Adopt an Animal: Keeper Notes about the adopted animal and window decal for donations up to $49; $50-$199 includes an adoption certificate, Zoo magazine, invitation to the annual Parents party, color photo; $200-$499 includes a poster of a painting of the Zoo's famous painting pachyderm, Ruby, and name recognition on Zoo grounds; $500-$999 includes invitations to exclusive Zoo events and your name in Arizoo magazine; $1000 includes a lithograph of a painting by Ruby the elephant, a wall plaque, a behind-the-scenes tour for up to six people and an invitation to the annual reception with the Zoo director

PITTSBURGH ZOO

Adopt An Animal Program   412-665-3640
One Hill Road
Pittsburgh PA 15206

Adopt An Animal: adoption certificate, an invitation to the
Zoo's annual Adopt An Animal Party, decal, animal fact sheet,
your name on a special recognition board-starting at $15;
Adopt Your Favorite Penguin Hockey Player and a Zoo
Penguin: adoption certificate for both your player and your
bird, photo of your player, decal, hockey schedule, penguin fact
sheet, invitation to the Zoo's annual Adopt An Animal Party,
your name on a special recognition board–starting at $25

POINT DEFIANCE ZOOLOGICAL SOCIETY

5400 North Pearl Street   206-591-5368
Tacoma WA 98407-3218   206-591-5448 fax

Adopt An Animal: adoption certificate, color photo, invitation
to a special event, animal fact sheet–starting at $25; other
benefits are included with higher donations

PUEBLO ZOO

3455 Nuckolls Avenue   719-561-9664
Pueblo CO 81005-1234

A.D.O.P.T. an Animal: adoption certificate, your name on the
A.D.O.P.T. Honor Roll, an invitation to visit anytime–starting at $25

RACINE ZOO
2131 North Main Street   414-636-9189
Racine WI 53402   414-636-9307 fax
Adopt An Animal: adoption certificate, photo of your animal,
letter about your animal–$25; T-shirts, sweatshirts, note cards,
cookbooks

REID PARK ZOO
900 South Randolph Way   520-881-1078
Tucson AZ 85716   (animal adoptions)
520-791-5378 fax   520-881-4753
Adopt An Animal: adoption certificate, animal fact sheet, your
name on the Parents' Recognition Board at the Zoo, an invitation to the annual Parents' Party, a behind-the-scenes
tour–starting at $25

RIVERBANKS ZOO & GARDEN
P.O. Box 1060   803-779-8717
Columbia SC 29202   803-256-6463
Zoo Parent: Zoo Parent certificate, window decal, T-shirt
iron-on, your name on the Zoo Parents honor roll, an invitation to the annual Zoo Parent "Breakfast With the Director"
at the Zoo– starting at $15

ROGER WILLIAMS PARK ZOO
Providence RI 02905   401-785-3510
Adopt An Animal: adoption certificate, animal fact sheet,
"I Have a Wild Child" bumpersticker, invitation to annual
Parent's Party–starting at $20

SACRAMENTO ZOO
3930 West Land Park Drive   916-264-5888
Sacramento CA 95822
Adopt An Animal: adoption certificate, animal fact sheet,
bumper sticker, your name on the VIP showcase board at the
Zoo, invitation to the Zoo Parents' Picnic–starting at $25

SAINT LOUIS ZOO
P.O. Box 790080   314-768-5450
St. Louis MO 63179
Zoo Parents Program: adoption certificate, decal, T-shirt
transfer, invitation to the annual Parents picnic, your name on
the Kiosk for one year–$15; $25-$99 includes a color photo
and an animal fact sheet; $100-$249 includes a frame for the
animal photo; $250 includes a listing in the Zoo's annual
report and an invitation to the Annual Appreciation Dinner

SALISBURY ZOO
P.O. Box 2979   301-548-3188
Salisbury MD 21802
Adopt An Animal: adoption certificate, animal fact
sheet–starting at $15

SAN ANTONIO ZOO
3903 N. St. Mary's Street   512-734-7183
San Antonio TX 78212
Adopt An Animal: adoption certificate, iron-on decal, your
name displayed on the Zoo Adoption Board–starting at $15;
$100 includes an autographed photo of your zoo animal

SAN DIEGO ZOOLOGICAL SOCIETY
Center for Reproduction of Endangered Species (CRES)
P.O. Box 271   619-557-3974
San Diego CA 92112   619-231-3954 fax
Adopt-an-Animal: adoption certificate, newsletter–$50; higher
donation amounts include free passes to the Zoo, color photos
and photo caravan tours at the Wild Animal Park;
T-shirts are also available for purchase by mail.

SAN FRANCISCO ZOO
1 Zoo Road   415-753-7117
San Francisco CA 94132-1098   415-681-2039 fax
Adopt An Animal: adoption certificate, color photo, nature
notes about the species, your name on the Parent Showcase at
the Zoo–starting at $25; donors of higher amounts may also
receive a T-shirt, a stuffed animal or private tour;
Adopt An Acre: honorary deed to the rainforest noting the
amount of the acreage purchased and the country of location
–starting at $15

SANTA ANA ZOO
1801 East Chestnut Avenue   714-953-8555
Santa Ana CA 92701
Adopt An Animal: adoption certificate, your name displayed
on the Zoo recognition board, "Something Wild" decal, invitation to the annual Something Wild Picnic, one year
subscription to the Zoo's newsletter–$50; $100 includes your
name displayed prominently in gold letters; $250 includes an
invitation to a Something Wild cocktail party with animal

SANTA ANA ZOO (CONT.)

experts, Zoo staff and other Zoo Parents; $500 includes a
meeting with the zookeepers who will design a personalized
"zoo experience" just for you; $1000 includes a day spent
touring three special exhibits at another area zoo

SANTA BARBARA ZOO

500 Ninos Drive   805-962-5339
Santa Barbara CA 93103-3798   805-962-1673 fax

Foster Feeders: adoption certificate, your own plaque on the
Foster Feeder Board, subscription to the Zoo newsletter, cards
sent on special occasions, birth announcements, invitation to a
special event for Foster Feeders and Zoo members–starting at $25

SEDGWICK COUNTY ZOO

5555 Zoo Boulevard   316-942-2212, ext. 204
Wichita KS 67212   316-942-3781 fax

Adopt-An-Animal: minimum benefits include an adoption
certificate, animal fact sheet, brief reading list, bookmark, your
name and species of animal printed on the adoption board at
the Zoo entrance, invitation to the annual Breakfast with the
Keepers–starting at $20

SENECA PARK ZOO

2222 St. Paul Street   716-336-7205
Rochester NY 14621

Zoo Parent Program (Adopt an Animal): adoption certificate,
photo, animal fact sheet, invitation to the annual Zoo Parent
party–starting at $30; $50 includes a Zoo Parent T-shirt; other
benefits are available to higher donors

SUNSET ZOO
2333 Oak Street   913-587-APES
Manhattan KS 66502

Zoo Parents: adoption certificate, animal fact sheet, free pass to the Zoo to visit the adopted animal, your name on the ZooParent adoption center board, invitation to the annual "family reunion," a Mother's or Father's Day card, sticker–starting at $10; $100 includes an 8x10 photo of the adopted animal

TOLEDO ZOO
P.O. Box 4010   419-385-5721
Toledo OH 43609-9988   419-385-6935 fax
                                   419-389-8670 fax

Adopt an Animal: adoption certificate, decal, T-shirt transfer, invitation to visit your adopted animal at a special Zoo PAL evening at the Zoo, your name on the Zoo PAL plaque –starting at $20; $100 includes an 8x10 color photo of the adopted animal; $200 includes your name displayed on a plaque placed at the animal's exhibit

TOPEKA ZOO
635 Gage Boulevard   913-272-5821
Topeka KS 66606-2066   913-272-7595
                                   913-272-2539

Adopt An Animal: official adoption papers, "My Family Tree Grew...At The Topeka Zoo" decal, your name in the Zooreka magazine, an invitation to the annual adoptive parents party – starting at $10

TULSA ZOO

5701 East 36th Street North   918-669-6601
Tulsa OK 74115-2100   918-669-6610 fax

Adopt An Animal: adoption certificate, animal fact sheet, your name on the Sponsor Board at the Zoo and in ZooNews, two passes to the Zoo, 10% discount at the Zoo gift shop, invitation to the ZooCare family night for you and your immediate family–starting at $25; $100 includes two Zoo passes good for one year, two family invitations to ZooCare family night; $500 includes a behind-the-scenes tour for ten people, four Zoo passes good for one year, four family invitations to ZooCare family night; $1000 includes eight Zoo passes good for one year, eight family invitations to ZooCare family night and the use of the grounds for a private picnic

UTAH'S HOGLE ZOO

P.O. Box 58475   801-582-1631
Salt Lake City UT 84158-0475   801-584-1770 fax

Adopt A Wild Child: adoption certificate, "Adopt A Wild Child" window decal, invitation to special Parent's Day events, recognition on "The Lion's Pride Donor Board," mention in The Safari Newsletter–starting at $20

WAIKIKI AQUARIUM

2777 Kalakaua Avenue   808-923-9741
Honolulu HI 96815-4027   808-923-1771 fax

T-shirts, golf shirts, earrings, bracelets, charms, pendants, note cards, prints, stuffed toys available by mail.

WASHINGTON PARK ZOO

Friends of the Washington Park Zoo
4001 SW Canyon Road   503-220-2493
Portland OR 97221   503-223-9323 fax

Sponsor An Animal: certificate, animal fact sheet, Zoo newsletter, an invitation to ZooParent Night–starting at $25; $50 includes a color photo of the sponsored animal; $100 includes your name on the ZooParent Recognition Board for one year; $250 includes an invitation to the Annual Breakfast with the Curator

ZOO ATLANTA

800 Cherokee Avenue, S.E   404-624-WILD
Atlanta GA 30315   404-624-5600
                                   404-627-7514 fax

Adopt-an-Animal: adoption certificate, color photo of your animal, animal fact sheet, Adopt-an-Animal decal, a year's subscription to the Zoo magazine–starting at $35; $100 includes recognition on the Adopt-an-Animal board at the Zoo and in the Zoo magazine; $300 includes invitations to quarterly events at the Zoo

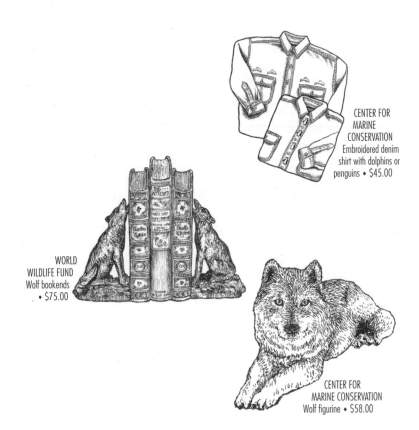

CENTER FOR
MARINE
CONSERVATION
Embroidered denim
shirt with dolphins or
penguins ♦ $45.00

WORLD
WILDLIFE FUND
Wolf bookends
♦ $75.00

CENTER FOR
MARINE CONSERVATION
Wolf figurine ♦ $58.00

What Area Of Animal Interest Would You Like To Support?

All organizations serve many needs of the animals. Each organization has been placed in the one or two categories that most represent its main purposes and activities.

ADVOCACY AND LEGISLATION

BATS

Bat Conservation International ◆ *page 40*

BEARS

Great Bear Foundation ◆ *page 87*
North American Bear Society ◆ *page 136*

BEAVERS

Friends of Beaversprite ◆ *page 79*

BIRDS, DOMESTIC

United Poultry Concerns ◆ *page 182*

BIRDS, WILD

American Birding Association ◆ *page 20*
Birds of Prey Rehabilitation Foundation ◆ *page 42*
Cape May Bird Observatory ◆ *page 44*
Delaware Valley Raptor Center ◆ *page 55*
Florida Audubon Society Center for Birds of Prey ◆ *page 73*
Free Flight Bird and Marine Mammal
  Rehabilitation ◆ *page 76*
Hawk Mountain Sanctuary ◆ *page 89*
Hawkwatch International ◆ *page 90*
International Bird Rescue Research Center ◆ *page 100*
International Crane Foundation ◆ *page 101*
International Osprey Foundation ◆ *page 104*
National Foundation to Protect America's Eagles ◆ *page 128*
North American Loon Fund ◆ *page 137*
Pelican Man's Bird Sanctuary ◆ *page 149*
Peregrine Fund ◆ *page 153*
Purple Martin Conservation Association ◆ *page 160*

EDUCATION (CONT.)

ELEPHANTS

FARM ANIMALS

GORILLAS

HABITAT PROTECTION

HORSES AND BURROS

HUMANE SOCIETIES

HUMANE SOCIETIES (CONT.)

INVERTEBRATES

KOALAS

MANATEES

MARINE ANIMALS, GENERAL

OPOSSUMS

ORANGUTANS

PIGS

PRIMATES

RABBITS

SEA LIONS

SEA OTTERS

TURTLES AND TORTOISES

**CENTER
FOR MARINE
CONSERVATION**
Timber wolf
stoneware stein
♦ $39.95

**CENTER
FOR MARINE
CONSERVATION**
Dolphin picture
frame ♦ $16.50

**INTERNATIONAL
WOLF CENTER**
Fleece pullover
♦ $97.00

Organizations By State

ALABAMA

Montgomery Area Zoological Society
Montgomery ✦ *page 219*

ALASKA

Alaska Wildlife Alliance, Anchorage ✦ *page 16*
North American Wolf Society, Fairbanks ✦ *page 139*
Wolf Song of Alaska, Anchorage ✦ *page 199*

ARIZONA

North American Bear Society, Scottsdale ✦ *page 136*
Phoenix Zoo, Phoenix ✦ *page 221*
Reid Park Zoo, Tucson ✦ *page 223*
Where Wolves Rescue, Sun City ✦ *page 187*

CALIFORNIA

Actors and Others for Animals
North Hollywood ✦ *page 12*
American Cetacean Society, San Pedro ✦ *page 21*
American Mustang and Burro Association
Lincoln ✦ *page 25*
American Wildlife Rescue Service
Scotts Valley ✦ *page 29*
Animal Protection Institute of America
Sacramento ✦ *page 31*
Charles Paddock Zoo, Atascadero ✦ *page 209*
Desert Tortoise Preserve Committee
San Bernardino ✦ *page 57*

CALIFORNIA (CONT.)

ILLINOIS

INDIANA

IOWA

KANSAS

KENTUCKY

```
. . . . . . . . . . . . . . . . . . . . . . . .
```

SECTION FOUR

```
. . . . . . . . . . . . . . . . . . . . . . . .
```

WASHINGTON

WEST VIRGINIA

WISCONSIN

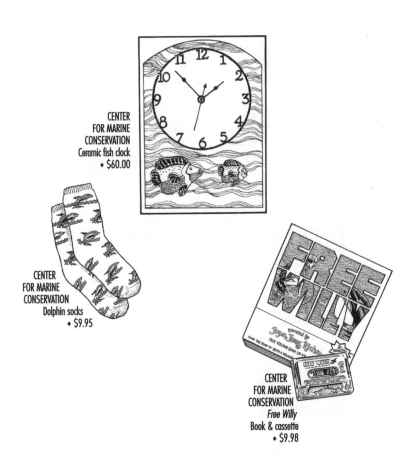

**CENTER
FOR MARINE
CONSERVATION**
Ceramic fish clock
♦ $60.00

**CENTER
FOR MARINE
CONSERVATION**
Dolphin socks
♦ $9.95

**CENTER
FOR MARINE
CONSERVATION**
Free Willy
Book & cassette
♦ $9.98

Gifts Available By Category

ADOPT-AN-ACRE

ADOPT-AN-ANIMAL

ADOPT
AN
ANIMAL

ART & ART OBJECTS

Including art bowls and plates, ceramic and decorative boxes, collector plates, figurines, lithographs, music boxes, nesting boxes, photographs, posters, prints, sculptures, sparkle globes, stained glass, statues, trinket boxes, wood carvings.

AFRICAN WILDLIFE FOUNDATION ♦ *page 15*
→ Posters: cheetah in Serengeti-$10.95 ♦ mountain gorillas in Parc de Volcans-$10.95 ♦ elephant in Amboseli-$10.95 ♦ crowned cranes in Lake Mburo-$10.95

ALASKA WILDLIFE ALLIANCE ♦ *page 16*
→ Prints: Arctic Wolves, color-$10

AMERICAN HORSE PROTECTION ASSOCIATION ♦ *page 22*
→ Prints: limited edition, of Secretariat, Northern Dancer and Man O'War, 19x13-$150 ($75 will benefit AHPA)

AMERICAN HUMANE ASSOCIATION ♦ *page 23*
→ Posters: "Making a World of Difference," full-color painting of numerous species-$12 ♦ "Get A Cat/Get A Life," 18x24-$6 ♦ "Finally Someone Who'll Treat You Like The God You Really Are," 17x25-$5 ♦ "Older Dogs Won't Give You Any Crap," 17x25-$5 ♦ "He'll Worship The Ground You Walk On. And Sniff It Too," 17x25-$5

AMERICAN MUSTANG AND BURRO ASSOCIATION ♦ *page 25*
→ Posters: limited editions, "Mustang Spring" and "Wild Horses of the Red Rock"-$40 each or $70 for both

ART
&
ART
OBJECTS

AMERICAN SOCIETY FOR THE PREVENTION OF CRUELTY TO ANIMALS ♦ *page 27*

� ➥ Posters: adoptions bus-$5 ♦ family dog-$10

ANIMAL WELFARE INSTITUTE ♦ *page 34*

➥ Prints: two cachalot whales, color, 20x26-$25

BAT CONSERVATION INTERNATIONAL ♦ *page 40*

➥ Posters: Bats of America-$9.95

CAMP FIRE CONSERVATION FUND ♦ *page 43*

➥ Limited edition prints: signed and numbered prints of the antelope in the Sonoran desert-$150 ♦ artist proofs of the antelope-$200; with black and white remarques-$500

CENTER FOR MARINE CONSERVATION ♦ *page 47*

➥ Figurines: handpainted resin of mother penguin and baby on base of simulated snow-$54 ♦ white polar bear and baby on "snow" base-$85 ♦ Venetian crystal dolphin, 6¼"-$28 ♦ two emperor penguin babies, handpainted resin-$15 ♦ hand-blown glass penguins with a base of natural amethyst crystal, 3" tall-$17.95 ♦ iridescent faceted crystal dolphin, 1¾" tall-$110 ♦ baby sea otter of cold cast resin-$32 ♦ penguin chick, polished marble composite, 4" tall-$16.95 ♦ green glass frog, 3½x3¼-$17 ♦ resting wolf in handcast stone, handpainted, 11x4⅞-$58 ♦ Galapagos turtle hatchling of gypsum stone, handpainted-$40 ♦ leaping dolphins in clear blue, green, or pink, 5" long-$14.50 ♦ turtle with babies in sand, handpainted ground hardwood fibers, 6x4½x1½-$45 ♦ mother and baby humpback handpainted on slate, signed by artist, 8x10-$86.50 ♦ crystal penguin on a frosty ice flow, 1⅞x2¼-$39.50

➥ Sculptures: sea otter pup and mother, detailed and hand

painted cast porcelain, 5x3³/₄-$37.50 ♦ sea otter and baby, handpainted and detailed, 5¹/₂" tall-$85 ♦ dolphin of smooth frosted glass, 6"-$24.50 ♦ lead crystal penguin, 2¹/₄x1⁷/₈, gift boxed-$47.50 ♦ crystal orca mother and baby, etched and sandblasted, 4x7¹/₂x2-$152 ♦ limited edition mother orca and baby, cold cast bronze, handpainted-$62.50 ♦ manatee and calf, handpainted sand sculpture, 6¹/₂x5-$20 ♦ molten glass manatee, 4" long-$20 ♦ three dolphins with undersea flora and fauna, porcelain and bronze, numbered with a certificate, 11x10¹/₂x6-$337.50 ♦ orca on wave sand sculpture, 5x4-$20 ♦ crystal breaching whale, 5³/₄x9¹/₄-$240 ♦ lead crystal dolphin, 4¹/₂x4-$98 ♦ two crystal dolphins with cobalt accents-$34.50 ♦ eight dolphins of cold rolled steel, sea green patina, 22x26-$78.50 ♦ lead crystal wolf, 6x4¹/₂-$120 ♦ underwater tropical fish on coral reef, 8¹/₂x9-$75 ♦ orca mother and baby with coral reef, porcelain, 8" tall-$175 ➝ Ceramic boxes: two dolphins, 2³/₄" diameter, white bisque finish-$12.50 ➝ Nesting boxes: handpainted penguins fit inside each other, largest is 5"-$15.95 ➝ Trinket boxes: pewter wolf with cub trinket box, 3" long-$42.50 ♦ pewter penguin and chick trinket box-$42.50 ➝ Music boxes: three dolphins ride the waves, plays "Ebb Tide"-$32.95 ➝ Sparkle globes: sea otter and sea shell in a clear globe of glitter, 3³/₄" high-$19 ♦ tropical fish globe-$20 ♦ mother turtle and coral on inside, baby turtles and eggs on base-$40 ➝ Art bowls: 24% lead crystal blue glass with raised design of dolphins, 7" diameter-$225 ➝ Prints: showering

ART & ART OBJECTS

CENTER FOR MARINE CONSERVATION (CONT)
turtles, 10x8, matted-$19.95 ♦ Orcinas Orca, 24x32-$28 ♦ set
of four seashell prints, double-matted in seafoam green and
mauve, white washed wood frames, 9x11, conch, sand dollar,
scallop, nautilus-$86.40 set; $26.50 each ♦ manatee and calf
photographic print, double-matted, gold frame with glass,
11x14-$34.95 ♦ waterproof laminated print with suction cups
to affix to bathroom wall, dolphin scene, 18½x28¾-$25 ♦ five
white baby seals, double-matted in blue and white, 9x21-$25
♦ sea otter watercolor, matted, wood framed, under plexiglass,
21½x23½-$74.95 ♦ emperor penguin chicks all in a row,
double-matted, 9x21-$25 ♦ golfing penguins, matted, 8x10-
$19.95 ♦ frogs frolicking in an old bathtub, matted, 8x10-
$19.95 ♦ red-eyed tree frogs in photograph, framed and
matted under glass, 13x23-$45 ♦ penguins stand in line for a
shower, matted, 8x10-$19.95 — Posters: sunlight filtering
through blue ocean to five humpback whales, 24x30, limited
edition-$35 ♦ Beauty and the Reef, 30x24-$25 ♦ The Earth Is
A House That Belongs To All Of Us, for children, 38x12¼-
$20 ♦ clown fish, 24x30-$25 ♦ "Megaptera" whale tail, 33x24-
$30 ♦ wolf in the snow, 24x36-$13.50 ♦ whale wall chart,
laminated, 27x40-$27.50

CHASE WILDLIFE FOUNDATION ♦ *page 49*
— Porcelain boxes: monkey, 3½"-$30 — Posters: Parrots of
Paradise-4 for $35 ♦ Jaguar Jungle-$30 ♦ Tiger Raj-$30

DALLAS ZOO ♦ *page 211*
— Small lithographs: panda bear or Siberian tiger-$35
— Large lithographs: with glass and wood frames-$300

DIAN FOSSEY GORILLA FUND ♦ *page 58*

ART
&
ART
OBJECTS

➥ Posters: "Give Me A Future"-$5 ♦ DFGF souvenir poster-
$17.25 ➥ Figurines: pewter gorilla, 2½" tall on ¼" base-$37.50

DOLPHIN RESEARCH CENTER ♦ *page 62*

➥ Prints: dolphin color photographs, 5x7 print in an 8x10 color
mat-$10.95 ➥ Posters: dolphin dancing, 18x20, "The greatest
festivals of our lives are those at which we dance ourselves."-$20

DORIS DAY PET FOUNDATION ♦ *page 64*

➥ Whimsical animal sculptures: steel with verdigris finish,
choose from three different animal poses, 4x6 to 6x6-$25 each
➥ Posters: Doris Day's "Dogs Allowed" Cypress Inn watercolor print, 19x24, signed by Doris-$29.95

FARM ANIMAL REFORM MOVEMENT ♦ *page 69*

➥ Posters: a variety of messages-$2 to $6

FARM SANCTUARY ♦ *page 70*

➥ Posters: Stop Farm Animal Abuse, color photos, 17x22-$4
♦ Cruelty in the Crate, two-color design, 17x22-$2

FRIENDS OF ANIMALS ♦ *page 78*

➥ Framable "Prayer for Animals": by Albert Schweitzer, 11x15-$7

FRIENDS OF BEAVERSPRITE ♦ *page 79*

➥ Prints: "Dorothy and the Beavers," limited edition-$6

FRIENDS OF CONSERVATION ♦ *page 80*

➥ Posters: elephant-$10

FRIENDS OF THE SEA OTTER ♦ *page 83*

➥ Glass art bowls: cobalt blue with brown otter, 14" across-
$148 ➥ Prints: signed and numbered watercolor otter by
Lo Schiavo-$22 ♦ mom and pup of soft charcoal, 17x11-$13

ART
&
ART
OBJECTS

FRIENDS OF THE SEA OTTER (CONT)

➥ Figurines: porcelain baby sea otter, 4¹/₂x3-$26.50 ♦ earth-enware otter, 8"-$39 ♦ ironwood sea otter, 6"-$24.95

➥ Decorative boxes: for pins, paper clips or a small gift, with a full color otter, black plastic-round for $4.50; square for $6.25

FRIENDS OF WASHOE ♦ *page 84*

➥ Posters: photos with information on each of the five chimps supported by contributions to Friends of Washoe-$4.95

GORILLA FOUNDATION ♦ *page 86*

➥ Posters: Koko the gorilla with her kitten-$15; autographed by Koko herself-$150 ➥ Color Prints: 3 different gorilla photos available-$25

GREAT BEAR FOUNDATION ♦ *page 87*

➥ Figurines: forepaw track cast of a 700 pound Yellowstone bear, almost 12"-$40 ➥ Prints: "The Long Trek," grizzly bear and cubs in Alaska-$150; artist proof commemorative-$500

HAWK MOUNTAIN SANCTUARY ♦ *page 89*

➥ Prints: Hawk Mountain North Lookout, breathtaking print encapsulating the aura of the mountain, 12x4-$20; 34x14-$125

HAWKWATCH INTERNATIONAL ♦ *page 90*

➥ Posters: twelve species of eagles, hawks and falcons, 24x36-$12

HOOVED ANIMAL HUMANE SOCIETY ♦ *page 94*

➥ Posters: full color horse portrait, 20x34, story and poem included-$6

HORSE POWER PROJECTS ♦ *page 95*

➥ Tonka sculptures: bronze, 7" high, edition of 125 (one half of purchase price is tax deductible)-$750 ➥ Uma sculptures:

(Japanese word for horse), bronze, 23" high x 18" long, edition of 25 (one half of purchase price is tax deductible)-$4200

HUMANE SOCIETY OF THE UNITED STATES ♦ *page 98*

➜ Posters: "Be A Pal. Prevent A Litter," Willard Scott with a dog and a cat, 18x24-$2 ♦ "Guess who pays?"-$1.50 ♦ "Animals ...It's their world too."-$2

IN DEFENSE OF ANIMALS ♦ *page 99*

➜ Posters: Lincoln and "Animal rights"-$6.25 ♦ Vivisection: Science Gone Mad-$6.25

INTERNATIONAL MARINE MAMMAL PROJECT ♦ *page 103*

➜ Posters: Earth Island-$9

INTERNATIONAL SOCIETY FOR ANIMAL RIGHTS ♦ *page 107*

➜ Posters: The Compassion Poster, Albert Schweitzer quote, 24x18-$20

INTERNATIONAL SOCIETY FOR ENDANGERED CATS ♦ *page 109*

➜ Posters: tiger, white tiger, cheetah or lion in stone-$20 ♦ miniatures available in 6 species-$6 each ♦ 3 different reclining wild cats-$10 each

INTERNATIONAL WOLF CENTER ♦ *page 111*

➜ Posters: Wolves of the High Arctic, mom and pups, 28x22-$15 ♦ Amber Eyes, wolf portrait, 24x36-$19.95 ♦ Winter Romp, wolves in the snow, 36x24-$9.95 ♦ Wolf Credo on black and white drawing, 11x17-$5.50 ♦ We Are One Family, a vision of man and wolf connected, 22x35-$25

ART
&
ART
OBJECTS

JANE GOODALL INSTITUTE ♦ *page 113*
➞ Prints: Anguish, a watercolor of a chimp and child in embrace, 24x32, numbered and signed by the artist and Jane Goodall-$450 ♦ Anguish, unnumbered, signed by the artist and Jane Goodall 24x32-$300 ♦ limited edition photo of an old zoo chimpanzee reaching out to Jane Goodall, embossed art print-$20 ➞ Posters: Anguish, with four paragraphs by Jane Goodall, 14x20-$35 ♦ Rainforests of the World, glow-in-the-dark, choose from four different regions-$12 each or $40 for all four ♦ Chimp Galahad with Jane Goodall quote-$6 ♦ Chimp Flo with offspring Flint and Fifi-$5 ♦ Fifi Termite Fishing-$6 ♦ Chimp Mike, formerly alpha male at Gombe-$6 ♦ "Protect Chimpanzees and their Environment," detailed drawing with maps and charts-$6 ♦ "The Last Tree," two chimps depicted in rain forest deforestation-$6 ♦ color your own posters: two different posters featuring 50 or 61 animals, each includes 15 non-toxic jumbo markers-$17 for each poster with markers

MISSION: WOLF ♦ *page 126*
➞ Posters: Snowdancer, color photo of Peaches, a resident wolf of Yellowstone-$25

MOUNTAIN LION FOUNDATION ♦ *page 127*
➞ Posters: mother cougar and cub-$5.95

NATURE CONSERVANCY ♦ *page 131*
➞ Prints: frogs-$50 ➞ Posters: frogs-$18 ➞ Sculptures: bear holding a candle-in-glass, natural fragrance-$34.95

NORTH AMERICAN BEAR SOCIETY ♦ *page 136*
→ Prints: "Confrontation" of bears, limited edition, 20x30-
$100; with frame-$225 ♦ "Discovering The Meadow," mother
and cub, 15x21-$25; with frame-$105

NORTH AMERICAN WOLF SOCIETY ♦ *page 139*
→ Prints: wolf portrait, 8½x11-$5 ♦ wolf and caribou in spruce
forest, 8½x11-$5

OPOSSUM SOCIETY OF CALIFORNIA ♦ *page 142*
→ Sculptures: hand-carved wooden opossum family, 4" long-$24
→ Decorative boxes: handpainted mother and baby opossum on
the front of a 9x6x8 wooden box, baby blue or beige-$33
→ Prints: black pencil drawing of an opossum, 9x12-$5

**ORANGUTAN FOUNDATION
INTERNATIONAL** ♦ *page 144*
→ Posters: featuring Camp Leakey resident, Mola, 17x22-$5
→ Prints: set of 4, 8½x11, orangutans, signed by the artist-$35
♦ Hearts of Borneo, 17½x20½-$25   → Figurines: 8" tall adult
male orangutan of natural ceramics-$25

PACIFIC WILDLIFE PROJECT ♦ *page 147*
→ Prints: "Fiesta De Las Golondrinas" (Return of the Cliff
Swallows), 8x10 matted-$20; 9x12 matted-$35

PEREGRINE FUND ♦ *page 153*
→ Crystal sculptures: falcon, 10x6-$250 ♦ peregrine falcon,
8x7-$180 ♦ baby owl, 3½"-$43.50   → Collector plates:
Cooper's hawk, peregrine falcon with chicks, bald eagle or
burrowing owls and chicks-$47.50   → Russian stacking owls:
five wooden owls nest inside each other-$25

ART
&
ART
OBJECTS

ART
&
ART
OBJECTS

PET PRIDE OF NEW YORK ♦ *page 154*
➥ Posters: Peter Berg Carousel-$15

PREDATOR PROJECT ♦ *page 157*
➥ Limited edition prints: grizzly bear or wolf, 20x24 lithograph -$100

PURPLE MARTIN CONSERVATION ASSOCIATION ♦ *page 160*
➥ Photographs: purple martins in color, eight different, unframed, 8½x11-$19.95 for the set of 8; $39.95 for any single photo framed

REDWINGS HORSE SANCTUARY ♦ *page 163*
➥ Posters: 11x17 color photo of adopted animals-$10

ROCKY MOUNTAIN RAPTOR PROGRAM ♦ *page165*
➥ Prints: limited edition prints of great horned owl, American kestrel or barn owl-$50 ♦ framed, limited edition peregrine falcon-$100

SAN FRANSCISCO SPCA ♦ *page 166*
➥ Posters: Computa-Cat-$12 ♦ Digital-Dog-$12

SANGRE DE CRISTO ANIMAL PROTECTION ♦ *page 167*
➥ Posters: Artists for Animals-$15 ♦ Wolf (supports wolf education)-$10

SAVE THE DOLPHINS PROJECT ♦ *page 169*
➥ Posters: Earth Island - Save It, 30x23-$9

SAVE THE WHALES ♦ *page 171*
➥ Posters: Kissing Dolphins, 24x33-$24.95 ♦ Megaptera, 33x24-$24.95 ♦ Orca Trio, 26x35-$24.95 ♦ La Petite Baleine, 33x24-$24.95 ♦ Maui Dawn, 35x26-$24.95

ART & ART OBJECTS

WILD HORSE SANCTUARY ♦ *page 191*
— Prints: The Mustangs, color-$85 — Posters: Wild Horse Sanctuary, black and white with varnish, 20x28-$15

WILDLIFE PRESERVATION TRUST INTERNATIONAL ♦ *page 195*
— Posters: Animals Of The Rainforest, 36x24, laminated-$8.50 ♦ Lemurs Of Madagascar, 18x24-$10 ♦ Wolf, 38½x27½, laminated-$10 ♦ Liberian Wildlife, 24x18-$1 ♦ Fragile Earth, 22x28, laminated, recycled paper-$9.50 ♦ The Big Cats, 26¾x38½, laminated-$10 ♦ Turtles And Tortoises, 26¾x38½, laminated-$10 ♦ Snakes, 26¾x38½, laminated-$10 ♦ Frogs And Toads, 26¾x38½, laminated-$10 ♦ Birds Of Prey, 26¾x38½, laminated-$10 ♦ Butterflies, 26¾x38½, laminated-$10 ♦ Birds Of The Woods, 26¾x38½, laminated-$10 ♦ The Tropical Rainforest, 26¾x38½, laminated-$10 ♦ Creatures Of The Forest, 26¾x38½, laminated-$10 — Prints: Lemurs Of Madagascar, 18x24, signed and numbered -$150 ♦ Liberian Wildlife, 24x18, signed and numbered-$150

WILLIAM HOLDEN WILDLIFE FOUNDATION ♦ *page 196*
— Posters: collage drawing of William Holden, Kenyan wildlife and Africa-$18

WOLF HAVEN INTERNATIONAL ♦ *page 197*
— Posters: set of three, 2 posters of a cub and another of an adult wolf which has educational information on the back, each measures 16x22-$6

WOLF SONG OF ALASKA ♦ *page 199*
— Prints: Spirit of the Wolf, limited edition print of a Northwestern

Indian symbol of the wolf, signed and numbered -$65 ◆ Eminent Domain, two wolf packs eye each other warily, signed and numbered edition,18x24-$195 ◆ Wilderness Nexus, wolves and a musher, signed and numbered limited edition, 18x24-$145
— Posters: Eyes of the Night, wolf and owl, signed, 16x24-$30

ART
&
ART
OBJECTS

WORLD BIRD SANCTUARY ◆ *page 201*
— Wood sculptures: eagles and owls, small-$12; large-$20; extra large-$40; custom order-$60

Books

BOOKS

Including blank books, bookmarks, book plates, cookbooks, diaries, field guides, journals.

ADOPT-A-COW ◆ *page 13*
— Cookbooks: vegetarian-$5

AFRICAN WILDLIFE FOUNDATION ◆ *page 15*
— Books: *The African Safari*, 750 color photos of African wildlife-$22.95

ALASKA WILDLIFE ALLIANCE ◆ *page 16*
— Books: *Wolf Zoobook*, for children-$3

ALLIED WHALE ◆ *page 18*
— Books: *The Field Guide to Whales*-$24

AMERICAN ANTI-VIVISECTION SOCIETY ◆ *page 19*
— Animal Rights Bookshelf: a large selection of over 35 books-$4.95 to $24.95

AMERICAN BIRDING ASSOCIATION ◆ *page 20*
— Books: large selection of atlases and field guides-$4.95 to $50

BOOKS

AMERICAN HORSE PROTECTION ASSOCIATION ♦ *page 22*

← Books: *To Love A Horse,* spiral-bound with illustrations-$20 ($10 benefits AHPA) ♦ *America's Last Wild Horses,* 320 pages and 60 photos-$14.95 ($7.95 benefits AHPA)

AMERICAN HUMANE ASSOCIATION ♦ *page 23*

← Bookmarks: black and white drawings on colorful bookmarks of a dog, cat, horse, fish, bird or small mammal-$2 for the set of six

AMERICAN LIVESTOCK BREEDS CONSERVANCY ♦ *page 24*

← Books: a variety of books available on rare breeds-$4 to $108

AMERICAN MUSTANG AND BURRO ASSOCIATION ♦ *page 25*

← Books: large selection of reference, training and care, stories and childrens' books-$3.95 to $27.50

AMERICAN SOCIETY FOR THE PREVENTION OF CRUELTY TO ANIMALS ♦ *page 27*

← Books: *For Kids Who Love Animals*-$6.95 ♦ *Complete Dog Training Manual*-$22.95 ♦ *Complete Dog Care Manual*-$24.95 ♦ *Complete Cat Care Manual*-$24.95 ♦ *ASPCA Pet Care Guide for Kids: Birds, Guinea Pigs, Kittens, Rabbits, Fish, Hamsters, Puppies*-$9.95

AMERICAN VEGAN SOCIETY ♦ *page 28*

← Cookbooks: over 60 cookbooks with vegan, near vegan, and vegetarian recipes-$1.75 to $25 ← Books: over 300 books on religion, nutrition, animal oppression, the environment, vivisection, travel and shopping-$3 to $25

ANIMAL RIGHTS COALITION ◆ *page 33*   BOOKS
— Books: *Diet for A New America*-$13.95 ◆ *Simply Vegan*-$12
◆ *The Power of the Plate*-$10.95 — Cookbooks: *New Farm
Vegetarian Cookbook* -$7.95 ◆ *ARC Cookbook II*-$2 ◆ *Tofu Cookery*-
$11.95

ANIMAL WELFARE INSTITUTE ◆ *page 34*
— Books: a large selection of books on animal rights and
endangered species-$5 to $16

BALTIMORE ZOO ◆ *page 205*
— Books: *Farmyard Animals*-$7.95 ◆ *A is for Animals*, pop-up
book-$15.95 ◆ *Who Comes To The Waterhole*-$13.95 ◆ *Journey
Of The Red-Eyed Tree Frog*-$16 ◆ *Big Cats*-$14.95 — Journals:
zebra or tiger-$9.50

BAT CONSERVATION INTERNATIONAL ◆ *page 40*
— Books: *Extremely Weird Bats*-$10.95 ◆ *Zoobooks/ Bats*, for
children-$3 ◆ *Bats: Mysterious Flyers of the Night*, for children-
$7.95 ◆ *It Goes eeeeeeeee!*, for children-$14.95 ◆ *Bats of the World*-
$20.95 ◆ *Golden Guide/Bats of the World*-$5.95 ◆ *The World of
Bats*-$30.95 ◆ *The Bat in My Pocket*-$10.95 ◆ *Bat Bomb: WW II's
Secret Weapon*-$25.95 ◆ *America's Neighborhood Bats*-$10.95 ◆ *Bat
House Builder's Handbook*-$6.95 ◆ *Stellaluna*, for children-$15.95 ◆
Taking Katy for a Nightride, for children-$5.95

**CARIBBEAN CONSERVATION
CORPORATION** ◆ *page 45*
— Books: 5 books on sea turtles and habitats by the CCC
founding director, Archie Carr-$19.95 to $31.50 ◆ *Turtles And
Tortoises*-$22.95 ◆ *The Quetzal And The Macaw*-$27.95

BOOKS **CENTER FOR MARINE CONSERVATION** ♦ *page 47*
➥ Books: *Nature Hide and Seek*, underwater wildlife for ages 5 to
9-$12.95 ♦ *Alpha-Books & Count With Us*, 36 little books of each
letter and number, for toddlers-$19.95 ♦ *Look Inside The Ocean*,
for children-$11.95 ♦ *Sam the Sea Cow*, ages 4 to 8-$7.95
♦ *Nature by the Numbers*, pop-up pictures, ages 2 to 5-$12.95
♦ *Sharks and Other Creatures of the Deep*-$11.95 ♦ *A Is For
Animals*, learn ABC's-$15.95

CENTER FOR WHALE RESEARCH ♦ *page 48*
➥ Books: *Killer Whales*-$20

**COMMITTEE TO ABOLISH SPORT
HUNTING** ♦ *page 51*
➥ Books: *The American Hunting Myth*-$14.95

DIAN FOSSEY GORILLA FUND ♦ *page 58*
➥ Journals: hard cover with blank pages-$10

DOLPHIN RESEARCH CENTER ♦ *page 62*
➥ Books: *A Charm of Dolphins*-$9.95

DORIS DAY ANIMAL LEAGUE ♦ *page 63*
➥ Books: *Pets-R-Permitted: Travel & Pets Directory*-$9.95

DORIS DAY PET FOUNDATION ♦ *page 64*
➥ Books: *Pet Heroes*-$6.59 ♦ *Butch's Biscuit Book*-$6 ♦ *Letters to
Strongheart*-$7.50 ♦ *Kinship All Her Life*-$7.50 ♦ *Doris Day: Her
Own Story*-$9.50 ➥ Canine cookbooks: *No Barking at the Table*,
canine recipes-$11.99

ELEPHANT RESEARCH FOUNDATION ♦ *page 66*
➥ Books: *Elephants: The Deciding Decade*-$20

FARM ANIMAL REFORM MOVEMENT ♦ *page 69*
➥ Books: *Animal Factories*-$13 ♦ *Diet For a New America*-$14

♦ *Vegan Nutrition*-$8 ♦ *Pregnancy, Children and the Vegan Diet*- BOOKS
$10 ‒ Cookbooks: *Cookbook for People Who Love Animals*,
vegan recipes-$10

FARM SANCTUARY ♦ *page 70*
‒ Books: *What's Wrong With Eating Meat?*-3.50 ♦ *`Twas The
Night Before Thanksgiving*, for children-$15.95 ♦ *The Chicken
Gave It To Me*, a story for children about a chicken on a
mission to make the world a more caring, sensitive and
humane place-$12.95 ‒ Cookbooks: *The High Road To Health*
by Lindsay Wagner, vegan recipes-$12 ♦ *The Uncheese
Cookbook*, dairy-free cheese recipes-$11.95 ♦ *The Low-Fat
Jewish Vegetarian*, 150 recipes-$15 ♦ *Famous Vegetarians and
Their Favorite Recipes*, includes Ghandi's chapatis and George
Harrison's lentil soup-$14.95 ♦ *The New Farm Vegetarian
Cookbook*-$8.95

FEMINISTS FOR ANIMAL RIGHTS ♦ *page 72*
‒ Cookbooks: *The Perennial Political Palate*-$16.95
‒ Books: *The Sexual Politics of Meat*-$14.95 ♦ *Ecofeminism:
Women, Animals, Nature*-$19.95

FLORIDA VOICES FOR ANIMALS ♦ *page 75*
‒ Books: many on animal welfare-$4 to $10

FRIENDS OF BEAVERSPRITE ♦ *page 79*
‒ Books: *The Beaver*, for young people-$6.95 ♦ *Lily Pond*-$17
for hardcover; $9 for softcover ♦ *Beaversprite, My Years Building
an Animal Sanctuary*-$15 for hardcover; $10 for softcover
♦ *Best of Beaver Defenders*-$10 ♦ *Hoofmarks*-$22.95
‒ Cookbooks: *Simply Vegan*-$12

BOOKS **FRIENDS OF THE SEA OTTER** ♦ *page 83*
➥ Bookplates: otter design-$12 for 4 ➥ Books: assorted sea otter titles for children and adults in hardback and paperback-$3.50 to $12.95

GORILLA FOUNDATION ♦ *page 86*
➥ Books: *The Education of Koko*-$15

GREAT BEAR FOUNDATION ♦ *page 87*
➥ Books: various books on bears, including coffee table books and children's books-$4.50 to $40

GREYHOUND FRIENDS ♦ *page 88*
➥ Books: *The Greyhound Who Wanted a Greyhound Friend*, an illustrated children's story-$5

HAWK MOUNTAIN SANCTUARY ♦ *page 89*
➥ Books: *The Mountain And The Migration*, a guide to the Sanctuary-$13.95

HAWKWATCH INTERNATIONAL ♦ *page 90*
➥ Books: a selection of field guides, raptor information, children's books, and coffee table books-$3 to $59.95

IN DEFENSE OF ANIMALS ♦ *page 99*
➥ Books and cookbooks: vegetarian cookbooks, childrens' books and animal rights issues-$4.95 to $19.95

INTERNATIONAL CRANE FOUNDATION ♦ *page 101*
➥ Books: *Reflections: The Story of Cranes*-$4.95

INTERNATIONAL FUND FOR ANIMAL WELFARE ♦ *page 102*
➥ Books: *Seasons Of The Seal*-$27.95 ♦ *Red Ice: My Fight To Save The Seals*-$7.95

INTERNATIONAL PRIMATE PROTECTION LEAGUE ♦ *page 105*

→ Books: *Baboon Orphan*, hardcover-$8 ♦ *The Apes*, hardcover -$16 ♦ *Among the Orangutans*, softcover-$8; hardcover-$15

INTERNATIONAL SOCIETY FOR ANIMAL RIGHTS ♦ *page 107*

→ Books and cookbooks: large selection of animal rights topics and vegetarian cookbooks-$4.95 to $20

INTERNATIONAL WOLF CENTER ♦ *page 111*

→ Books: *Following The Pack*-$19.95 ♦ *Society Of Wolves: National Parks and the Battle Over the Wolf*-$29.95 ♦ *Out Among The Wolves*, essays-$14.95 ♦ *Of Wolves And Men*-$17 ♦ *Wolves of the Minong: The Isle Royal's Wild Community*-$18.95 ♦ *Zoobooks: Wolves*, grades 5 to 12-$2.95 ♦ *Wolves*, for the young reader-$4.95 ♦ *Wolves for Kids*, ages 3 to 5-$6.95 ♦ *Timber Wolf in Wisconsin*-$17.95 ♦ *The Wolf*-$15.95 ♦ *The Arctic Wolf: Living With The Pack*-$19.95 ♦ *The Way of the Wolf*-$29.95

INTERSPECIES COMMUNICATION ♦ *page 112*

→ Books: *Dolphin Dreamtime*-$8.25 ♦ *Why We Garden*-$4.25

JANE GOODALL INSTITUTE ♦ *page 113*

→ Books authored by Jane Goodall: *Grub, The Bush Baby*-$14 ♦ *In The Shadow of Man*-$15 ♦ *My Life With The Chimpanzees*-$3.50 ♦ *The Chimpanzee Family Book* (UNICEF and UNESCO Children's Book of the Year for 1989)-$18 ♦ *Through A Window* (sequel to In The Shadow of Man)-$10 ♦ *Visions of Caliban* (written with Dale Peterson)-$23

BOOKS **JUSTICE FOR ANIMALS** ♦ *page 115*
→ Bookmarks: magnetic, animal designs-$4 → Books: various titles available-$8.95 to $12.95

LEND-A-PAW RELIEF ORGANIZATION ♦ *page 116*
→ Books: *All I Need to Know I Learned From My Cat*-$5 ♦ *Cat Owner's Manual*-$6.98

LOS ANGELES AUDUBON SOCIETY ♦ *page 117*
→ Books: large selection of birding topics around the world-$1.95 to $295

MAINE ANIMAL COALITION ♦ *page 119*
→ Books: *Old McDonald's "Factory Farm"*-$14 ♦ *Animal Liberation* ♦ *The Vegetarian Self-Defense Manual*-$5 ♦ *Kids Can Save The Animals*-$7 ♦ *Animals, Nature and Albert Schweitzer*-$5
→ Cookbooks: *Total Vegetarian Cooking*-$3

MID-ATLANTIC GREAT DANE RESCUE LEAGUE ♦ *page 125*
→ Cookbooks: $7.50

MOUNTAIN LION FOUNDATION ♦ *page 127*
→ Books: *Cougar: The American Lion*-$19.95 ♦ *Crimes Against the Wild*, about poaching in California-$10

NATURE CONSERVANCY ♦ *page 131*
→ Books: *Two Eagles/Dos Auguilas*, captures the rich habitats of the wildlife of the 2,000 mile U.S./Mexico borderlands-$55 ♦ *Return of the Eagle*-$19.95 ♦ *Preserving Eden*-$39.95 ♦ *Tallgrass Prairie*-$29.50 ♦ *Heart of the Land*-$24

NETWORK FOR OHIO ANIMAL ACTION ♦ *page 132*
→ Books: a variety of animal rights issues-$2 to $12

NEW ENGLAND ANTI-VIVISECTION SOCIETY ♦ *page 133*

BOOKS

➤ Books: *The Cat Who Came for Christmas,* Cleveland Amory-$18.50 ♦ *The Cat and the Curmudgeom,* Cleveland Amory-$18.50 ♦ *The Best Cat Ever,* Cleveland Amory-$18.50 ♦ *The Compassionate Cook*-$8.99 ♦ *Food for Life*-$13 ♦ *The Power of Your Plate*-$12.50 ♦ *A Physicians Slimming Guide*-$5.95 ♦ *Free the Animals*-$13.95 ♦ *The Cruel Deception*-$14 ♦ *The Rights of Nature*-$12.95 ♦ *Kids Can Save the Animals*-$6.99

NORTH AMERICAN BEAR SOCIETY ♦ *page 136*

➤ Books: *The Last Grizzly*-$22 ♦ *The Grizzly in the Southwest*-$22 ♦ *King of the Ice*-$12.95

NORTH AMERICAN LOON FUND ♦ *page 137*

➤ Books: *Loon Lake,* for children-$13.95 ♦ *Love of Loons*-$14.95 ♦ *The Common Loon: Spirit of Northern Lakes*-$35 ♦ *Loon Notes*-$3.95 ♦ *Loon Magic*-$19.95; $50 for cloth

NORTH AMERICAN VEGETARIAN SOCIETY ♦ *page 138*

➤ Cookbooks: over 30 cookbooks with vegetarian recipes-$5 to $26.95 ➤ Books: over 70 books on vegetarianism, nutrition, animal rights, health, vivisection, philosophy, religion, natural gardening, natural child bearing and rearing, children's books, dining-out guides-$2.50 to $24.95

OCEANIC PROJECT DOLPHIN ♦ *page 140*

➤ Books: *Oceanic Society Field Guide to the Gray Whale*-$5.95 ♦ *Oceanic Field Guide to the Humpback Whale*-$5.95

BOOKS

ORANGUTAN FOUNDATION INTERNATIONAL ♦ *page 144*
➥ Books: *Reflections of Eden: My Life in Borneo with the Orangutans* by Dr. Birute Galdikas-$25 ♦ *Among the Orangutans,* for children-$7/paperback

PACIFIC WHALE FOUNDATION ♦ *page 146*
➥ Books: *Hawaii's Humpback Whales*-$15 ♦ *Humpback Whales of Australia*-$19.95

PAWS WITH A CAUSE ♦ *page 148*
➥ Cookbooks: T*oastin' the Dogs: Recipes of the Famous and Distinguished*-$16.95

PEOPLE FOR ANIMAL RIGHTS ♦ *page 151*
➥ Books: *Beyond Beef*-$21 ♦ *Free The Animals*-$13.95

PEOPLE FOR THE ETHICAL TREATMENT OF ANIMALS ♦ *page 152*
➥ Cookbooks: *The Compassionate Cook,* a vegetarian cookbook serves up the favorite recipes of PETA staff and members that make cooking fun and easy, 224 pages-$9.95

PEREGRINE FUND ♦ *page 153*
➥ Books: over 45 books for children and adults about birds

PET PRIDE OF NEW YORK ♦ *page 154*
➥ Books: *Good Bye My Friend,* dealing with the loss of an animal friend-$5 ➥ Cat cookbooks: *Cookbook for Cats: Recipes for a Healthy Cat*-$8.50

PROGRESSIVE ANIMAL WELFARE SOCIETY ♦ *page 159*
➥ Books: over 200 books on animal rights, activism, pet care, anti-vivisection, endangered species, factory farming, animals in entertainment, health, feminism, non-violence, religion, poetry,

reference, vegetarianism and children's books-$1.25 to $23.95   BOOKS
→ Cookbooks: over 80 books with vegan, vegetarian and vegetarian catering recipes-$3.50 to $26.95

PURPLE MARTIN CONSERVATION ASSOCIATION ♦ *page 160*
→ Books: over 35 books on bird house construction, bird behavior, bird feeding, the environment, Peterson field guides to plants and animals-$5.95 to $25.95

RACINE ZOO ♦ *page 223*
→ Cookbooks: 100 pages, includes favorite recipes from Racine area restaurants-$12

RAPTOR CENTER AT THE UNIVERSITY OF MINNESOTA ♦ *page 161*
→ Books: over 50 books for adults and children including educational, scientific and coffee table color photo books; the most popular titles are: *Raptor Rescue! An Eagle Flies Free*, the story of an eagle's recovery from admission to the raptor center to rehabilitation to release, color photos for elementary school age-$16.95 ♦ *Return of the Eagle*, celebrates the upgrading of the bald eagle from endangered to threatened, 100 color photos-$19.95 ♦ *Raptors: Birds of Prey*, intimate portraits, personal vignettes and revealing statistics, over 100 color photos, for teens and adults-$18.95 ♦ *Owls: Their Lives and Behavior*, coffee table book with color photos-$38

ROAR FOUNDATION ♦ *page 164*
→ Books: *The Cats of Shambala* by Tippi Hedren and Ted Taylor, recounts the history of Shambala and big cat behavior-$23 ♦ *The World According to Natasha* tells of Tippi Hedren's

BOOKS **ROAR FOUNDATION** (CONT)

philosophies and her beloved Siberian tiger-$20 ♦ *Lion Tales*, a love story about the lions of Shambala-$20

ROCKY MOUNTAIN RAPTOR PROGRAM ♦ *page 165*

— Books: *Zoobooks of Eagles, Owls, Birds of Prey or Endangered Animals*-$3.50 each ♦ *Birds of Prey*-$7.95

SANGRE DE CRISTO ANIMAL PROTECTION ♦ *page 167*

— Cookbooks: *Country Kitchen*, vegetarian-$11.95 — Books: over a dozen books on animal rights and animal care-$3.95 to $28

SAVE THE MANATEE CLUB ♦ *page 170*

— Books: *Manatees and Dugongs*-$27.95 ♦ *Sam The Sea Cow*, for children-$12.50 ♦ *The Manatee*, an introduction to manatees for young readers-$15.95

SAVE THE WHALES ♦ *page 171*

— Books: *Humphrey, The Humpback Whale*, for children-$5.50

SEA TURTLE RESTORATION PROJECT ♦ *page 173*

— Books: *The Turtle And The Island*, children's folk tale from Papua New Guinea-$13.95 ♦ *Tracks In The Sand*, life cycle of the loggerhead sea turtle for children-$14.95 ♦ *The Sea Turtle: So Excellent A Fish*-$15.95

SUNCOAST SEABIRD SANCTUARY ♦ *page 175*

— Books: a variety of books on birds, manatees, shells etc.-$4 to $12

SUPRESS ♦ *page 176*

— Books: *Slaughter of the Innocent*, proves the fraud of animal experimentation-$8.95 ♦ *Naked Empress*, an exposé on the corruption of the chemical and pharmaceutical industries-$16

♦ *1000 Doctors Against Vivisection*, doctors and scientists around BOOKS
the world speak out against the medieval ritual of animal
experimentation-$19

SUTTON AVIAN RESEARCH CENTER ♦ *page 177*
➤ Books: *Hawks in Flight*-$9.95 ♦ *Eagles, Hunters Of The Sky*,
children's story and activities-$6.95 ➤ Bookmarks: eagles or
flowers, plastic coated-$1

TIMBER WOLF PRESERVATION SOCIETY ♦ *page 179*
➤ Books: *Never Cry Wolf*-$14 ♦ *Wolf Pack*-$13.60

TRUMPETER SWAN SOCIETY ♦ *page 181*
➤ Books: *Swans of the World in Nature, History, Myth and Art*-
$26.95 ♦ *Koog and Tina*-$10

UNITED POULTRY CONCERNS ♦ *page 182*
➤ Cookbooks: *Instead of Chicken, Instead of Turkey: A Poultryless
"Poultry" Potpourri*, vegetarian recipes-$9.95 ➤ Books: *Nature's
Chicken, The Story Of Today's Chicken Farms*, for children-$5.95
♦ *Animal Place: Where Magical Things Happen*, for children-$8.99
♦ *A Boy, A Chicken & The Lion Of Judah: How Ari Became A
Vegetarian*, for children-$8

VEGETARIAN RESOURCE GROUP ♦ *page 183*
➤ Books: *A Vegetarian Sourcebook*-$13 ♦ *The Vegetarian's Self-
Defense Manual*-$6 ♦ *Vegetarian Journal Reports*-$12 ♦ *Judaism And
Vegetarianism*-$14 ♦ *Raising Your Family Naturally*-$15 ♦ *Vegetarian
Journal's Guide to Natural Foods Restaurants in the U.S. and Canada*-
$15 ➤ Cookbooks: *Meatless Meals For Working People*-$6 ♦ *Simply
Vegan*-$12 ♦ *Tofu Cookery*-$17 ♦ *Ecological Cooking*-$12.50 ♦ *The
New Laurel's Kitchen*-$24 ♦ *No Cholesterol Passover Recipes*-$15

BOOKS **VEGETARIAN RESOURCE GROUP (CONT)**

• *Lean And Luscious And Meatless*-$18 • *Vegetarian Quantity Recipes*-$15 • *The New Farm Vegetarian Cookbook* -$9.50 • *Leprechaun Cake And Other Tales: A Vegetarian Story-Cookbook* -$12 • *Simple, Lowfat & Vegetarian*-$15 • *The Lowfat Jewish Vegetarian Cookbook*-$15

WHALE ADOPTION PROJECT • *page 184*

– Books: *I Wonder If I'll See A Whale*, for children-$14.95 • *Baby Whale*, children's color paperback-$1.95 • *Where the Whales Are*-$12.95 • *Elephants, The Deciding Decade*-$35 • *New England Whales*, color paperback-$6.95 • *Sierra Club Handbook of Whales and Dolphins*-$16.95 • *Crystal: The Story of a Real Baby Whale*, children's-$12.95 • *Wings in the Sea, The Humpback Whale*-$10.05

WHALE CONSERVATION INSTITUTE • *page 185*

– Bookmarks: southern right whale, humpback or orca, 24k gold finish-$5.95 – Books: *The Whale Watcher's Guide Book*-$12.95

WHALE MUSEUM • *page 186*

– Books: *A Guide To Marine Mammals Of Greater Puget Sound*-$14.95 • *Whales For Kids*-$6.95 • *Zoobooks*, whales, dolphins and porpoises or seals and sea lions-$3.25 • *Sitiwi-A Whale's Story*, first year of an orca's life, for children-$9.95 • *Whale In The Sky*, Northwest native legend-$4.99 • *Whales-Gentle Giants*, grades 1 to 3-$3.50• *Orca's Song*, a retelling of a Northwest native myth-$5.95 • *Davy's Dream*, a young boy's adventures with wild orcas-$9.95 • *A Whale Named Henry*-$8.95 • *A Look Inside the Ocean*, a poke-and-look learning book-$11.95 • *Ocean Facts*-$5.95 • *Orca-The Whale Called Killer*-$12.95 • *Killer Whales*, light text with

photos-$14.95 ♦ *Killer Whales*, by three regional researchers-   BOOKS
$19.95 ♦ *Sierra Club Handbook of Whales and Dolphins*-$18
♦ *Meeting the Whales-Equinox Guide To The Giants of the Deep*-
$9.95 ♦ *The Book Of Whales*, reference book of all species-$35
♦ *Dolphins & Porpoises*, reference of all species-$24.95 ♦ *Guardians
of the Whales*, a quest to study whales in the wild-$34.95 ♦ *Orcas,
Eagles & Kings-The Natural History of Puget Sound & Georgia Strait*,
coffee table book-$29.95

WILD CANID SURVIVAL AND RESEARCH
CENTER ♦ *page 189*
— Books: over 15 children's books-$3.50 to $14.95 ♦ over 25
adults' books-$3.95 to $29.95 — Bookmarks: "Save A Place
For Me-Extinction Is Forever," Mexican wolf-25¢ each
— Blank books: 5x7 spiral-bound-$10

WILDLIFE HABITAT ENHANCEMENT
COUNCIL ♦ *page 194*
— Field guides: (Roger Tory Peterson basic series): *Eastern
Birds*-$15.95 ♦ *Western Birds*, third edition-$16.95 ♦ *Mammals*-
$14.95 ♦ *Reptiles & Amphibians of Eastern/Central North America*-
$16.95 ♦ *Western Reptiles & Amphibians*-$16.95 ♦ *Eastern Trees*
-$14.95 ♦ *Western Trees*-$15.95

WILDLIFE PRESERVATION TRUST
INTERNATIONAL ♦ *page 195*
— Books: *Birds Of Prey*-$35 ♦ *State Of The Ark*-$13 ♦ *Durrell In
Russia*-$15 ♦ *The Ark's Anniversary*-$15 ♦ *My Family And Other
Animals*-$8 ♦ *Finding Out About...Jungles, Mountains or Deserts*,
age 7 to 9-$4.50 for softcover ♦ *Toby The Tortoise*, for children-
$14 ♦ *Conservation Guides, Endangered Species, Trees And Forests*

BOOKS **WILDLIFE PRESERVATION TRUST INT'L (CONT)**
or *Rivers And Seas*, for children-$4.50 each; $10.95 for a com
bined volume ♦ *Mysteries And Marvels*, amazing aspects of
nature series for ages 8-10, *Animal World, Bird Life, Reptile
World, Insect Life, Ocean Life, Plant Life*-$5.95 each for soft-
cover; $21.95 for the combined volume ♦ *World Wildlife*,
habitats series for ages 8-12, *Rainforest, Polar, Mountain or
Grasslands*-$6.95 each for softcover; $13.95 each for hardcover
♦ *Hook-A-Book*, for ages 18 months to 3 years, books that hook
onto each other, Lemur, Monkey, Opossum or Bat-$3.99 each
♦ *Junkyard Bandicoots*, tales of endangered species for age 10
up-$9.95

WOLF HAVEN INTERNATIONAL ♦ *page 197*
→ Books: *Discovering Wolves*, illustrated activity book for grades 2
to 5-$4.95 ♦ *Wild Wolves*, for early readers in grades 1 to 3-$3.50

WOLF SONG OF ALASKA ♦ *page 199*
→ Books: *Brother Wolf*, a narrative of the kinship of wolves and
humans, 140 photos-$19.95 and $40 ♦ *Eyes of the Gray Wolf*, for
all ages, 13 pages, hardcover-$13.95 ♦ *White Wolf*-$40 ♦ *Of
Wolves and Men*-$17 ♦ *Wolves*-$20 ♦ *The Return of the Wolf*-$16.95

**WOODSTOCK ANIMAL RIGHTS
MOVEMENT** ♦ *page 200*
→ Cookbooks: many cookbooks available, including *Simply
Vegan*-$12 ♦ *Ecological Cooking*-$10.95 ♦ *The Gradual Vegetarian*-
$12 ♦ *Friendly Foods Cookbook*-$16.95 ♦ *The Compassionate Cook*-
$8.99 ♦ *Tofu Cookery*-$14.95 ♦ *The Vegan Cookbook*-$10.95
♦ *Famous Vegetarians And Their Recipes*-$14.95 ♦ *The Cookbook For*

People Who Love Animals-$9.95 ♦ *The Single Vegan*-$9 ♦ *Eat For* BOOKS
Strength-Oil Free-$7.95 ♦ *The Vegetarian Times Cookbook*-$13
♦ *I Can't Believe This Has No Sugar Cookbook*-$9.95 ➡ Books:
many available including *Kids Can Save The Animals*-$6.99 ♦
Brother Eagle, Sister Sky: A Message From Chief Seattle, all ages-
$16 ♦ *A Squirrel's Tale*, children-$9.95 ♦ *There's A Mouse About
The House*, children-$9.95 to $14 ♦ *The New Natural Cat: A
Complete Guide For Finicky Owners*-$14 ♦ *Dr. Pitcairn's Complete
Guide To Natural Health For Dogs and Cats*-$12.95 ♦ *Vegetarian
Cats And Dogs*-$13.95 ♦ *Diet For A New America*-$13.95 ♦ *Dr.
Dean Ornish's Program For Reversing Heart Disease*-$15 ♦ *Animal
Liberation*-$9.95 ♦ *Save The Animals*-$4.95 ♦ *Radical
Vegetarianism*-$9.95 ♦ *Vegan Nutrition: Pure And Simple*-$10

XERCES SOCIETY ♦ *page 203*
➡ Journals: *Conversations with Bugs*, hardcover, featuring decorative drawings of invertebrates, 128 pages-$15.35 ➡ Books:
Naturalist, a memoir by Harvard biologist and Pulitzer prize-
winning author Edward O. Wilson who writes of his passion for
science and his commitment to conservation-$29.20

Calendars
CALENDARS

ALASKA WILDLIFE ALLIANCE ♦ *page 16*
➡ Alaska wildlife-$10

ALLIANCE AGAINST ANIMAL ABUSE ♦ *page 17*
➡ Horse photos-$11

**AMERICAN MUSTANG AND BURRO
ASSOCIATION** ♦ *page 25*
➡ Wild horses-$9.95

CALENDARS **ANIMAL ALLIES** ♦ *page 30*
— Color photos of cats and dogs-$5.95

ANIMAL RESCUE ♦ *page 32*
— $7.50

CENTER FOR MARINE CONSERVATION ♦ *page 47*
— Perpetual calendar of handpainted resin features month, day, and special occasion pieces which attach with Velcro, penguin design, 17x13¼-$65

DALLAS ZOO ♦ *page 211*
— "Great Apes"-$8.95 ♦ "Big Cat"-$9.95 ♦ "Wolfsong"-$10.95

DOLPHIN RESEARCH CENTER ♦ *page 62*
— Dolphin photography-$10.99

FRIENDS OF THE SEA OTTER ♦ *page 83*
— Otter design-$7.95

GREYHOUND FRIENDS ♦ *page 88*
— Museum quality photographs-$10

INTERNATIONAL MARINE MAMMAL PROJECT ♦ *page 103*
— Dolphins-$11

INTERNATIONAL WOLF CENTER ♦ *page 111*
— Color wolf photos-$9.95

JUSTICE FOR ANIMALS ♦ *page 115*
— Full color with animal pictures-$5

MOUNTAIN LION FOUNDATION ♦ *page 127*
— Full color photos of the great cats of North America-$10.95

NORTH AMERICAN LOON FUND ♦ *page 137*
— Loon color photos-$9.95

PET PRIDE OF NEW YORK ♦ *page 154*
→ Photos of Pet Pride adoptees-$7.50

PROGRESSIVE ANIMAL WELFARE SOCIETY ♦ *page 159*
→ Animal stories and photos-$7

RAPTOR CENTER AT THE UNIVERSITY OF MINNESOTA ♦ *page 161*
→ Bald eagles or owls, for wall-$10.99

REDWINGS HORSE SANCTUARY ♦ *page 163*
→ Color photos of horse scenes at Redwings-$6.95

SAVE THE DOLPHINS PROJECT ♦ *page 169*
→ Color photos of marine mammals-$10

SUTTON AVIAN RESEARCH CENTER ♦ *page 177*
→ Bald eagle photographs-$9.95

WILDLIFE HABITAT ENHANCEMENT COUNCIL ♦ *page 194*
→ Full color glossy photos from member sites, weekly appointment calendar, 6x9-$9.95

WORLD WILDLIFE FUND ♦ *page 202*
→ WWF offers 4-5 calendars each year-$12 to $15

Clothing

Including aprons, baby bibs, bandanas, belts, bolo ties, bow ties, boxer shorts, button covers, caps, children's wear, hats, jackets, jogging suits, leggings, neckties, nightshirts, pants, polo shirts, ponchos, robes, scarves, shawls, shirts, shoelaces, shoes, shorts, slippers, socks, suspenders, sweaters, sweatsuits/pants/jackets/shirts, tank tops, T-shirts, vests, visors, windbreakers.

CLOTHING **ACTORS AND OTHERS FOR ANIMALS** ♦ *page 12*
➜ Celebrity autographed T-shirts: black with 66 names in white-$17; white with 66 names in black-$17 ➜ Celebrity autographed sweatshirts: with 129 names; black with white names, white with 4 colors, pink with 2 colors, or red with white-$30 ➜ Bandanas: pawprints of Beethoven, Dreyfus, Benji, Lassie and Eddie-$4.95

ADOPT-A-COW ♦ *page 13*
➜ T-shirts: adult-$12; child-$10 ♦ Baseball caps-$6

ALASKA WILDLIFE ALLIANCE ♦ *page 16*
➜ T-shirts: "The Wolf-Spirit of Wild Alaska"-$15.50
➜ Sweatshirts: "The Wolf-Spirit of Wild Alaska"-$25.00; hooded with hand-warmer pockets-$30.00

ALLIANCE AGAINST ANIMAL ABUSE ♦ *page 17*
➜ T-shirts: Horse Force-$10 ➜ Sweatshirts: horse design-$20

AMERICAN ANTI-VIVISECTION SOCIETY ♦ *page 19*
➜ T-shirts: "Animal experiments are a dying tradition."-$13
♦ "Speciesism"-$13

AMERICAN BIRDING ASSOCIATION ♦ *page 20*
➜ T-shirts: ABA logo, short sleeve-$9.50; long sleeve-$12.95
♦ "You're probably Birding, but I'm just Winging It"-$9.95
➜ Caps: ABA logo-$7.95

AMERICAN CETACEAN SOCIETY ♦ *page 21*
➜ T-shirts: gray whale spyhopper on front and back, aqua-$12
♦ whales in a circle, color design on white, long sleeve-$14
♦ whale species of the world, black and white wraparound design on white-$10 ♦ swimming dolphins on blue-$12

➤ Sweatshirts: grey whale spyhopper on front and back, aqua-$20 ◆ whale species of the world, black and white wraparound design on white-$18

CLOTHING

AMERICAN HORSE PROTECTION ASSOCIATION ◆ *page 22*

➤ T-shirts: white with black horse and royal blue print-$12
➤ Baseball caps: royal blue with white imprint-$8
➤ Sweatshirts: white with black horse and royal blue print-$12

AMERICAN HUMANE ASSOCIATION ◆ *page 23*

➤ T-shirts: "Making a World of Difference," full-color painting of numerous species, white-$12 ◆ "Get A Cat/Get A Life," colorful cat face graphic on black-$12; $7 for child's ◆ "Who Says Neutered Dogs Have No Balls?" bull dog graphic with black lettering on tropical pink, bright yellow or aqua-$12; $7 for child's ➤ Sweatshirts: "Making a World of Difference," full color painting of numerous species, white-$15

AMERICAN LIVESTOCK BREEDS CONSERVANCY ◆ *page 24*

➤ T-shirts: ALBC logo in brick with lettering on unbleached cotton-$12 ◆ Dominique Chicken, red and black print on grey heather-$12 ◆ William Beebe quote, black print on unbleached cotton, design on back, "...when the last individual of a race of living things breathes no more, another heaven and another earth must pass before such a one can be again."-$12

AMERICAN MUSTANG AND BURRO ASSOCIATION ◆ *page 25*

➤ T-shirts: "Wild and free: Protect the mustang"-$15
➤ Sweatshirts: "Wild and free: Protect the mustang"-$20.50

CLOTHING **AMERICAN RESCUE DOG ASSOCIATION** ♦ *page 26*
→ T-shirts: -$10 to $15 according to size

AMERICAN SOCIETY FOR THE PREVENTION OF CRUELTY TO ANIMALS ♦ *page 27*
→ T-shirts: Puppy Mills, red-$14 ♦ "Share the Earth"-$14
→ Caps: ASPCA logo, navy-$8

AMERICAN WILDLIFE RESCUE SERVICE ♦ *page 29*
→ T-shirts: black AWRS logo on royal blue or red-$15
→ Sweatshirts: black AWRS logo on royal blue or red-$25

ANIMAL PROTECTION INSTITUTE OF AMERICA ♦ *page 31*
→ T-shirts: API logo-$15 ♦ "Who Will Speak For Me?"-$15
♦ "Focus on Animals - While There's Still Time"-$15
♦ "Premarin: Just Say No!"-$15

ANIMAL RIGHTS COALITION ♦ *page 33*
→ T-shirts: "Respect All Life," featuring a cat, dog, rat or pig with ARC logo on sleeve-$12 ♦ "Animal Liberation"-$15
♦ "Vivisection"-$15 ♦ "Choose Vegetarian"-$15 ♦ "Hunt each other, leave the animals alone"-$15 ♦ "Humans aren't the only species...We just act like it"-$15 ♦ cow diagram-$15 ♦ "Thanks, but no tanks," (dolphin)-$15

ANIMAL WELFARE INSTITUTE ♦ *page 34*
→ T-shirts: "Save the Whales and Protect the Dolphins from Pollution and Profiteering."-$12 ♦ "Save the Elephants," long sleeve-$14

ANIMAL WELFARE SOCIETY OF SOUTHEASTERN MICHIGAN ♦ *page 35*
→ T-shirts: "Jack," a dog-$7; XXL-$8 ♦ Miss Kitty," a cat-$10;

XXL-$11 ◂ Sweatshirts: "Everyone Deserves A Second Chance"-$20 to $23

CLOTHING

ANTI-CRUELTY SOCIETY ◆ *page 36*
◂ T-shirts: "The Anti-Cruelty Society"-$11 ◂ Sweatshirts: $20
◂ Caps: $8

ASSISI ANIMAL FOUNDATION ◆ *page 37*
◂ T-shirts: Christmas kitties-$15 ◆ Christmas puppies-$15
◆ Cat person-$15 ◆ Dog person-$15 ◆ Horse person-$15
◆ Assisi design-$15 ◆ Pumpkin with kitty-$15 ◆ Sweatshirts:
Christmas kitties-$25 ◆ Christmas puppies-$25 ◆ Cat person-
$25 ◆ Dog person-$25 ◆ Horse person-$25 ◆ Assisi design-$25
◆ Pumpkin with kitty-$25

BALTIMORE ZOO ◆ *page 205*
◂ T-shirts: African watering hole design with imprint on
sleeve-$15.95 ◂ Sweatshirts: glow-in-the-dark-$17.95 ◆ rain
forest design-$29.95 ◂ Aprons: Baltimore Zoo logo-$19.95

BAT CONSERVATION INTERNATIONAL ◆ *page 40*
◂ T-shirts: three different styles-$17.95 ◂ Caps: BCI-$17.95

BEST FRIENDS ANIMAL SANCTUARY ◆ *page 41*
◂ T-shirts: Best Friends cats, colorful art on white-$18
◆ cougar or wolf, black on white-$18

**BIRDS OF PREY REHABILITATION
FOUNDATION** ◆ *page 42*
◂ T-shirts: raptor designs, long sleeved or short sleeved,
assorted colors-$10 to $20 ◂ Sweatshirts: raptor designs,
assorted colors-$10 to $20

CLOTHING **BROOKFIELD ZOO** ♦ *page 208*

➤ T-shirts: Siberian tiger-$15.95; child's-$10.95 ➤ Sweatshirts: "One Earth"-$18.95 ➤ Hats: zebra or tiger with 3D ears-$8.95

CARIBBEAN CONSERVATION CORPORATION ♦ *page 45*

➤ T-shirts: Sea Turtle Survival League, teal/purple logo design on white, grey or terracotta-$18.95

CENTER FOR MARINE CONSERVATION ♦ *page 47*

➤ T-shirts: two embroidered dolphins swim through sunlit waters, design on front and back, deep teal-$28 ♦ turtle on a sand-colored background-$22 ♦ Sea Turtles of the World on spruce green-$22 ♦ sea otters screen-printed in natural tones on moss green-$18.50 ♦ sea otters on front and back, navy blue-$19 ♦ three shimmering dolphins on black, front and back design-$22.50 ♦ "Don't Say Goodbye..." colorful manatee design on white-$18.95 ♦ dolphins wrap around a black tee-$18.95 ♦ all-around sea life scene, white-$20 ♦ glow-in-the-dark dolphin scene, gray, youth sizes-$12.95 ♦ colorful frog alphabet, for children, white-$13 ♦ glow-in-the-dark dolphins, navy-$12.50 ♦ vivid fish on white-$18 ♦ penguins with inner tube, white-$16.50 ♦ purple/green dolphins on blue-$19 ♦ frogs on all-around design, navy-$19; child's-$14.50 ♦ colorful frogs on white-$21.50; youth-$15.50 ♦ red-eyed tree frog, hand painted front and back-$21 ♦ wolves on front and back, white-$18.95 ♦ large white wolf portrait on black-$18.50 ♦ glow-in-the-dark shark, black, youth sizes-$14 ♦ baby wolves, black, youth sizes-$14 ♦ sea life on gray, blue-banded neck and sleeves, youth

sizes-$16.95 ♦ tropical fish on white-$22; youth sizes-$17
♦ tie-dyed dolphins-$21.50 ♦ loon on a moonlit lake, black-
$19.50 ♦ loon design on light tan-$26 ⟶ Sweatshirts: two
embroidered dolphins swim through sunlit waters, design on
front and back, deep teal-$41 ♦ turtle on a sand-colored back-
ground-$46 ♦ sea otters screen-printed in natural tones on
moss green, hooded with pouch pocket-$52 ♦ sea otter silk
screened on black-$32.50 ♦ sea otters on front and back, navy
blue-$33 ♦ "Don't Say Goodbye..." colorful manatee design on
white-$34.95 ♦ dolphins wraparound design, black-$33.50
♦ for toddlers, hooded, "Little Squirt" on back, navy-$16
♦ dolphin design glows in the dark, gray, youth sizes-$20
♦ colorful frog alphabet, white, youth sizes-$21 ♦ glow-in-the-
dark dolphins, navy-$19.50 ♦ vivid fish on white-$33 ♦ penguins with inner tube, white-$24.50 ♦ purple/green dolphins
on blue-$22.50 ♦ frogs on all-around design, navy-$33; child's-
$22 ♦ frogs completely cover white sweat-$36 ♦ wolves on
front and back, white-$33.50 ♦ large wolf portrait on black-
$29.50 ♦ canyon wolf scene on front, back and sleeves, double-
collared, black-$35.50 ♦ glow-in-the-dark shark, black, youth
sizes-$20.50 ♦ baby wolves, black, youth sizes-$20 ♦ sea life on
gray, youth sizes-$18.95 ♦ sharks on front and back, black,
youth sizes-$18.95 ♦ sea turtle embroidered on blue with
collar-$62.50 ♦ loon on a moonlit lake, black-$33 ♦ mother and
baby loon on navy, fuchsia inner collar-$34 ⟶ Shirts: whale tail
embroidered on navy fleece, drawstring neck and waist-$59.95
♦ embroidered dolphins or penguins, two front flap pockets,

CLOTHING

CENTER FOR MARINE CONSERV. (CONT)

wood-toned buttons-$45 • "Dolphins of the World Unite" on natural cotton twill, drawstring waist-$49.95 • white turtleneck with embroidered sea turtle on neck-$26.50 • light tan fleece pullover with loon design, drawstring neck and waist, long sleeve-$55 ➝ Boxer shorts: humpback whales on dark blue-$14 • red/white/black penguins on white-$15.50 • frogs on white-$15.95 ➝ Jogging suits: royal blue knit, cotton/poly, dolphin motif, two pieces-$48 ➝ Sweatshirts: embroidered white tail on left chest of the navy fleece jacket with green sleeves-$78; matching navy drawstring pants-$49.50 • puffy white seal pups, navy, youth sizes -$36 • moss green with dolphin design on pullover front, drawstring at both waist and neck, pullover-$62.50; pants-$49.50 ➝ Jackets: dancing dolphins, windbreaker-$39.95 ➝ Neckties: beige sea otter on navy or wine -$18.50 • white dolphins on wine or navy-$18 • underwater scene of tropical fish against a dark blue background, silk-$40 • penguins on wine-$18.50 • frogs on navy, silk-$40 ➝ Belts: tropical fish on dark blue background, adjustable web, leather tabs, brass buckle-$19.95 ➝ Vests: pastel shells on periwinkle background-$38.95 • brightly colored fish on aqua-$27.50 ➝ Socks: bright dolphins on white nylon/spandex, men's or women's-$9.95 • black and white penguins on knee socks, acrylic nylon/spandex, two pair-$19.95 • colorful frogs on white-$10.50 • wolves howl at the moon, denim blue, men's or women's-$13 • black and white penguins on red, two pair-$19.95 ➝ Caps: colorful frogs on white-$15.50 • brightly

colored tropical fish-$15.50 ▬ Suspenders: penguins of red-$14 CLOTHING
♦ brightly colored sea life swimming on a blue/green background, 1¼" wide straps-$12.50 ♦ loons on pale green-$14
▬ Nightshirts: black and white -$42 ♦ frogs on white-$29.95
▬ Robes: black and white penguins on white-$47.59 ♦ tropical
fish on white, terry, 48" long-$56

COLORADO HORSE RESCUE ♦ *page 50*
▬ Sweatshirts: mountain/horse logo-$25; child's-$18
♦ horse/heart logo $20 ♦ hooded, royal blue-$25 ▬ T-shirts:
long sleeve, collared, royal blue-$18; XXL for $23 ♦ horse
logo-$15; XXL for $18 ▬ Hats: CHR logo-$10 ▬ Visors:
CHR logo-$10

COMMITTEE TO ABOLISH SPORT HUNTING ♦ *page 51*
▬ Hats: C.A.S.H logo-$6.95

CONCERN FOR CRITTERS ♦ *page 52*
▬ T-shirts: two-colored logo-$9; child's-$5 ♦ black logo-$9
▬ Sweatshirts: red with black hearts down both sleeves-$19

CONCERN FOR HELPING ANIMALS IN ISRAEL ♦ *page 53*
▬ T-shirts: "Animals Are For Loving" with cat picture on
front, light blue, mint green, yellow or pink-$12; child's-$10

DALLAS ZOO ♦ *page 211*
▬ T-shirts: long sleeve with zoo insignia-$24.99 ♦ baby zoo
animal design for kids-$9.99 ▬ Sweatshirts: zoo imprint-
$49.99 ♦ V-necked knit pullover shirt with zoo imprint-$51.99
▬ Safari hats: animal print band-$22.99

CLOTHING **DAYS END FARM HORSE RESCUE** ♦ *page 54*
➥ T-shirts: DEFHR logo-$15   ➥ Tank tops: DEFHR logo-$12

DELAWARE VALLEY RAPTOR CENTER ♦ *page 55*
➥ T-shirts: owls, eagles or hawks-$13; XXL for $16

DELTA SOCIETY ♦ *page 56*
➥ T-shirts: white or blue with colorful artwork-$12
➥ Sweatshirts: white or blue with colorful artwork-$22

DESERT TORTOISE PRESERVE COMMITTEE ♦ *page 57*
➥ T-shirts: "I may be slow..but I get there," design on front and back, blue-$9; $7 for child's ♦ "Desert Tortoise Natural Area," mint, youth sizes-$7 ♦ Committee logo, jade with tan tortoise-$11 ♦ desert tortoise with wildflowers, multi-color design on white-$12   ➥ Caps: jade with beige design-$6

DIAN FOSSEY GORILLA FUND ♦ *page 58*
➥ Boxer shorts: repeating black gorilla pattern-$12
➥ Sweatshirts: monogrammed front and logo on back-$25
➥ T-shirts: mother and baby gorilla-$17 ♦ white gorilla on green-$17

DOGS FOR THE DEAF ♦ *page 59*
➥ Polo shirts: jade green, logo on left breast-$19.50
➥ T-shirts: Dogs for the Deaf, royal blue-$10 ♦ designer style grey with white/green/blue/orange logo-$14 ♦ long sleeve, forest green with white, design on front and back-$16
➥ Sweatshirts: designer style, black with white/green/blue and orange logo-$20; XXL for $22   ➥ Windbreakers: unlined nylon, royal blue-$20; XXL for $22   ➥ Caps: royal blue-$6

DOLPHIN ALLIANCE ♦ *page 60*
➥ T-shirts: Bogie and Bacall dolphins-$12 ♦ Welcome Home-$15

DOLPHIN FREEDOM FOUNDATION ♦ *page 61*
➥ T-shirts: dolphins, light blue, dark blue, white or black-$25

DOLPHIN RESEARCH CENTER ♦ *page 62*
➥ T-shirts: logo on neon colors (pink, yellow, mango or lime) or stone-washed colors (turquoise, navy, dark green or purple) with large turquoise/white/navy logo on back-$20; on white-$15 ♦ one of-a-kind art tees painted by the DRC dolphins-$35; child's-$30 ➥ Sweatshirts: suede embroidered applique logo, stone-washed blue or emerald with red lettering-$52
➥ Baseball shirts: navy DRC logo on ash gray, large turquoise/navy /white logo on back-$28 ➥ Shorts: logo on knit with pockets in stone-washed colors (turquoise, navy, dark green or purple)-$22 ➥ Hats: adjustable, logo on long-billed in turquoise, navy or purple-$12; short-billed on navy, white or khaki-$10

DORIS DAY ANIMAL LEAGUE ♦ *page 63*
➥ T-shirts: "I Love Dogs" or "I Love Cats," white-$13.95
➥ Sweatshirts: "Handle With Care," a basket full of cats or dogs, white-$19.50

DORIS DAY PET FOUNDATION ♦ *page 64*
➥ T-shirts: logo with bright red, navy, white w/red or white w/navy or white w/black-$9.95 ➥ Sweatshirts: logo on red, navy, white w/red or white w/navy-$15 ➥ Aprons: adjustable with pockets, red with white logo-$11.95

CLOTHING **EARTHTRUST** ♦ *page 65*

→ T-shirts: Flipper-$15; child's-$12 ♦ leaping dolphin-$15
♦ Save the Whales-$15 ♦ "Treasures" by Mark McKay-$20
→ Polo shirts: "Treasures" by Mark McKay-$25

ELEPHANT RESEARCH FOUNDATION ♦ *page 66*
→ T-shirts: Asian and African elephant designs-$10 to $12

EQUINE RESCUE LEAGUE ♦ *page 67*
→ T-shirts: horse logo-$12 → Sweatshirts: horse logo-$22

FARM ANIMAL REFORM MOVEMENT ♦ *page 69*
→ T-shirts: several designs available-$10 → Aprons: several
designs available-$8

FARM SANCTUARY ♦ *page 70*
→ T-shirts: "If You Love Animals Called Pets...Why Do You
Eat Animals Called Dinner?" black and white animals nestled
in green grass on white-$11; $10 for child's; long sleeve-$15
♦ Please Don't Eat The Animals, Berkeley Breathed multi-
colored cartoon of Opus carrying a rescued lamb, white $12;
$10 for child's; long sleeve-$17 ♦ Join Farm Sanctuary...Go
Vegetarian! multi-colored graphic of farm animals and dinner
plate, white-$18 → Sweatshirts: "If You Love Animals Called
Pets...Why Do You Eat Them For Dinner?" black and white
animals nestled in green grass on white-$18 ♦ Please Don't Eat
The Animals, Berkeley Breathed multi-colored cartoon of
Opus carrying a rescued lamb, white-$20 ♦ Join Farm
Sanctuary...Go Vegetarian! multi-colored graphic of farm
animals and dinner plate, white-$20 → Bandanas: spotted cow
with Farm Sanctuary logo-$3.50

CLOTHING

FELINES ♦ *page 71*
➞ T-shirts: $11 ➞ Sweatshirts: $20.75 ➞ Nightshirts: $15

FEMINISTS FOR ANIMAL RIGHTS ♦ *page 72*
➞ T-shirts: FAR logo-$10

FLORIDA VOICES FOR ANIMALS ♦ *page 75*
➞ T-shirts: logo-$10

**FREE FLIGHT BIRD AND MARINE MAMMAL
REHABILITATION** ♦ *page 76*
➞ T-shirts: seal, brown pelican, hawk and handler silhouette-
$12; long sleeve-$22 ➞ Sweatshirts: seal, brown pelican, hawk
and handler silhouette-$25

FREE WILLY FOUNDATION ♦ *page 77*
➞ T-shirts: Kieko design-$15

FRIENDS OF ANIMALS ♦ *page 78*
➞ T-shirts: elephant-$14 ♦ wolf-$14 ♦ cat and dog-$14

FRIENDS OF BEAVERSPRITE ♦ *page 79*
➞ T-shirts: "Beavers Build Beautiful Habitats"-$12 ♦ Dorothy
and the Beavers"-$12 ➞ Sweatshirts: "Beavers Build Beautiful
Habitats"-$20 ♦ "Dorothy and the Beavers"-$20

**FRIENDS OF THE AUSTRALIAN KOALA
FOUNDATION** ♦ *page 81*
➞ T-shirts: koala-$12.50

FRIENDS OF THE SEA OTTER ♦ *page 83*
➞ Boxer shorts: unisex, adult for $14.95; kid's for $12.95
➞ Sweatshirts: holiday otter design-$24 ♦ white otter on black-
$29 to $32 by size ♦ eight color otter design on white, teal or
royal blue-$24; youth for $18 ➞ T-shirts: eight-color otter
design on white, teal or royal blue-$16; youth for $11 ♦ otters

CLOTHING

FRIENDS OF THE SEA OTTER (CONT)

front and back-$20 ♦ otters in kelp on ash background-$16; youth for $11 ➞ Sweaters: navy and white with FSO design-$54 ➞ Neckties: otter design, silk, navy or red-$45 ➞ Aprons: sea otter-$13.95 ➞ Baby bibs: terry cloth with otter scene-$7.99

FRIENDS OF WASHOE ♦ *page 84*

➞ Sweatshirts: five-chimpanzee logo, cream or green-$25.95; youth for $10.95 ➞ T-shirts: five-chimpanzee logo, white or grey-$10.99

FUND FOR ANIMALS ♦ *page 85*

➞ T-shirts: "Support Your Right to Arm Bears," white or ash-$12; long sleeve-$17; XXL-$19 ♦ "Animals have Rights, Too!" black, royal blue or fuchsia-$12; child's-$10 ♦ "Bovine, Feline, Canine...Asinine," (Silhouettes of animals; last silhouette is that of a hunter.)-$10 ♦ moose, wolf or elephants in various colors-$18 ➞ Sweatshirts: "Support Your Right to Arm Bears," white or ash-$25 ♦ "Bovine, Feline, Canine...Asinine," orange or grey-$22

GORILLA FOUNDATION ♦ *page 86*

➞ T-shirts: logo on white, black or purple-$17 ♦ oversized wildlife designs; gorilla, lion, white tiger or giant panda; shirt back reads "Extinction is Forever"-$20 ♦ long sleeved in teal with white logo-$22 ♦ gold foil logo on back-$20 ♦ children's, red with white logo, indigo with white logo, white with black logo or black with white logo-$12 ➞ Sweatshirts: blue with white logo or heather grey with black logo-$27

GREAT BEAR FOUNDATION ♦ *page 87*

➞ T-shirts: GBF color logo, ash-$15 ♦ "Moonlight Bears,"

five-color scene on purple-$16 ✦ "Sleeping Grizzly," white on   CLOTHING
pigment-dyed sage shirt-$20 ✦ "The Eight Bears of North
America," ash-$18 ✦ "Spirit Bear," color design on white,
children's only-$12 ⇀ Sweatshirts: GBF color logo, ash-$24
⇀ Caps: GBF logo on royal blue-$12

GREYHOUND FRIENDS ✦ *page 88*
⇀ T-shirts: silhouette logo or brindle standing greyhound in
color-$18; child's for $11 ⇀ Sweatshirts and sweatshirt
cardigans: six different greyhound designs-$25 ⇀ Hats: grey-
hound silhouette-$8

HAWK MOUNTAIN SANCTUARY ✦ *page 89*
⇀ Shirts: embroidered logo on left breast, natural color cotton
twill with knit collar and waistband-$42.50 ✦ embroidered logo
on hooded long sleeve cotton twill, front pouch pocket and
knitted waistband, stone-washed moss green or tan-$47
✦ embroidered logo on left breast, cotton twill with low drawstring neck and waist, black-$42.50 ✦ Migration, hawks soaring
on front and back, white cotton twill with high tunnel neck
drawstring collar and knitted waistband-$49 ⇀ T-shirts: Still
Climbing At 60, mint green or dark gray-$18; hooded, long
sleeve, stone gray-$29 ✦ Migration, hawks soaring on front and
back, white-$19; long sleeve-$25 ✦ Soar, contemporary design
in turquoise/olive/red on white-$19 ✦ Hawk Mountain, with
contemporary eagle graphic in gold/red/black on light gray or
sage green-$18 ⇀ Sweatshirts: Migration, hawks soaring on
front and back, white-$30 ⇀ Caps: poly/cotton twill with
embroidered logo in black-$9 ✦ tan embroidered logo on

CLOTHING

HAWK MOUNTAIN SANCTUARY (CONT)
forest green, suede bill-$19 ◆ natural with chestnut embroidered logo and suede bill-$19 ⇀ Bandanas: Hawk Mountain with raptor silhouettes, includes identification key, assorted colors; name your favorite color-$6.95

HAWKWATCH INTERNATIONAL ◆ *page 90*
⇀ T-shirts: Raptor Rapture, five raptor species in multi-colors on the front and a bald eagle on the back, unbleached cotton-$16; XXL-$17 ◆ logo with Cooper's hawk in flight on light blue, mint green, red, white or ash grey-$12 ⇀ Sweatshirts: Silent Watch, raptors on grey-$24; XXL-$26 ⇀ Caps: logo embroidered in gold on nylon cap with Velcro closure, black, eggplant or navy-$12

HELEN WOODWARD ANIMAL CENTER ◆ *page 91*
⇀ T-shirts: HWAC logo-$10 ⇀ Sweatshirts: HWAC logo-$20

HELPING HOMELESS CATS ◆ *page 92*
⇀ T-shirts: black and white, kitten and teardrop design-$12; $10 for child's ⇀ Sweatshirts: white cat face logo on black, emerald green or red-$20

HEMLOCK HILL FARM SANCTUARY ◆ *page 93*
⇀ T-shirts: hand painted, may be painted to order-$15 to $50

HOOVED ANIMAL HUMANE SOCIETY ◆ *page 94*
⇀ T-shirts: teal or maroon design on grey-$15; XXL-$18
◆ logo, grey, tan, red, light blue or navy-$6

HORSE POWER PROJECTS ◆ *page 95*
⇀ T-shirt dress/nightshirts: $19 ⇀ T-shirts: Just Say Whoa!-$13 ◆ Horse Power logo-$13

CLOTHING

HUMANE EDUCATION COMMITTEE ♦ *page 96*
— T-shirts: "Humane Education Now," L or XL-$9
— Sweatshirts: "The Humane and Educated Cat"-$17

HUMANE FARMING ASSOCIATION ♦ *page 97*
— T-shirts: 3 designs of pigs or cows-$12

HUMANE SOCIETY OF THE UNITED STATES ♦ *page 98*
— T-shirts: "Animals...It's their world too."-$11 ♦ HSUS animals in colorful artwork-$12

IN DEFENSE OF ANIMALS ♦ *page 99*
— T-shirts: "Please Don't Buy Fur," with black and white raccoon on black-$15 ♦ Geckos with Darwin quote "The love for all living creatures is the greatest attribute of man."-$15 ♦ "Shop Cruelty Free. Boycott Procter & Gamble," black and red on white-$15 ♦ "Why Jail Whales?/ Dying to Amuse you"-$9.95 ♦ "ACT! In Defense of Animals," red and gray on black-$15 ♦ "Animal liberation," long sleeve-$18 ♦ Abraham Lincoln profile and quote, purple and green on white-$15
— Sweatshirts: "Please Don't Buy Fur," with black and white raccoon on black-$20 ♦ "ACT NOW! In Defense of Animals," black and red on white-$20 ♦ "Shop Cruelty Free. Boycott Procter & Gamble," black and red on white-$20

INTERNATIONAL BIRD RESCUE RESEARCH CENTER ♦ *page 100*
— T-shirts: pelican and murre-$17 ♦ flying pelican, jade or gray-$17; long sleeve-$20 ♦ Santa Clara River, commemorative, white or gray-$20 ♦ Apollo Sea, commemorative-$20
— Sweatshirts: logo, kids logo or pelicans-$22; $17 for kids

CLOTHING **INTERNATIONAL CRANE FOUNDATION** ♦ *page101*
➥ T-shirts: whooping crane on aqua-$12.50; $11.50 for child's

INTERNATIONAL MARINE MAMMAL PROJECT ♦ *page103*
➥ T-shirts: Earth Island-$13; $11 for child's ♦ Save the Dolphin
-$13; $11 for child's ♦ three dolphins-$13 ♦ Save the Whales-$13

INTERNATIONAL OSPREY FOUNDATION ♦ *page 104*
➥ T-shirts: TIOF logo with osprey portrait-$10

INTERNATIONAL PRIMATE PROTECTION LEAGUE ♦ *page 105*
➥ T-shirts: silverback mountain gorilla with baby-$14
♦ gorilla family, white or aqua-$14 ♦ gibbon family, silver,
beige, aqua or pink-$14 ♦ chimpanzee on both sides, white or
aqua-$14 ➥ Sweatshirts: gorilla designs on front and back-$25

INTERNATIONAL SNOW LEOPARD TRUST ♦ *page 106*
➥ Sweatshirts: snow leopard against snow-clad mountains-$28

INTERNATIONAL SOCIETY FOR ANIMAL RIGHTS ♦ *page 107*
➥ T-shirts: "Too much of a good thing"-$12 ♦ "Spay/Neuter. It
stops the killing!"-$12 ♦ children's "Share the Earth"-$9 ♦ Save
the Dolphins-$12 ♦ Elephant/Ban Ivory-$12 ♦ children's "Share
the Earth," to color themselves with a package of washable
markers included-$12 ➥ Sweatshirts: "Too much of a good
thing"-$15.99 ♦ children's, African environment-$13.95
➥ Nightshirts: cats with "Happiness is being with you"-$13

INTERNATIONAL SOCIETY FOR COW PROTECTION ♦ *page 108*
➥ T-shirts: "Be udderly cool: Protect Cows"-$10 ♦ ISCOWP

logo-$10 ♦ "Stop the murder"-$10 ♦ Ox power-$10 ♦ "Seed   CLOTHING
to Sustenance"-$10 ♦ Kiss My Ox-$10

INTERNATIONAL SOCIETY FOR ENDANGERED CATS ♦ *page 109*

➛ T-shirts: Endangered cats, Lynx kittens, Lion and Leopard-
$17; XXl-$19 ♦ Golden Kingdom-$29; child's for $13
♦ Cheetahs-$15; $16 for XXL ♦ 37 species-$10; XXL for $11
♦ snow leopard-$11.50; $12.50 for XXL   ➛ Sweatshirts: endangered cats & Lynx kittens-$27; XXL-$29 ♦ snow leopard-$25;
$28 for XXL ♦ 37 species-$25; XXL for $28

INTERNATIONAL WILDLIFE REHABILITATION COUNCIL ♦ *page 110*

➛ T-shirts: IWRC logo on black, white, dark green or light
blue-$17

INTERNATIONAL WOLF CENTER ♦ *page 111*

➛ T-shirts: wolf pups, for children, gray, pink or over-dyed
blue-$10 ♦ logo with Run With These Wolves, colorfast brick,
denim blue and deep green-$16   ➛ Shirts: long sleeve Henley,
three buttons at top, natural tone body and green sleeves, logo
on sleeve and left chest-$23 ♦ long sleeve, zip to center chest,
crew neck, fleece of recycled plastic soda bottles, black, green
or cranberry, embroidered trim with wolf design-$97   ➛
Sweatshirts: IWC logo on deep green, denim, white or gray-
$33   ➛ Jackets: fleece made from recycled plastic soda bottles,
green or cranberry-$110   ➛ Caps: logo on denim blue,
moss or brown canvas-$9.95   ➛ Bandanas: wolf logo on
natural, black, navy, turquoise, purple or wine-$3.50

CLOTHING **JANE GOODALL INSTITUTE** ♦ *page 113*

→ T-shirts: three different designs of Jane Goodall's various chimp friends, available in many colors-$14 ♦ Chimp Fifi's second-born, Frodo-$25 ♦ Far Side cartoon, 'Well, well - another blond hair...Conducting a little more "research" with that Jane Goodall tramp?'-$14 ♦ Color-your-own T-shirts, includes six colorfast fabric paints with instructions to paint the wildlife scene-$18; $17 for child's → Sweatshirts: Chimp FiFi's second-born, Frodo-$12

JUST CATS ♦ *page 114*

→ T-shirts: I Spayed a Stray Today-$15 → Sweatshirts: Just Cats logo-$20

JUSTICE FOR ANIMALS ♦ *page 115*

→ T-shirts: various designs and sayings-$8 to $12 ♦ handmade, decorated front and back-$20

LEND-A-PAW ORGANIZATION ♦ *page 116*

→ T-shirts: Socks cat-$10 ♦ Lend-A-Paw-$10 → Sweatshirts: Lend-A-Paw-$20

LOS ANGELES AUDUBON SOCIETY ♦ *page 117*

→ T-shirts: L.A. Audubon Society-$9.95; long sleeved-$12.95 → Sweatshirts: L.A. Audubon Society-$16.95 → Aprons: L.A. Audubon Society-$10.95 **LYNX EDUCATIONAL**

FUND FOR ANIMAL WELFARE ♦ *page 118*

→ T-shirts: 3 different colorful designs-$20 ♦ "It takes up to 40 dumb animals to make a fur coat. But only one to wear it."-$15 ♦ "Yuck your disgusting fur coat"-$15

MAINE ANIMAL COALITION ♦ *page 119*
━ T-shirts: The Way Life Should Be "HuMaine," natural, green and red-$10

MARINE MAMMAL STRANDING CENTER ♦ *page 120*
━ T-shirts: "Cupid" The Seal, seal face on front with tail on back, white print on navy, fuchsia, turquoise, black, white, grey or green-$10; XXL for $12; $7 for child's ━ Sweatshirts: "Cupid" The Seal, seal face on front with tail on back in navy, royal, white, grey or green-$20; XXL for $32

MEOW ♦ *page 121*
━ T-shirts: MEOW logo-$10 to $13 ━ Sweatshirts: MEOW logo-$18 to $22

MEXICAN WOLF COALITION OF TEXAS ♦ *page 122*
━ T-shirts: Mexican wolf-$15

MICHIGAN ANTI-CRUELTY SOCIETY ♦ *page 123*
━ T-shirts: animal designs with MACS logo-$10
━ Sweatshirts: animal designs with MACS logo-$20

MICHIGAN HUMANE SOCIETY ♦ *page 124*
━ T-shirts: MHS logo with red heart on cream or black-$10; XXL-$12 ━ Sweatshirts: MHS logo with red heart on cream or black-$20; XXL-$22 ━ Shorts: knit jersey, MHS logo on cream or black-$20 ━ Baseball hats: unbleached cotton twill with black accents and embroidered MHS logo, adjustable-$16

MID-ATLANTIC GREAT DANE RESCUE LEAGUE ♦ *page 125*
━ T-shirts: three Dane heads logo-$13.50 ♦ "Danes Are Great. Bet You Can't Just Have One."-$13.50 ♦ "Friendship

CLOTHING

MID-ATLANTIC GREAT DANE RESCUE LEAGUE (CONT)

for a gentler, kinder world"-$13.50 ◆ "Who Me?" Dane puppy sitting in front of torn-up sofa and shoe-$13.50

MISSION: WOLF ◆ *page 126*
— T-shirts: Circle Of Wolves-$15; long sleeve-$18
— Sweatshirts: Circle Of Wolves-$25

MOUNTAIN LION FOUNDATION ◆ *page 127*
— T-shirts: Endangered, design of all endangered cats in North America-$12.95

NATIONAL FOUNDATION TO PROTECT AMERICA'S EAGLES ◆ *page 128*
— T-shirts: Save America's Eagles-$15 — Sweatshirts: Save America's Eagles-$20 — Caps: adjustable-$10

NATIONAL WOLF HYBRID ASSOCIATION ◆ *page 130*
— T-shirts: NWHA logo in black with shining gold wolf eyes, gray-$10 — Caps: summer baseball caps with mesh back, NWHA logo, gray-$8

NATURE CONSERVANCY ◆ *page 131*
— T-shirts: endangered birds of the Americas, front and back design-$21.95 ◆ habitats of North and South America and the Pacific; choose rain forest, coral reef, desert or mountain-$17.95 ◆ The Last Great Places, a tapestry-style celebration of unique ecosystems, TNC logo on back-$13.95 ◆ bison-$19.95 ◆ pronghorn antelopes-$19.95 ◆ wild cats of America featured on this all-over design-$21.95 ◆ endangered turtles, all-over design, teal-$21.95 ◆ jaguar and cubs on white-$19.95 ◆ TNC

logo on white-$14.95 ♦ youth sizes, choose bald eagle, polar bears, Florida panther, wolf-$14.95 ⬏ Sweatshirts: embroidered logo on denim-look or purple-$39.95 ⬏ Caps: TNC logo embroidered, purple/black or forest green-$12

NETWORK FOR OHIO ANIMAL ACTION ♦ *page 132*
⬏ T-shirts: Animals have rights!-$8; $12.50 for long sleeve;
♦ anti-fur statement-$8

NEW ENGLAND ANTI-VIVISECTION SOCIETY ♦ *page 133*
⬏ T-shirts: Blinded for Beauty, slogan in shocking pink with black logo of a cruelty-free rabbit-$8 ♦ Rats Rights, slogan in neon pink with a white rat, NEAVS logo on sleeve-$8

NEW YORK TURTLE AND TORTOISE SOCIETY ♦ *page 134*
⬏ T-shirts: NYTTS logo, black lettering and art on silver-$18
♦ sea turtle, black lettering and art on turquoise or raspberry-$18
♦ turtle collage, green lettering and art on light tan-$18 ♦ turtle egg nest, black lettering and art on turquoise-$18

NOAH'S FRIENDS ♦ *page 135*
⬏ T-shirts: Your Fur Coat Is Almost Ready-$15 ♦ The Fur Industry Says It's Okay To Use Animals Raised On A Ranch. What They Don't Tell You Is A Ranch Measures 28"x10"x16"-$16 ♦ The Shocking Truth Behind Ranched Furs-$16 **NORTH AMERICAN BEAR SOCIETY** ♦ *page 136*
⬏ T-shirts: NABS logo on white-$10; XXL$11 ⬏ Hats: NABS logo on white-$7 ⬏ Suspenders: leather embossed logo, red or camouflage-$18

CLOTHING

NORTH AMERICAN VEGETARIAN SOCIETY ♦ *page 138*

➞ T-shirts: Vegetarianism Is Serious Environmental Action-$15
♦ The New Four... What For? The Vegetarian Answer-$15
➞ Sweatshirts: Vegetarianism Is Serious Environmental Action-
$25 ♦ The New Four ...What For? The Vegetarian Answer-$25

OPOSSUM SOCIETY OF CALIFORNIA ♦ *page 142*

➞ T-shirts: opossum, "Native marsupial of the Americas. We
outlived the dinosaurs. Can we survive man?" ash, green, red
or black-$13 ♦ logo on fuchsia-$11 ♦ logo design on front and
back, ash, white or beige-$14.50 ➞ Sweatshirts: logo design
on front and back, ash, white or beige-$20 ➞ Tank tops:
opossum, native marsupial of the Americas, "We outlived the
dinosaurs. Can we survive man?" large, cranberry only-$5; XL
plum only-$5

ORANGE COUNTY PEOPLE FOR ANIMALS ♦ *page 143*

➞ T-shirts: OCPA logo on black/grey/white with Abraham
Lincoln quote-$15

ORANGUTAN FOUNDATION INTERNATIONAL ♦ *page 146*

➞ T-shirts: "Orangutan: Person of the forest-Vanishing as the
rainforest falls," beige-$15 ♦ multi-color drawing of mother
and baby-$20 ♦ OFI logo, beige or blue-$10

PACIFIC WHALE FOUNDATION ♦ *page 146*

➞ Sweatshirts: PWF logo and "Save The Whales," with drawstring collar and pockets, purple or green-$63 ♦ PWF logo and
"Save The Whales," with button collar, periwinkle or white-$58

PACIFIC WILDLIFE PROJECT ♦ *page 147*

➛ T-shirts: PWP pelican and seabird logo-$15 ♦ "Return of the Swallows 1995," commemorative with PWP logo-$10 ♦ "Fiesta De Las Golondrinas," commemorative with PWP logo-$10 ♦ "Mr. P," American white pelican portrait-$30 ➛ Sweatshirts: PWP pelican and seabird logo-$25

PAWS WITH A CAUSE ♦ *page 148*

➛ T-shirts: PAWS logo-$8.50; $10 for XXL; $11 for XXXL ♦ PAWS designer logo-$9; $10.50 for XXL; $11 for XXXL ➛ Sweatshirts: PAWS logo-$16; $19 for XXL; $20 for XXXL ♦ PAWS designer logo with a doberman or rottweilers-$20; $24 for XL; $27 for XXL and XXXL ♦ PAWS logo, short sleeve-$16; $19 for XXL; $20 for XXXL ♦ PAWS designer logo with rottweilers-$20; XL for $24 ➛ Jackets: stadium pullover I, stand up zip-through collar with contrasting lining, embroidered logo, navy/jade or ice/navy-$86 ♦ stadium pullover II, stand-up zip-through collar with contrasting heavy, four-color knit trim at collar, wrists and waist, embroidered logo, navy or heather-$80 ♦ voyager, winter, embroidered logo, teal/green or burgundy /blue-$80.05 ♦ mariner, light winter, hidden hood, embroidered logo, burgundy/teal-$108.75 ➛ Caps: cream with teal/maroon embroidered logo and green visor-$17 ➛ Golf hats: white with teal/maroon embroidered logo-$17

PEOPLE FOR ABANDONED PETS ♦ *page 150*

➛ T-shirts: C.A.T.S or D.O.G.S. with paw prints, white w/navy design, grey w/navy design, forest green w/light grey design or navy w/light grey, XL only-$14; long sleeved mock turtleneck-$22

CLOTHING

PEOPLE FOR ANIMAL RIGHTS ♦ *page 151*
➞ T-shirts: black and white logo on white or black-$15
➞ Sweatshirts: black and white logo on black-$20 ➞ Caps:
black and white logo on black and white cap-$6

PEOPLE FOR THE ETHICAL TREATMENT OF ANIMALS ♦ *page 152*
➞ T-shirts: Respect Your Fellow Earthlings, exclusive artwork
by Berkeley Breathed-$16.75

PEREGRINE FUND ♦ *page 153*
➞ Scarves: silk falcon scarf, 36"square, rust or navy-$95
➞ Neckties: silver flying falcons on blue silk-$25 ➞ Caps:
Peregrine Fund logo on tan or green-$7

PIGS, A SANCTUARY ♦ *page 155*
➞ T-shirts: sanctuary logo, white or gray-$15

PIONEERS FOR ANIMAL WELFARE ♦ *page 156*
➞ T-shirts: black PAWS logo "Pets Are Worth Saving" on
white-$6.50; XL, 1X, 2X, 3X-$8; child's-$5.50 ➞ Sweatshirts:
black Paws logo "Pets Are Worth Saving" on white $6.50; XL,
1X, 2X, 3X-$16.50

PRESERVATION OF THE AMAZON RIVER DOLPHIN ♦ *page 158*
➞ Belts: handwoven from the Shambira palm, some with
seeds-$10 to $20

PROGRESSIVE ANIMAL WELFARE SOCIETY ♦ *page 159*
➞ T-shirts: Neuter is Cuter, orange/black cat on white-$12
♦ Find The Love Of Your Life At PAWS, multi-colored panel

on white-$12 ➞ Sweatshirts: Neuter is Cuter, orange/black cat
on white-$22.50 ✦ PAWS For All Animals, fuchsia/red/purple/
green on black and white-$22.50 ✦ Find The Love Of Your
Life At PAWS, multi-colored panel on white-$22.50

PURPLE MARTIN CONSERVATION ASSOCIATION ✦ *page 160*
➞ T-shirts: I'm Out Of My Gourd Over Purple Martins, on
heather gray-$9.95 ✦ PMCA logo on 2 different shirts, heather
gray-$9.95 ✦ Purple Martins Make Great Neighbors, on
white-$9.95 ✦ collage of native birds, including the purple
martin, white-$11.95 ➞ Sweatshirts: Purple Martins Make
Great Neighbors, gray-$19.95; XXL-$21.95

RACINE ZOO ✦ *page 223*
➞ T-shirts: Zoo logo-$10; child's-$9 ➞ Sweatshirts: Zoo logo
-$18; child's-$14

RAPTOR CENTER AT THE UNIVERSITY OF MINNESOTA ✦ *page 161*
➞ T-shirts: many styles of North American birds of prey
designs, child and adult sizes-$18 to $24 ✦ most popular shirt:
"Can you find nine eagles?" in tan or black-$18

RAPTOR EDUCATION FOUNDATION ✦ *page 162*
➞ T-shirts: life-size elf owl in color on white-$12 ✦ eagle
motifs on black or white-$12 to $15 ➞ Sweatshirts: eagle
motifs-$18 to $20 ➞ Neckties: embroidered peregrine falcon,
red, blue, green-$35

CLOTHING **REDWINGS HORSE SANCTUARY** ♦ *page 163*

➡ T-shirts: children's, purple logo on ash-$10 ♦ colored paintings of rescued animals on natural, ash or dark turquoise-$15

➡ Sweatshirts: RHS logo on black, forest green, or slate blue-$30 ➡ Caps: RHS logo embroidered on black poplin-$10

ROCKY MOUNTAIN RAPTOR PROGRAM ♦ *page 165*

➡ T-shirts: three great horned owls, various colors-$12; long sleeve-$15 ♦ red-tailed hawk, natural-$10; long sleeve-$12 ♦ snowy owl, white-$15 ♦ peregrine falcon, ash or natural-$15

➡ Sweatshirts: three great horned owls, various colors-$20; hooded-$22 ♦ bald eagle, white-$20 ♦ red-tailed hawk, natural-$18

SAN DIEGO ZOO ♦ *page 225*

➡ T-shirts: CRES logo-$11.95; child's-$9.95

SANGRE DE CRISTO ANIMAL PROTECTION ♦ *page 167*

➡ T-shirts: Animal Damage Control Likes Wildlife...Dead -$15 ♦ We Need A Safe Town Near Your Town, prairie dog -$15 ♦ Factory Farming-From The Torturehouse To The Slaughterhouse-Last Stop... Your Plate, maroon chicken design on white-$15 ♦ Please ...Don't Buy Fur, raccoon face, black shirt w/white artwork or white shirt w/black artwork-$15 ♦ Say "No" To Dissection, white with red and black design-$15 ♦ SdeCap logo in white on colored shirt-$12

SAVE THE DOLPHINS PROJECT ♦ *page 169*

➡ T-shirts: Save The Dolphins, four-color design on white-$13; $11 for child's ♦ Earth Island - Save It, 4-color design on white -$13; $11 for child's

SAVE THE WHALES ◆ *page 171*
→ T-shirts: Save The Whales, dark blue logo on light blue or white-$9.95; child's in white only-$6.95; baby's in white, pink, mint green, yellow, blue-$5.95 ◆ Save The Whales, Mary Engelbreit design, white-$16.95 ◆ grey whale head on white, lavender, silver, peach, watermelon or mint green-$10 ◆ orca breaching to the sun with splashes of water, white-$10; child's-$7.95 ◆ humpback whale breaking the ocean's surface with design on back and one sleeve-$20.95 → Shoes: hand painted whales on canvas tennis shoes-$49.95

SEA SHEPHERD CONSERVATION SOCIETY ◆ *page 172*
→ T-shirts: SSCS whale logo, blue or black on white-$15 ◆ penguin cartoon with "Back Off Jack"-$18

SEA TURTLE RESTORATION PROJECT ◆ *page 173*
→ T-shirts: colorful turtle design with Viva La Tortuga! on white-$15; child's-$12 ◆ colorful turtle design with Save The Sea Turtles on white-$15; child's-$12

SINAPU ◆ *page 174*
→ T-shirts: "Colorado's Ecosystems Need Wolves" on back with a variety of wolf art on front-$13

SUNCOAST SEABIRD SANCTUARY ◆ *page 175*
→ T-shirts: Sanctuary logo in blue lettering on white-$12
→ Sweatshirts: white Sanctuary logo on navy blue-$20

SUPRESS ◆ *page 176*
→ T-shirts: Teach Your Teacher A Lesson: Say NO To Dissection!-$15 ◆ Animal Research: Scientific Fraud, gray-$15

CLOTHING **SUTTON AVIAN RESEARCH CENTER** ♦ *page 177*
⇒ T-shirts: adult bald eagle in flight on back with chick on front, white-$12 ♦ southern bald eagle, white-$12 ♦ American bald eagle in flight, gray-$12 ♦ bald eagle in three poses with native Indian beadwork design, four colors-$16.95

TIMBER WOLF ALLIANCE ♦ *page 178*
⇒ T-shirts: line drawing collage of wolves, gray or mint green-$12 ⇒ Sweatshirts: line drawing collage of wolves, gray or mint green-$24

TIMBER WOLF PRESERVATION SOCIETY ♦ *page 179*
⇒ T-shirts: logo with wolf pictures of individuals at the farm-$12.85 ⇒ Sweatshirts: logo with wolf pictures of individuals at the farm-$23 ⇒ Summer jackets: logo, flannel lining, wolf on back, footprints on front-$58

TREE HOUSE ANIMAL FOUNDATION ♦ *page 180*
⇒ T-shirts: "Life Is Short. Pet Hard," red lettering and smiling kitty face on white-$16 ⇒ Sweatshirts: "Have A Heart For Animals," athletic grey with bright blue lettering-$21.95 ⇒ Polo shirts: burgundy with Tree House logo-$19.95

TRUMPETER SWAN SOCIETY ♦ *page 181*
⇒ T-shirts: three-color logo on white cotton-$12 ♦ three-color logo on wedgwood blue, cotton/poly-$12 ⇒ Sweatshirts: three-color logo on white and blue, heavyweight-$22

UNITED POULTRY CONCERNS ♦ *page 182*
⇒ Shirts: black & white photographic images of factory-farmed chickens, cotton-$24 ⇒ Leggings: black & white photographic images of factory-farmed chickens, cotton-$20

CLOTHING

WAIKIKI AQUARIUM ♦ *page 228*

→ T-shirts: black and blue illustrations of ocean life, choose humu-humu fish or nautilus design, white or ash-$12.75 ♦ crop top, black and blue illustrations of ocean life on white or ash -$11.75; one size fits all-$12.75 ♦ jellyfish on black-$16.75 ♦ barracuda on blue-$16.75 ♦ nautilus on turquoise-$15 ♦ butterfly fish on red-$15 ♦ puffer fish on blue-$15 ♦ monk seal on turquoise -$15 ♦ humu-humu fish on burgundy-$15 → Golf shirts: embroidered logo on left breast, blue, white, mint or pink-$26.50

WHALE ADOPTION PROJECT ♦ *page 184*

→ Sweatshirts: red crew neck with WAP logo-$28.95 ♦ hooded red crew neck with WAP logo-$34.95 ♦ white with colorful WAP logo-$22.95 ♦ with black and white WAP logo-$21.95 ♦ hooded with pocket, white with black & white WAP logo-$26.95 → T-shirts: gray with colorful WAP logo-$13.95 ♦ marine life on front and back, white-$13.95 ♦ endangered wildlife on front and back, white-$13.95 ♦ "Save the Humans," green whale on white-$11.95 ♦ "I love my humpback whale"-$8.95 for child's; $10.95 for adult → Neckties: silvery dolphin pairs on navy blue-$10.95 ♦ white whales on burgundy or navy-$9.95 → Caps: corduroy with WAP logo-$9.95

WHALE CONSERVATION INSTITUTE ♦ *page 185*

→ Caps: WCI logo, white-$12

WHALE MUSEUM ♦ *page 186*

→ T-shirts: K-Pod (16 black orca fins) on white-$17.95; child's-$10.95; long sleeve-$19.95 ♦ Orca Trio, white, red, ash or teal-$17.95; child's in white, red, ash, or teal-$10.95 ♦ two

CLOTHING **WHALE MUSEUM** (CONT)

orcas with ORCA printed below, red, teal ash or white-$17.95; child's in same colors-$10.95

WHERE WOLVES RESCUE ♦ *page 187*

— T-shirts: hand painted wolf on white-$35 ♦ three wolves hand painted on white-$40 ♦ two howling pups and WWR name, fuchsia, coral, yellow or light blue-$13

WILD BURRO RESCUE ♦ *page 188*

— T-shirts: mother and baby burros on jade, fuchsia, ash, teal or natural-$17.50 ♦ herd of wild burros running, coral, moss green, oatmeal or purple-$17.50

WILD CANID SURVIVAL AND RESEARCH CENTER ♦ *page 189*

— T-shirts: Northern Lights, black-$16 ♦ all-over design, heather blue-$24 ♦ wolf pack, blue spruce-$16 ♦ red wolf art on back, white-$16 ♦ Mexican wolf photo on natural-$20
— Sweatshirts: "Each Day Wolves Touch And Caress One Another to Re-establish And To Re-affirm Their Close Relationships. A Warm And Loving Reminder For All Mankind...," with wolf family on gray-$24 — Caps: Wolf Sanctuary logo, brown, black or blue-$6.50 — Nightshirts: Night Howl, white with black howling wolf and neon moon and stars-$15 — Ponchos: long, yellow, hooded WCSRC logo on front or back-$10 — Bow ties: for ladies, burgundy or navy with stripes and walking wolves-$14 — Socks: white tube socks with black paw prints-$4 — Shoestrings: white with Wolf Sanctuary and paw prints in black, 36½"-$2.50 per pair

WILDCARE ♦ *page 190*
➤ T-shirts: logo-$12 ➤ Sweatshirts: logo-$17

WILD HORSE SANCTUARY ♦ *page 191*
➤ T-shirts: Wild Horse Sanctuary logo on navy with red design, or red with navy design or pink with teal green design-$10

WILDLIFE PRESERVATION TRUST INTERNATIONAL ♦ *page 195*
➤ T-shirts: Belize Zoo, a colorful macaw on off-white-$15; youth sizes-$10 ♦ Color Your Own, set includes T-shirt, non-toxic neon fabric paints, brush and color mixing chart, choose either monkeys and apes or wild cats-$18; $17 for youth ♦ thick-billed parrot on front and back on egg-shell color-$15 ♦ golden lion tamarin on front and back on black or white-$15; $10 for youth, white ➤ Sweatshirts: black-footed ferret on white-$24

WILLIAM HOLDEN WILDLIFE FOUNDATION ♦ *page 196*
➤ T-shirts: white or powder blue in small, safari green or black in large and XL-$12

WOLF HAVEN INTERNATIONAL ♦ *page 197*
➤ T-shirts: wolf design in white on purple, burgundy or black, paw print on left sleeve-$16.50; XXL-$18.50

WOLF HOLLOW WILDLIFE REHABILITATION CENTRE ♦ *page 198*
➤ T-shirts: Wolf Hollow logo on black, bright blue or cream, unbleached cotton-$20; child's-$14

WOLF SONG OF ALASKA ♦ *page 199*
➤ T-shirts: Wolf Song of Alaska screened logo in blue, green or wine, one-size-fits-all-$17 ➤ Caps: blue and white embroidered logo on creme-grey corduroy-$12

CLOTHING

WOODSTOCK ANIMAL RIGHTS MOVEMENT ♦ *page 200*

← T-shirts: Endangered Means There Is Still Time, white, youth sizes-$13 ♦ Baby Wolves, black, youth sizes-$13 ♦ Celebrate Life, green-$17 ♦ dolphins, turquoise-$17 ♦ Chief Seattle, turquoise-$17 ♦ whales, navy blue-$17 ♦ Compassion For All Beings, black-$17 ♦ Animal Research-Too Much Pain And Torture For Too Little Knowledge, black-$17 ♦ two iguanas on black-$18 ← Sweatshirts: Celebrate Life, green-$25 ♦ white wolf on black-$25 ♦ two iguanas on black-$25

WORLD BIRD SANCTUARY ♦ *page 201*

← T-shirts: thick-billed parrots, colorful design on white, Preserve Habitat to Preserve Diversity on back-$12 ♦ red-tailed hawk, white design on black, World Bird Sanctuary on sleeve-$12; XXL for $14 ♦ great horned owl, white design on black, eyes are bright yellow, World Bird Sanctuary on sleeve-$12; XXL for $14; child's for $8.50 ♦ peregrine falcons on white-$12; XXL for $14 ♦ bald eagles, five-color design on white or gray-$12; XXL-$14; child's-$8.50 ♦ Harris' hawk, five color design on natural, long sleeved, mock tee or three button Henley collar-$22; XXL-$24 ♦ hummingbird, seven-color design on white-$14 ♦ owls of the Midwest, black design with red lettering on white-$12; XXL-$14 ♦ barn owl, WBS logo on white-$12; XXL $14 ♦ short-eared owl, color design on unbleached cotton-$12; XXL-$14 ♦ birds of the world, colorful design on white-$14 ← Sweatshirts: bald eagle on white, gray or yellow-$18 ♦ great horned owl on back-$18; XXL-$20 ← Shirts: teal fleece pullover, WBS logo embroidered on

breast, zipper front-$50 ➞ Jackets: red-tailed hawk coach
jacket, white design on black-$36 ➞ Ponchos: with WBS
logo, hooded with Velcro tabs, vinyl storage pouch, black
design on aqua-$12 ➞ Caps: bald eagle on red, gray or white-
$8 ✦ black WBS logo design on gray, red or white-$8 ✦ peregrine falcon, black design on gray, red or white-$8

WORLD WILDLIFE FUND ✦ *page 202*
➞ T-shirts: giraffe-$20 ✦ black-footed ferret-$16 ✦ iguana
-$16.95 ➞ Sweatshirts: midnight cat-$35 ➞ Nightshirts:
panda babies, adult sizes-$22.50; youth sizes-$12 ➞ Slippers:
frog design-$12.95 ➞ Vests: jungle safari-$45

XERCES SOCIETY ✦ *page 203*
➞ T-shirts: Monarch butterfly alighting on milkweed flowers,
white-$16.95

Computer Software & Supplies
Including CD-ROMs, mousepads, screen savers, software, video games

AMERICAN BIRDING ASSOCIATION ✦ *page 20*
➞ Software: five different bird databases-$49.95 to $125.00
➞ CD-Roms: birds, birdsongs and street atlases-$69.95 to
$150.00

BAT CONSERVATION INTERNATIONAL ✦ *page 40*
➞ Computer screen savers: Masters of the Night Skies-$19.95

JANE GOODALL INSTITUTE ✦ *page 113*
➞ Mousepads: four different rain forest scenes-$17 each

CLOTHING

COMPUTER
SOFTWARE
&
SUPPLIES

COMPUTER
SOFTWARE
&
SUPPLIES

LOS ANGELES AUDUBON SOCIETY ♦ *page 117*
➥ Software: bird databases for IBM and MAC-$59.95 to
$174.95 ➥ CD-Roms: four versions of Birds of North
America-$59 to $195 ➥ Video games: Gone Birding!-$44.95

NATURE CONSERVANCY ♦ *page 131*
➥ Computer screen savers: each has 22 photographs; choose
from five different themes (needs Microsoft Windows 3.1 and
a 256 color VGA)-$14.95 or 2 for $26

WHALE CONSERVATION INSTITUTE ♦ *page 185*
➥ CD-Roms: In The Company of Whales CD-ROM, by
WCI and Discovery Channel-$50

CRAFTS ## Crafts
Including cross-stitch kits and designs, flower and leaf press sets.

FRIENDS OF THE SEA OTTER ♦ *page 83*
➥ Cross-stitch kits: mother and pup, 10³/₄x9-$10.95 ✦ otter
pup, 9x7-$13.95

**WILD CANID SURVIVAL AND RESEARCH
CENTER** ♦ *page 189*
➥ Cross-stitch designs: booklet of two timber wolf designs-$4.95

**WOODSTOCK ANIMAL RIGHTS
MOVEMENT** ♦ *page 200*
➥ Flower & leaf press sets: $17.95

Desk Supplies & Accessories

Including desk sets, erasers, letter openers, memo pads, name/address labels, note cubes, notepads, note paper, pencils, pens, Post-It® notes, rulers

DESK
SUPPLIES
&
ACCES-
SORIES

AMERICAN BIRDING ASSOCIATION ♦ *page 20*

– Ballpoint pen/flashlights: -$4

BALTIMORE ZOO ♦ *page 206*

– Note cubes: zebra design-$9.95

CENTER FOR MARINE CONSERVATION ♦ *page 47*

– Letter openers: pewter humpback whale-$11.50

– Notepads: 3x4 light blue sticker notes with penguins, 50 sheets per pad, 10 pads-$13.50 ♦ turtle Post-It® notes, ten pads, 50 sheets each-$13.50 ♦ dolphin Post-It notes, ten pads, 50 sheets each-$13.50 – Note cubes: 3½" cubes of 350 pages, shell design-2 for $15 ♦ 3½" cubes, tropical fish design-2 for $15 ♦ 3½" cubes, penguins-2 for $15 ♦ frog scenes-2 for $18 ♦ dolphin note cubes, two of 350 pages-$17.50

DORIS DAY PET FOUNDATION ♦ *page 64*

– Memo pads: 5x7 white sheets with logo in red, 25 sheets-4 for $4.50 – Magnetic memo pad holders: with cartoon cat and dog, 4x5 holds 3x5 sheets-$14.95

INTERNATIONAL SOCIETY FOR ENDANGERED CATS ♦ *page 109*

– Pens: ultrafine point in your choice of 5 wildcats-$2

JUSTICE FOR ANIMALS ♦ *page 115*

– Memo pads: different animal rights quotes with artwork, 50 sheets-$3 – Pens: "Justice for Animals"-50¢ – Pencils: "Justice for Animals"-50¢ – Name/address labels: full color with different animal designs available-$6 for 200

DESK
SUPPLIES
&
ACCES-
SORIES

MID-ATLANTIC GREAT DANE RESCUE LEAGUE ◆ *page 125*

➤ Notepaper: head or body of Danes, four different designs-10 for $4.50

PEOPLE FOR ANIMAL RIGHTS ◆ *page 151*

➤ Pens: black and white logo on black and white ballpoint-$1

SAVE OUR STRAYS ◆ *page 168*

➤ Pens: ballpoint-5 for $3

SAVE THE WHALES ◆ *page 171*

➤ Pencils: neon colors of green, yellow, orange, pink or red-75¢ each or two for $1

TREE HOUSE ANIMAL FOUNDATION ◆ *page 180*

➤ Notepads: gray tabby magnetic-backed notepad, 100 sheets-$5.95   ➤ Letter openers: 8½", wooden with carved cats of orange, black or white-$5.95

WILD CANID RESEARCH AND SURVIVAL CENTER ◆ *page 189*

➤ Desk sets: pewter wolf statue mounted on wooden base with pen-$30   ➤ Pencils: Wolf Sanctuary, bright neons-30¢; wolf head, pencil toppers-30¢   ➤ Pens: ivory with brown Wolf Sanctuary lettering, retractable-$1.50   ➤ Letter openers: ivory with brown Wolf Sanctuary lettering-$1.50   ➤ Rulers: Wolf Sanctuary, white with black type, 6"-50¢

WORLD BIRD SANCTUARY ◆ *page 201*

➤ Pencils: WBS logo, assorted neon colors-25¢   ➤ Erasers: barn owls to fit pencils-50¢

Foods

Including chocolates, coffees.

CENTER FOR MARINE CONSERVATION ♦ *page 47*

→ Chocolate eggs: with chocolate turtle or penguin hatchlings inside-$17.50

FRIENDS OF WASHOE ♦ *page 84*

→ Coffees: Washoe blend, 20 oz.-$3.99

Gift Baskets

FARM SANCTUARY ♦ *page 70*

→ Gift baskets: includes four different vegetarian burger mixes, BBQ Fib Rib, Veggie Jerkey, educational literature on vegetarianism, a farm animal photo gift card, vegetarian cookbook-$30; without cookbook-$22

INTERNATIONAL SOCIETY FOR ENDANGERED CATS ♦ *page 109*

→ Gourmet gift baskets: Ohio-shaped basket with goodies for chocolate lovers and 2 black and gold ISEC mugs-$32 ♦ Deli basket with cookies, candies, Cocoa Amore and an ISEC mug-$20 ♦ Afternoon delight: mug with teas and cookies (may choose coffee or cocoa instead of tea)-$10 ♦ Gourmet jelly beans (or red and green jelly beans with Christmas wrap or blue and white jelly beans in Hanukkah wrap) in an ISEC mug-$12 ♦ Country basket with Cocoa Amore (may have herbal tea or coffee instead), cookies, gingerbread mix, two cookie cutters and an ISEC mug-$25

GIFT
WRAP

Gift Wrap

Including gift bags, gift wrap, gift enclosure cards.

FRIENDS OF THE SEA OTTER ♦ *page 83*

‑ Gift bags: holiday otter design-mini for $1.85; small for $2.85; medium for $3.85 ‑ Gift wrap: mother and pup design-3 sheets for $3.75 ‑ Gift enclosure cards: -5/$2.25

INTERNATIONAL PRIMATE PROTECTION LEAGUE ♦ *page 105*

‑ Gift wrap: gibbons-$4.50 for 3 packs

PIONEERS FOR ANIMAL WELFARE ♦ *page 156*

‑ Gift wrap: paw print with PAWS logo, red/green or black/white, 5 sheets of 19x28-$3; 10 sheets for $5

WILD CANID SURVIVAL AND RESEARCH CENTER ♦ *page 189*

‑ Gift bags: recycled brown paper with handles, stamped with paw prints or howling wolf-80¢; matching gift tags-40¢ ♦ color photo of grey wolf on glossy paper, matching gift tag, black woven handles, wolf information on side-$3.50

HOLIDAY
ITEMS

Holiday Items

Including holiday cards, tree ornaments, wreaths

BALTIMORE ZOO ♦ *page 205*

‑ Tree ornaments: rain forest tree, handcrafted aluminum-$19.95 ‑ Holiday cards: Baltimore Zoo-15 for $9.95

BROOKFIELD ZOO ♦ *page 208*

‑ Holiday cards: animal and nature messages-10 for $9
‑ Holiday fold-up note cards: -10 for $8 ‑ Tree ornaments: tiger-$2.95

BIRDS OF PREY REHABILITATION FOUNDATION ♦ *page 42*
— Holiday cards: snowy owl drawing-6 for $5

DALLAS ZOO ♦ *page 211*
— Tree ornaments: Dallas Zoo logo-$15.99

FARM SANCTUARY ♦ *page 70*
— Holiday cards: Frances the pig on front, Merry Oink inside-20 for $7

FRIENDS OF THE SEA LION ♦ *page 82*
— Holiday cards: -16 for $12.50

FRIENDS OF THE SEA OTTER ♦ *page 83*
— Tree ornaments: lacquered wheatstraw otter-$5.99 ♦ clay sea otter with starfish-$15 — Holiday cards: black and white, mother and pup otter-20 for $14.95 ♦ colorful otters-10 for $13.95

MICHIGAN ANTI-CRUELTY SOCIETY ♦ *page 123*
— Holiday cards: animal designs-20 for $10

MOUNTAIN LION FOUNDATION ♦ *page 127*
— Holiday greeting cards: holiday message with cougar-12 for $7.95

OPOSSUM SOCIETY OF CALIFORNIA ♦ *page 142*
— Holiday cards: "Happy O' Holidays, Gentle Blessings for All Creatures of the Earth," amused opossum design, red/green/black design on white-20 for $10 ♦ "Happy O'Holidays" on front with amused opossum design, blank inside, antique grey-tones on white-$1 each — Wreaths: wooden hand painted mother and baby opossum surrounded by floral cloth ribbon and silk leaves, 10" diameter (specify Christmas, Valentines Day, Easter, July 4th, Halloween or Thanksgiving)-$33

HOLIDAY
ITEMS

PELICAN MAN'S BIRD SANCTUARY ♦ *page 149*
➛ Holiday greeting cards: specially designed-20 for $10

**PROGRESSIVE ANIMAL WELFARE
SOCIETY** ♦ *page 159*
➛ Holiday cards: cow, Happy Moo Year-12 for $8.50 ♦ Peace
On Earth-And Goodwill to All-18 for $8.50

REDWINGS HORSE SANCTUARY ♦ *page 163*
➛ Holiday cards: featuring rescued animals; mother and foal or
donkeys-10 for $7.95

WHALE CONSERVATION INSTITUTE ♦ *page 185*
➛ Tree ornaments: southern right whale, humpback whale or
orca, 24K gold finish-$9.95

**WILD CANID SURVIVAL AND RESEARCH
CENTER** ♦ *page 189*
➛ Tree ornaments: rolled paper quilling, brown, white, red,
black or tan, 3"-$6

**WILDLIFE PRESERVATION TRUST
INTERNATIONAL** ♦ *page 195*
➛ Holiday cards: whimsical dodo drawing-12 for $8 ♦ thick-
billed parrot-12 for $8 ♦ sifaka (Madagascan primate) photo-12
for $8 ♦ golden-headed lion tamarin-12 for $8 ♦ variety of
dodos, sifkas, parrots and tamarins-12 for $8

Housewares & Home Accessories

Including baskets, bath mats, bathroom accessories, bookends, bowls, candles, canisters, children's training dishes, clocks, coasters, coat hooks, cookie cutters, cotton throws, crystal, dinnerware, door knockers, door mats, fans, glasses, key racks, lamps, magnets, mirrors, mobiles, mugs, night-lights, picture frames, pillow covers, pillows, platters, potpourri, potpourri bowls, rugs, salt and pepper sets, shower curtains, serving trays, soap dispensers, steins, stencils, switch plates, teapots, telephones, tiles, tissue boxes, towels, vases, wall hangings, wallpaper borders, wall plaques, welcome plaques, window gardens

HOUSE-
WARES
&
HOME
ACCESS-
ORIES

ACTORS AND OTHERS FOR ANIMALS ◆ *page 12*
➤ Celebrity autographed mugs: black and gold metallic, 66 names or 63 names-$7.20 each

ADOPT-A-COW ◆ *page 13*
• Mugs: travel-$2

AMERICAN ANTI-VIVISECTION SOCIETY ◆ *page 19*
➤ Mugs: royal blue, "Animals have Rights"-$6

AMERICAN HORSE PROTECTION ASSOCIATION ◆ *page 22*
➤ Mugs: white ceramic with royal blue imprint-$6.50; set of 4 for $20 ◆ travel mugs of white plastic with royal blue fitted lid and base with royal blue imprint-$5

AMERICAN RESCUE DOG ASSOCIATION ◆ *page 26*
➤ Tiles: -$8 ➤ Mugs: -$8

AMERICAN SOCIETY FOR THE PREVENTION OF CRUELTY TO ANIMALS ◆ *page 27*
➤ Mugs: ASPCA logo, white with navy type-$7 ➤ Umbrellas: navy, brown, forest green, black-$16

ANIMAL PROTECTION INSTITUTE OF AMERICA ♦ *page 31*

→ Mugs: glass, "Wild and running free"-$5; 4 for $20

ANIMAL RESCUE LEAGUE ♦ *page 32*

→ Photo mugs: send a photo to be imprinted on the mug, gift box included-$12.95

BALTIMORE ZOO ♦ *page 205*

→ Picture frames: animals carved by Arthur Court-$34.95

→ Rugs: handwoven children's rugs-$29.95

CARIBBEAN CONSERVATION CORPORATION ♦ *page 45*

→ Mugs: teal and purple CCC logo on white-$7.95

CENTER FOR MARINE CONSERVATION ♦ *page 47*

→ Candles: Earth globe which reveals three treasures when candle burns down-sterling whale tail pendant, a crystal, small pewter tree-$29.95 → Picture frames: dolphins surround this 3x2 frame, easel back-$16.50 ♦ collage of 3D sea life, 3½x5 -$19.95 → Lamps: sea life surrounds a coral reef, fish swimming on white shade 11½" tall-$56 → Vases: white opalescent with shimmering etched whales, 5" high-$54 → Potpourri bowls: penguin-shaped pewter lid-$18.50 → Glasses: 14 oz. double old fashioned drink glasses, each etched with a different dolphin, set of four-$28; set of four matching shot glasses-$16.50 ♦ 14 oz. double old fashioned drink glasses, each etched with a different whale, set of four-$28 ♦ different sea turtles etched on 14 oz. drink glasses, set of four-$28 → Child's training dishes: melamine set of divided plate, bowl, training cup, fork, spoon, vinyl placemat, all with endangered portraits-$24.94 → Mugs:

blue and white whale design on glazed stoneware, 10 oz.-$13.50
♦ manatees swimming through sunlit waters-$8 ♦ dolphin scene,
set of four stoneware mugs-$30 ♦ trumpet-shaped orca mug,
blue/black/white, hand painted glazed porcelain-$13.50
♦ dolphin mug, 12 oz. stoneware, may be personalized with 15
letters-$18.50 ♦ stoneware steins, pewter lids, wolf design, 7½"
tall, 10 oz.-$39.95 ♦ trumpet-shaped mug with humpback,
blue/white/black, glazed porcelain-$13.50 ➤ Teapots: green
porcelain with lobster handle, dolphin lid, fish spout, 16 oz.-
$32.50 ➤ Salt-and-pepper sets: black and white mother and
baby orcas, ceramic-$14.50 ♦ turtles-$17.95 ➤ Telephones: orca
with a splash-sound ringer-$79.95 ➤ Clocks: diving dolphins-
$22 ♦ hand painted fish on ceramic, 10½x7½-$60 ♦ hand painted
dolphins on ceramic, 8x11-$60 ♦ loon hand painted on ceramic,
3¾x7¾-$60 ➤ Cotton throws: sea turtle motif in green/blue/
natural, three layer fringe, 46x67-$60 ♦ manatees on pastel
shades of blue, pink, green and natural, fringed-$60 ♦ whales on
natural, green, navy and wine, fringed 46x67-$42.50 ♦ penguins,
navy and natural, fringed, 46x67-$43.50 ♦ dolphins on blue and
white, reversible, fringed, 46x67-$43 ♦ wolves in natural colors,
fringed, 67x46-$57 ➤ Rugs: colorful stenciled penguins, 2x3
-$29 ➤ Pillows: shell tapestry, 9" square-$16 ♦ three shell
shapes: pink starfish, 18x18; blue scallop, 14x18; green sand
dollar, 14x14-$27.50 each ♦ portrait of two wolves on black, 17"
square-$34 ➤ Door mats: hand painted with turtle hatchlings,
tan, 18x24-$24 ♦ coral reef, blue background 20x30-$27.95
♦ "Welcome" leaping dolphins, taupe/black, 18x24-$22.50

HOUSE-
WARES
&
HOME
ACCESS-
ORIES

HOUSE-
WARES
&
HOME
ACCESS-
ORIES

CENTER FOR MARINE CONSERVATION (CONT)

• "Welcome" with turtles on tan cut pile, 18x24-$23 ⟵ Door knockers: wooden loon, pull the string and it knocks-$34.50 ⟵ Shower curtains: clear vinyl with colorful turtle hatchlings-$19.95 • clear vinyl with whales-$16 • clear vinyl with sea shells-$25 • colorful starfish on blue background-$24 • blue dolphins on clear vinyl-$25 • black and white orcas against blue/green/white waves-$17.95 • colorful large tropical fish on clear vinyl-$25 • colorful smaller tropical fish on clear vinyl-$25 • penguins on clear vinyl-$25 ⟵ Bath mats: sea turtle on green deep soft nylon pile, 21x34-$29.95 • whale on deep pile, non-skid, 21x34-$22.50 • colorful sea shells on white, 21x43-$29.50 • scallop shape in sea mist green, 32x28-$35 • blue dolphin on white mat, 21x43-$25.50 • fish- shaped, primary colors, 22x34-$42 • penguin on gray background, 21x34-$24 ⟵ Towels: green sea turtle applique on white, bath-$18.50; hand-$13.50; fingertip-$8.50 • sea shells on blue or rose, bath-$11; hand-$8; fingertip-$5.50 • embroidered shells on sea mist green, hand-$14.50; fingertip-$10.50 • green dolphin applique on white, bath-$18.50; hand-$13.50; fingertip-$8.50 • colorful fish on white, bath-$15; hand-$12; wash cloth-$5.50 • beach towel, tropical fish, 50x31-$16.50 • loons on green or ivory, bath-$18.50; hand-$14.50; fingertip-$9.50 • penguins appliqued on white, bath-$18.50; hand-$13.50; fingertip-$8.50 ⟵ Soap dispensers: penguin in tuxedo, hand painted ceramic, 8" high-$21.50 • black and white orca, ceramic, 8" high-$21.50 ⟵ Tissue boxes: hand painted paper maché light blue whale-$34.50 ⟵ Welcome plaques:

"Welcome Friends" woodgrain design with sea turtle, hand cast of synthetic resin, hand painted, 11x8½-$29.95 ♦ "Welcome Friends" hand painted resin with dolphin, 14x7-$29.96
— Umbrellas: red with black and white penguins-$22 ♦ colorful whales in an ice blue sea-$22 ♦ coral reef with tropical fish, scalloped edges-$29 ♦ turtles, 3D head and tail, wood shaft and handle-$32

HOUSE-WARES & HOME ACCESS-ORIES

CHASE WILDLIFE FOUNDATION ♦ *page 49*
— Coasters: parrots of paradise-4 for $35

COLORADO HORSE RESCUE ♦ *page 50*
— Mugs: CHR logo-$7

COMMITTEE TO ABOLISH SPORT HUNTING ♦ *page 51*
— Pillow covers: owl-$24 — Wall hangings: owl-$24

CONCERN FOR HELPING ANIMALS IN ISRAEL ♦ *page 53*
— Picture frames: fabric covered, animal motif, small-$25; large-$30

DALLAS ZOO ♦ *page 211*
— Mugs: "Big Cat"-$6.99 ♦ Gray wolf-$7.99 — Teapots: monkey-$22.99; matching mugs-$6.99 each — Children's dinner sets: six pieces-$7.49

DESERT TORTOISE PRESERVE COMMITTEE ♦ *page 57*
— Mugs: beige with jade design-$7.50

DIAN FOSSEY GORILLA FUND ♦ *page 58*
— Mugs: gorillas-$5 ♦ Fossey Fund-$5 — Cookie cutter sets: gorillas, recipes, gift card -$5 — Steins: 25 ounces-$7

HOUSE-
WARES
&
HOME
ACCESS-
ORIES

DOGS FOR THE DEAF ♦ *page 59*
→ Mugs: insulated for hot or cold, granite gray with red lid and logo, 22 oz.-$5 ♦ 15 oz. ceramic blue with logo in white-$10 → Sports tumblers: 46 oz., granite grey with red flip-up lid, straw and logo-$7.50

DOLPHIN RESEARCH CENTER ♦ *page 62*
→ Magnets: dolphin color photographs, 3x4-$4.95

DORIS DAY PET FOUNDATION ♦ *page 64*
→ Key racks: rainbow, 3 hooks-$19.95 ♦ fence, 4 hooks-$19.95

EQUINE RESCUE LEAGUE ♦ *page 67*
→ Mugs: horse logo-$6

FRIENDS OF CONSERVATION ♦ *page 80*
→ German crystal with wildlife engraving: brandy snifters, champagne glasses, fruit bowls, tankards, tumblers, water pitchers, wine glasses, wine decanters-$50 to $325

FRIENDS OF THE SEA OTTER ♦ *page 83*
→ Serving trays: hand-inlaid sea otter-large for $47.50; medium for $37.50 → Dinnerware: otter designs-small plate for-$14.50; large plate for $45; mug for $7.95 → Mugs: colorful otters, travel-$12.50 ♦ tankard mugs, navy with gold trim mother and pup, 4½" high-$10.25 → Platters: glazed pottery, sea otter design, 16¾x5½-$76 → Coaster sets: sea otter design-4 for $29.95 → Canisters: glazed pottery with handpainted otter-$72 → Tiles: decorative with sea otter, hanger, two designs-$16 → Switch plates: otter mother and pup-$10.95 → Pillows: 22" otter-$82 ♦ decorative silver otters on blue, purple, and green waves, 14x14-$26 → Magnets: otter design, reproduction

scrimshaw, 2¼"-$3 ♦ ceramic sea otter, 2"-$6 → Clocks: ceramic with hand painted otter-$37 → Child's dish sets: melamine with otter designs includes bowl, training cup, spoon, fork, vinyl placemat, divided plate-$21.95 → Wall hangings: "Welcome," earthenware sea otter with blue or green ribbon-$46 → Picture frames: ceramic, mother and pup-$14.95

HOUSE-
WARES
&
HOME
ACCESS-
ORIES

GORILLA FOUNDATION ♦ *page 86*
→ Mugs: cobalt blue with white logo, 11 oz.-$10

HAWK MOUNTAIN SANCTUARY ♦ *page 89*
→ Mugs: "The World's First Sanctuary For Birds Of Prey" on one side and logo on the other, white stoneware-$8.50

HAWKWATCH INTERNATIONAL ♦ *page 90*
→ Mugs: white ceramic with logo in black, 11 oz.-$5

HELEN WOODWARD ANIMAL CENTER ♦ *page 91*
→ Mugs: white ceramic with blue logo-$5; larger blue mug-$61

HORSE POWER PROJECTS ♦ *page 95*
→ Mugs: heart tonka-$9.50

IN DEFENSE OF ANIMALS ♦ *page 99*
→ Mugs: Act! In Defense of Animals, with Harriet Beecher Stowe quote "It is a matter of taking the side of the weak against the strong, something the best people have always done," gray and red on white, 11 oz.-$7.50 ♦ Geckos with the Darwin quote "The love for all living creatures is the greatest attribute of man."-$7.50 ♦ Dalmatian on white, 14 oz. mug-$12

INTERNATIONAL MARINE MAMMAL PROJECT ♦ *page 103*
→ Mugs: dolphin or whale-$7.95

HOUSE-
WARES
&
HOME
ACCESS-
ORIES

INTERNATIONAL SNOW LEOPARD TRUST ♦ *page 106*

➞ Mugs: snow leopard-$7

INTERNATIONAL SOCIETY FOR ANIMAL RIGHTS ♦ *page 107*

➞ Mugs: ISAR logo-$5.95

INTERNATIONAL SOCIETY FOR ENDANGERED CATS ♦ *page 109*

➞ Mugs: ISEC logo in black with gold trim-$6 ➞ Magnets: ceramic tiger, white tiger or cheetah-$5 each

INTERNATIONAL WOLF CENTER ♦ *page 111*

➞ Mugs: logo on travel mug-$6.50 ♦ running wolves in iridescent gold or cobalt blue-$6 ➞ Night-lights: howling wolf handcast of resin-$34.95 ➞ Magnets: logo-$1

JANE GOODALL INSTITUTE ♦ *page 113*

➞ Magnets: mother chimp snuggles with baby, 2x2-$1 each

JUSTICE FOR ANIMALS ♦ *page 115*

➞ Mugs: animal designs and sayings-$6

MARINE MAMMAL STRANDING CENTER ♦ *page 120*

➞ Mugs: Cupid the Seal on front and back, ceramic, cobalt, 11 oz.-$6

MEOW ♦ *page 121*

➞ Mugs: MEOW logo-$6

MICHIGAN ANTI-CRUELTY SOCIETY ♦ *page 123*

➞ Mugs: cat and dog designs-$5

MICHIGAN HUMANE SOCIETY ♦ *page 124*

➞ Mugs: logo on cream-$7

**MID-ATLANTIC GREAT DANE RESCUE
LEAGUE** ◆ *page 125*

→ Mugs: various puppy postures-$10

**NATIONAL WILDLIFE REFUGE
ASSOCIATION** ◆ *page 129*

→ Mugs: blue and green logo on white porcelain, 11 oz.-$10;
2 for $18; 4 for $34

NATURE CONSERVANCY ◆ *page 131*

→ Mugs: logo on blue-$8.95 → Potpourri: natural fragrance,
5.5 oz.-$13.50 → Candle-in-glasses: natural fragrance-$34.95

**NEW YORK TURTLE AND TORTOISE
SOCIETY** ◆ *page 134*

→ Magnets: logo-$2

OPOSSUM SOCIETY OF CALIFORNIA ◆ *page 142*

→ Magnets: detailed polymer clay opossum-$10

PAWS WITH A CAUSE ◆ *page 148*

→ Mugs: ceramic beige with teal/maroon logo-$7.40 ◆ clear
acrylic with teal/maroon logo-$9 ◆ beige cooler cup with teal
or maroon logo-$5.40 ◆ clear grabber stein with teal/maroon
logo-$12 → Magnets: PAWS logo-$1 → Towels: golf, gray
with teal/maroon logo-$9

**PEOPLE FOR THE ETHICAL TREATMENT OF
ANIMALS** ◆ *page 152*

→ Humane mousetraps: catches mice alive and unharmed so
they can be released outdoors, 7x3x2½-$11.50

**PURPLE MARTIN CONSERVATION
ASSOCIATION** ◆ *page 160*

→ Mugs: 15 oz. with martin alone or PMCA logo-$7.95; 2 for
$13.95; 4 for $23.95

HOUSE-
WARES
&
HOME
ACCESS-
ORIES

RAPTOR CENTER AT THE UNIVERSITY OF MINNESOTA ♦ *page 161*

← Mobiles: four raptors for punch out, for children-$5 ← Mugs: full color bald eagle-$8

TREE HOUSE ANIMAL FOUNDATION ♦ *page 180*

← Mugs: maroon Tree House Foundation logo on grey travel mug with lid-$6.95 ← Magnets: fridge frames, colorful cat faces or dogs with bones-$5.95

WHALE ADOPTION PROJECT ♦ *page 184*

← Mugs: Whale Adoption Project, 10 oz., set of 2-$11.95 ♦ 12 oz., dolphin or whale-$6.95 ← Mobiles: six species of whales-$9.95

WHALE MUSEUM ♦ *page 186*

← Mugs: The Whale Museum with two orcas in black, white or almond-$6.95 ♦ The Whale Hotline design in white or almond-$6.95

WILD CANID SURVIVAL AND RESEARCH CENTER ♦ *page 189*

← Mugs: Inca portrait in green on white plastic, 12 oz.-$4.25 ♦ Mexican wolf-$5 ♦ howling wolf on ivory with brown design-$5 ← Clocks: two resting wolves etched in smoked acrylic, simulated walnut base-$50 ← Magnets: Wolf Sanctuary-$1 ♦ full wolf body, white, black or grey-$4.50 ♦ three styles of rectangular Leanin' Tree magnets-$3 ← Mobiles: endangered species punchout-$5

WILDLIFE PRESERVATION TRUST INTERNATIONAL ♦ *page 195*

← Mugs: red and green thick-billed parrot on white-$7.50; $14 for two ♦ WPTI red dodo logo on white-$7.50; $14 for two

WOLF HOLLOW WILDLIFE REHABILITATION CENTRE ♦ *page 198*

➞ Mugs: Wolf Hollow logo and animal tracks, brown on cream-$10

WOLF SONG OF ALASKA ♦ *page 199*

➞ Mugs: blue logo on white ceramic-$8 ➞ Clocks: a moose and wolves decorate this wooden wall clock in the shape of Alaska, brass accents, 17x13-$135 ♦ romancing wolves look out into a blue sky of starry constellations-$125

WOODSTOCK ANIMAL RIGHTS MOVEMENT ♦ *page 200*

➞ Shower curtains: dolphins, tropical fish or world map-$25 ♦ Earth From Space-$28 ♦ Rainbow Sea-$30 ➞ Mugs: Animals Have Rights-$6.50 ♦ Stop Animal Testing-$7.95 ♦ Rats Have Rights-$7.95 ♦ Fur Is Dead-$7.95 ♦ Eat Your Vegetables-$7.95 ♦ oversized, tuskers with elephant handle-$10.95 ➞ Candles: eagle-$25 ♦ whale-$13 ♦ dolphin-$13 ➞ Wall plaques: terra cotta ceramic sun and moon designs, small-$7.95; medium-$25; large-$49.95 ➞ Window gardens: Purrfect gardens, catgrass and catnip-$14

WORLD BIRD SANCTUARY ♦ *page 201*

➞ Mugs: owl, hawk, or falcon, ceramic-$5 ♦ WBS barn owl logo, ceramic, white on black or black on white-$4
➞ Magnets: owl, hawk, or falcon, ceramic-$4

WORLD WILDLIFE FUND ♦ *page 202*

➞ Cotton throws: animal print, 46x67-$52.50 ➞ Clocks: frog-sound alarm clocks-$25 ➞ Bookends: wolf design-$75
➞ Telephones: panda design-$50 ➞ Mirrors: open mouth frog mirror-$25

HOUSE-
WARES
&
HOME
ACCESS-
ORIES

Jewelry

Including belt buckles, bolos, bracelets, brooches, charms, earrings, jewelry boxes, money clips, necklaces, pendants, pins, rings, tie tacks, watches.

ALASKA WILDLIFE ALLIANCE ◆ *page 16*
→ Pins: 11 different wildlife designs, enameled-$13 to $16
→ Watches: wolf on the face, with Citizen quartz movement in brass with gold plating-$59.95

AMERICAN CETACEAN SOCIETY ◆ *page 21*
→ Pendants: sterling silver fluke-$24 ◆ sterling dolphin-$18
→ Tie tacks: hand painted pewter, killer whale, sperm whale, humpback whale or sea turtle-$8

AMERICAN LIVESTOCK BREEDS CONSERVANCY ◆ *page 24*
→ Earrings: handcrafted pewter, choose from three different pig breeds or a Dominique chicken-$10 → Pins: handcrafted pewter, choose from three different pig breeds or a Dominique chicken-$15 → Tie tacks: handcrafted pewter, choose from three different pig breeds or a Dominique chicken-$10

AMERICAN RESCUE DOG ASSOCIATION ◆ *page 26*
→ Tie tack/lapel pins: -$5

BALTIMORE ZOO ◆ *page 205*
→ Earrings: penguin-$14.95 ◆ turtle-$13.95 ◆ bear-$9.95
→ Necklaces: African animals, brass with gold plate-$59.95
◆ six different wooden African animals-$12.95 → Pins: elephant, solid brass with gold plate-$24.95

BEST FRIENDS ANIMAL SANCTUARY ◆ *page 41*
→ Pins: handcrafted porcelain cat, monkey, fox, horse or lizard-$15

CARIBBEAN CONSERVATION CORPORATION ♦ *page 45*

JEWELRY

━ Earrings: sterling silver drop sea turtles-$49.95 ♦ sterling silver sea turtles with green gemstones-$37.50 ━ Bracelets: sterling silver sea turtles with green gemstones-$75
━ Charms: sterling silver CCC logo charm-$32.95
━ Rings: sterling silver turtle, men's-$39.95; women's-$26.95
━ Pins: sterling silver sea turtle-$12

CENTER FOR MARINE CONSERVATION ♦ *page 47*

━ Pendants: 14K gold heart-shaped dolphin pendant with a genuine diamond-$186.50 ♦ 14K gold sea turtle-$100 ♦ sterling silver humpback whale with 18" silver chain-$36.50 ♦ whale tails in amethyst accented by sterling, 18" chain-$22.50 ♦ sterling mother nuzzles 14K gold calf, 18" sterling chain-$65 ♦ 14K gold and diamond whale tail-$175 ♦ 14K gold humpback whale-$110 ♦ 14K gold whale tail-$54 ♦ 14K gold mother and calf-$164.50 ━ Earrings: 14K gold heart-shaped dolphin posts-$135 ♦ sterling silver sea turtles with blue glass beads-$22.50 ♦ 14K gold sea turtles-$24.50 ♦ sterling silver humpback whales for pierced-$36 ♦ whale tails in amethyst accented by silver-$25 ♦ sterling silver dolphins dangle from lapis and silver beads-$32.50 ♦ sterling silver whale tails on sterling wires-$24 ♦ delicate nautiluses on wires-$20 ♦ 14K gold dolphins, posts-$50 ♦ sterling dolphin hoops with azurite and malachite beads-$14.50 ♦ 14K gold whale tails on wires-$90 ♦ polished brass dolphins play against teal and purple disks, wires-$19.95 ♦ sterling silver dolphins on spheres of aqua aura-$19.95 ♦ brass frog and deep turquoise

JEWELRY **CENTER FOR MARINE CONSERVATION (CONT)**

disk hang from ear wires-$16.50 • nickel/silver wolves on wires-$14.95 • sterling silver turtles with blue and silver beads, wires-$28.95 — Rings: sterling silver turtles, sizes 5,6,7,8-$20 • sterling silver humpback whale, adjustable-$34.50 • sterling silver procession of dolphins, sizes 5,6,7,8-$37.50 • sterling silver parade of dolphins, sizes 5,6,7,8-$42.50 • silver dolphin-$80 • 14K gold humpback whale-$250 • 14K gold dolphin-$295 • sterling silver swimming dolphins, sizes 5,6,7,8-$14 • 14K gold whale tail and wave, sizes 5,6,7,8,9-$235 — Bracelets: sterling silver sea turtles, adjustable-$36.50 • sterling silver humpback whales, adjustable-$45 • sterling silver mother nuzzling a baby, 7"-$47.50 • 14K gold humpback whales, 7"-$380 • 14K gold dolphins, 7"-$475 — Necklaces: green aventurine stone turtle wrapped in sterling silver, 18" sterling box chain-$22.50 • dolphin harmony ball, 1" silver ball with brass dolphin, 30" black cord-$32 • sterling silver penguin, 18" chain-$13.50 • sterling silver whale tail on 26" black cord-$32 • sterling silver mother manatee and baby, 18" chain-$34.95 • sterling silver dolphin on aqua aura ball, 18" chain-$18.95 • sterling silver dolphins on rose quartz heart on 18" chain-$55 — Pins: sterling silver sea otter holding a cultured pearl-$40 — Tie tacks: 14K gold whale tail-$55 — Watches: diving penguin-$37.50 • wolf on face, 3/4" wide black band-$49.95 • dolphins dive into waves, quartz, black leather band-$37.50 — Money clips: pewter humpback whale-$11.50

JEWELRY

COMMITTEE TO ABOLISH SPORT HUNTING ♦ *page 51*

➡ Necklaces: sterling silver and cloisonné Canada goose-$175 ♦ sterling silver and cloisonné deer-$195 ♦ sterling silver handmade links, 23"-$125   ➡ Pins: C.A.S.H. logo-$1.50 ♦ "Hunting sucks"-$2 ♦ "Fur sucks"-$7.95

DALLAS ZOO ♦ *page 211*

➡ Necklaces: Handmade miniature perfume bottles, from Africa-$6.99

DELTA SOCIETY ♦ *page 56*

➡ Pins: enamel cloisonné with multicolor logo-$7

DESERT TORTOISE PRESERVE COMMITTEE ♦ *page 57*

➡ Pins/tie tacks: enamel desert tortoise-$2.85   ➡ Pendants/ bolos: ceramic and leather tortoise design-$2.35

DIAN FOSSEY GORILLA FUND ♦ *page 58*

➡ Pins: pewter silverback gorilla-$6 ♦ Fossey Fund logo-$6

DOGS FOR THE DEAF ♦ *page 59*

➡ Pins: 1" lapel pin-$3 ♦ 1½" colorful lapel pin-$5

DOLPHIN RESEARCH CENTER ♦ *page 62*

➡ Earrings: dolphins on 14K gold posts-$26 ♦ 14K gold hoops-$36   ➡ Rings: sterling silver dolphin, adjustable-$14 ➡ Charms: 14K gold dolphin charm or pendant-$38 ➡ Pendants: 14K gold tail fluke pendant or charm-$32 ➡ Pins: gold-washed dolphin with poem, lapel pin-$5.95

ELEPHANT RESEARCH FOUNDATION ♦ *page 66*

➡ Pendants: silver elephant with ERF insignia-$40

FRIENDS OF ANIMALS ♦ *page 78*

➡ Pins: FoA logo-$5

JEWELRY **FRIENDS OF CONSERVATION** ♦ *page 80*
→ Pendants & pins: 14K and 18K gold cheetah logo-$350 to $495

FRIENDS OF THE SEA OTTER ♦ *page 83*
→ Pins: sterling silver sea otters-$38 ♦ sterling silver mother
otter and sleeping pup-$34.95 ♦ sea otter of gold or silver-
$12.50 ♦ sterling silver and amethyst sea life-$57 ♦ pewter sea
otter lapel pin-$3 → Earrings: sterling silver sea otters-$40
♦ gold or silver-plated otters-$16 ♦ gold-plated otter swing-
$36 → Watches: otter design, leather wristband-$59

GORILLA FOUNDATION ♦ *page 86*
→ Pendants /charms: sterling silver gorilla-$8

GREAT BEAR FOUNDATION ♦ *page 87*
→ Earrings: grizzly and salmon, gold plate-$18 ♦ grizzly and
salmon, sterling silver-$20 → Necklaces: grizzly, gold plate or
sterling silver-$30 → Pins: gold-plate grizzly tack pin-$16
♦ antique finish pewter grizzly tack pin-$8 → Bolos: pewter
grizzly bear-$30 → Belt buckles: bronze grizzly bear-$60
♦ pewter grizzly bear-$50

HAWK MOUNTAIN SANCTUARY ♦ *page 89*
→ Pins: silver bald eagle or golden eagle-$30 ♦ silver redtail,
redshoulder goshawk, osprey or harrier-$28 ♦ silver broadwing
or peregrine-$22 ♦ silver kestrel, merlin, sharpshin or small
broadwing-$15

HAWKWATCH INTERNATIONAL ♦ *page 90*
→ Earrings: handmade brass perched hawk on wires-$12
→ Pins: handmade brass soaring hawk-$20 → Bolos:
handmade brass Cooper's hawk-$24

HEMLOCK HILL FARM SANCTUARY ✦ *page 93*   JEWELRY
- Earrings: hand-beaded in your choice of colors, clip or pierced, some with semi-precious stones-$3 to $15

HOOVED ANIMAL HUMANE SOCIETY ✦ *page 94*
- Charms: HAHS logo, rose gold electroplate with blue enamel-$20

INTERNATIONAL CRANE FOUNDATION ✦ *page 101*
- Pins: logo-$2.50

INTERNATIONAL SOCIETY FOR ANIMAL RIGHTS ✦ *page 107*
- Pins: "I respect all creation"-$5 ✦ elephant or butterfly-$14 ✦ pig, bronze colored-$9 ✦ whale, black and white-$12

INTERNATIONAL SOCIETY FOR ENDANGERED CATS ✦ *page 109*
- Earrings: small cheetah in gold or silver plate-$12 ✦ jaguar in gold or silver plate-$20 ✦ bobcat in gold or silver plate-$12 ✦ leopard in gold or silver plate-$18 — Necklaces: leopard, choker length in gold or silver plate-$32 — Pins: ISEC spell cat in cloisonné in gold or silver plate outline-$5 ✦ two lions in gold or silver plate-$18 ✦ Amboseli/Kilimanjaro-$24 ✦ ceramic tiger, white tiger or cheetah-$5 each

INTERNATIONAL WOLF CENTER ✦ *page 111*
- Pins: running wolves-$10.95 ✦ wolf howling at the moon, carved from antler-$24.9 — Earrings: running wolves-$20 ✦ lone wolf-$18 ✦ coyote howling-$15 ✦ sterling silver wolf track-$22.95 — Necklaces: sterling silver wolf track-$18

JUST CATS ✦ *page 114*
- Pins: clay paw print-$12

JEWELRY **LEND-A PAW RELIEF ORGANIZATION** ♦ *page 116*
➜ Pins: bear design-$1 ➜ Watches: Lend-A-Paw logo on red
and white face-$24.95; black and gold face-$29.95

LOS ANGELES AUDUBON SOCIETY ♦ *page 117*
➜ Pins: assortment of bird and animal designs available-$11.95

MARINE MAMMAL STRANDING CENTER ♦ *page 120*
➜ Pins: silver, MMSC's First Aid logo, ³/₄"-$2

**MID-ATLANTIC GREAT DANE RESCUE
LEAGUE** ♦ *page 125*
➜ Jewelry: sterling silver and semi-precious stones by a Navajo
artist based on pre-historic cave drawings-$10.50 to $300

MISSION: WOLF ♦ *page 126*
➜ Bracelets & necklaces: handspun friendship bracelets and
necklaces from naturally shed wolf fur-$10 to $100

**NATIONAL WILDLIFE REFUGE
ASSOCIATION** ♦ *page 129*
➜ Pins: blue and gold on white cloisonné shield design-$3.50

NATURE CONSERVANCY ♦ *page 131*
➜ Pins: TNC logo, bronzed-$3

NORTH AMERICAN WOLF SOCIETY ♦ *page 139*
➜ Pins: pewter logo lapel pin-$5

OPOSSUM SOCIETY OF CALIFORNIA ♦ *page 142*
➜ Earrings: opossums with sterling silver findings, drop or
post, hand-sculptured detailed polymer clay, glows in the dark
-$15 ♦ gold plated opossum suspended in a hoop with a pink
pearl set on his belly, pierced ears-$15 ➜ Pins: detailed
polymer clay opossum, glows in the dark-$15 ➜ Tie tacks:
detailed polymer clay opossum, glows in the dark-$10

PACIFIC WHALE FOUNDATION ♦ *page 146*
— Pendants: sterling silver whale tail-$15

PAWS WITH A CAUSE ♦ *page 148*
— Pins: beige with teal/maroon logo-$3

PRESERVATION OF THE AMAZON RIVER DOLPHIN ♦ *page 158*
— Necklaces: from the Shambira palm, made with colorful seeds-$4 to $25 — Bracelets: from the Shambira palm, some with seeds-$5 to $10

PURPLE MARTIN CONSERVATION ASSOCIATION ♦ *page 160*
— Earrings: flying birds in niobium-$15.95 ♦ flying birds in sterling silver-$16.95 — Tie tacks: flying bird in niobium-$11.95 ♦ flying bird in sterling silver-$12.95

RAPTOR CENTER AT THE UNIVERSITY OF MINNESOTA ♦ *page 161*
— Earrings: many styles of pierced earrings in birds of prey designs-$12 to $21

RAPTOR EDUCATION FOUNDATION ♦ *page 162*
— Pins: pewter or gold, hand painted-$3 to $20

ROCKY MOUNTAIN RAPTOR PROGRAM ♦ *page 165*
— Pins: enamel great horned owl-$14 ♦ enamel bald eagle-$14 ♦ enameled American kestrel-$11 ♦ enameled peregrine-$9
— Earrings: single feather-$24 ♦ double feather-$42 ♦ sterling spring-$48 ♦ bear paw-$50

SANGRE DE CRISTO ANIMAL PROTECTION ♦ *page 167*
— Pendants: sterling silver with SdeCAP logo-$25 — Pins: sterling silver with SdeCAP logo-$25

JEWELRY **SAVE THE WHALES** ♦ *page 171*
➤ Earrings: sterling silver whales for pierced-$17.95

TIMBER WOLF PRESERVATION SOCIETY ♦ *page 179*
➤ Belt buckles: pewter wolf-$23.75 ♦ brass on copper wolf-$26.75 ➤ Pins: cloisonné pin of TWPS wolves, Cleo-$3.95; Boltar-$7.65 ➤ Bolos: Cinnamon the wolf-$11.95
➤ Brooches: Cinnamon the wolf-$11.95

WAIKIKI AQUARIUM ♦ *page 228*
➤ Earrings: nautilus, 14k gold-$145 ➤ Bracelets: sterling silver dolphin-$113 ♦ 14k gold fish-$910 ➤ Charms/pendants: sterling silver whale tail, large-$51; medium-$27; small-$12 ♦ 14k gold whale tail, large-$128.50; medium-$59.50; small-$30

WHALE ADOPTION PROJECT ♦ *page 184*
➤ Watches: WAP logo on white 1⅛" dial, black band-$31.95 ♦ WAP logo on white ¾" dial, black vinyl band-$29.95 ➤ Pins: 1⅛" enamel humpback whale-$4.95 ➤ Tie tacks: hand painted pewter humpback whale, orca killer whale or sea turtle-$10.95

WHALE MUSEUM ♦ *page 186*
➤ Pins: round enamel TWM logo-$4.95 ♦ gold and black spy hopping orca bar pin-$8.95

WHERE WOLVES RESCUE ♦ *page 187*
➤ Earrings: sterling silver or gold plate wolfhead-$48
➤ Pendants: sterling silver or gold plate wolfhead-$24
➤ Pins: sterling silver or gold plate wolfhead-$24

WILD CANID SURVIVAL AND RESEARCH CENTER ♦ *page 189*
➤ Tie tacks: enamel wolf-$4.50 ♦ wolf profile, silver-$18
➤ Earrings: cloisonné wolf face, for pierced-$5 ♦ sterling silver

circle with wolf, for pierced-$42.50 ♦ wolf face, silver, for pierced-$36 → Pendants: sterling silver circle with wolf, 18" chain-$42.50 ♦ howling wolf, silver-$32 → Belt buckles: wolves in 3-D, fits 2" belt, pewter-$10; enameled-$13

JEWELRY

WILDLIFE PRESERVATION TRUST INTERNATIONAL ♦ *page 195*
→ Pins: red and gold enamel dodo lapel pin or tie tack-$4
→ Bracelets: silver pewter alloy motifs on a soft durable cord; choose a bird of prey, rhinoceros, tiger, gecko, snake or elephant-$6.99

WOLF HAVEN INTERNATIONAL ♦ *page 197*
→ Pins: logo pin of green/silver/gray/white-$4 ♦ gray or black wolf head-$4

WOLF SONG OF ALASKA ♦ *page 199*
→ Pins: colorful logo on cloisonné pin-$5.95

WOODSTOCK ANIMAL RIGHTS MOVEMENT ♦ *page 200*
→ Pendants: pewter Earth on a black satin cord-$13 ♦ sterling silver dolphin-$28 ♦ sterling silver whale tail-$36 → Bracelets: sterling silver African elephants-$48 ♦ sterling silver endangered species charm bracelet-$76 ♦ sterling silver dolphin link bracelet-$76 ♦ sterling silver dolphin-$110 → Pins: sterling silver dolphin-$56 ♦ sterling silver whale and calf-$76
→ Earrings: pewter lizards, tree frog, dolphin, pig or Earth-$13 ♦ sterling silver whale tail-$28

WORLD BIRD SANCTUARY ♦ *page 201*
→ Pins: WBS logo-$3.50

LUGGAGE ## Luggage

Including backpacks, briefcases, drawstring bags, duffel bags, hip/fanny packs, luggage tags, school bags, shoulder bags, tote bags.

AMERICAN LIVESTOCK BREEDS CONSERVANCY ♦ *page 24*

→ Tote bags: William Beebe quote "...when the last individual of a race of living things breathes no more, another Heaven and another Earth must pass before such a one can be again." on natural canvas-$10

AMERICAN SOCIETY FOR THE PREVENTION OF CRUELTY TO ANIMALS ♦ *page 27*

→ Tote bags: ASPCA logo, navy-$12

ANIMAL PROTECTION INSTITUTE OF AMERICA ♦ *page 31*

→ Tote bags: canvas, "Who will speak for me?"-$10 → Fanny packs: "Big or Small, Short or Tall...API Protects Them All."-$10

BALTIMORE ZOO ♦ *page 205*

→ Duffel bags: jungle safari design-$17.95 ♦ rain forest design-$24.95 → Drawstring bags: jungle safari design-$14.95 → School bags: jungle safari design-$19.95 → Tote bags: African waterhole design-$18.50

CENTER FOR MARINE CONSERVATION ♦ *page 47*

→ Tote bags: colorful Emperor penguins, white cotton-$18.95 ♦ over-all orca scene silkscreened on canvas, zippered top-$22.50 ♦ red-eyed tree frog design on black canvas-$18.95 ♦ penguins on white, black handles-$22 → Duffel bags: colorful tropical fish all over, 20x9½-$21.50 → Backpacks: frogs on blue and green, durable water repellent vinyl, 14x10½-$11

....

```
┌─────────────────────────────┐
│        SECTION FIVE          │
└─────────────────────────────┘
```

....

COMMITTEE TO ABOLISH SPORT HUNTING ◆ *page 51*
→ Tote bags: owl-$24

DELAWARE VALLEY RAPTOR CENTER ◆ *page 55*
→ Tote bags: eagle design-$10

DIAN FOSSEY GORILLA FUND ◆ *page 58*
→ Tote bags: Fossey Fund logo-$10 → Luggage tags: DFGF logo in green and black on white, sized to hold standard business card-$2.75

DOGS FOR THE DEAF ◆ *page 59*
→ Tote bags: black with colorful design-$15

DOLPHIN RESEARCH CENTER ◆ *page 62*
→ Fanny packs: colorful canvas, kids' size, dark blue and turquoise with stuffed dolphin on front-$12

DORIS DAY ANIMAL LEAGUE ◆ *page 63*
→ Tote bags: "I Love Cats" or "I Love Dogs," white with red handles-$15

DORIS DAY PET FOUNDATION ◆ *page 64*
→ Fanny packs: nylon with zipper pouch, black w/white logo or red w/black logo-$8.95

EARTHTRUST ◆ *page 65*
→ Tote bags: Flipper-$15

FARM ANIMAL REFORM MOVEMENT ◆ *page 69*
→ Tote bags: several designs available-$15

FARM SANCTUARY ◆ *page 70*
→ Tote bags: If You Love Animals Called Pets...Why Do You Eat Animals Called Dinner? natural color with green handle and graphic-$8

LUGGAGE **FRIENDS OF THE SEA OTTER** ♦ *page 83*
→ Tote bags: canvas with FSO design-$14.95

FRIENDS OF WASHOE ♦ *page 84*
→ Tote bags: Institute logo with chimp profile, green/black-brown-$6.95

FUND FOR ANIMALS ♦ *page 85*
→ Tote bags: "Protect Wildlife," turquoise on beige-$17.00

HAWK MOUNTAIN SANCTUARY ♦ *page 89*
→ Tote bags: natural canvas with HM logo-$9.95

HUMANE EDUCATION COMMITTEE ♦ *page 96*
→ Tote bags: -$7

HUMANE SOCIETY OF THE UNITED STATES ♦ *page 98*
→ Tote bags: "Animals..It's their world too."-$16.95

IN DEFENSE OF ANIMALS ♦ *page 99*
→ Tote bags: Shop Cruelty Free, with Darwin quote "The love for all living creatures is the greatest attribute of man."-$12.95

INTERNATIONAL MARINE MAMMAL PROJECT ♦ *page 103*
→ Tote bags: dolphin design-$9

INTERNATIONAL SOCIETY FOR ANIMAL RIGHTS ♦ *page 107*
→ Tote bags: "Animals Don't Smoke; Animals Don't Drive; Animals Don't Wear Makeup; Animals Don't Use Paint; Animals Don't Drink Alcohol; Animals Don't Drop Bombs; Because you do, why should they suffer?"-$10

INTERNATIONAL WILDLIFE REHABILITATION COUNCIL ♦ *page 110*
→ Tote bags: large, IWRC logo on heavy canvas-$15

INTERNATIONAL WOLF CENTER ♦ *page 111*   LUGGAGE
➝ Tote bags: IWC logo on canvas-$15.95
LEND-A-PAW RELIEF ORGANIZATION ♦ *page 116*
➝ Tote bags: cat design-$10
MEOW ♦ *page 121*
➝ Tote bags: MEOW logo-$7 to $18
MICHIGAN HUMANE SOCIETY ♦ *page 124*
➝ Tote bags: unbleached canvas with cream shoulder straps,
MHS logo-$13
MISSION: WOLF ♦ *page 126*
➝ Tote bags: Circle Of Wolves, canvas-$15
MOUNTAIN LION FOUNDATION ♦ *page 127*
➝ Tote bags: cougar drawing, teal and violet on natural cotton
canvas-$11.95
NATURE CONSERVANCY ♦ *page 131*
➝ Tote bags: logo on unbleached canvas-$7.95; 2 for $12.95
♦ canvas, choose bison, Florida panther, coral reef, polar bears,
wolf, bald eagle-$18.95 ♦ embroidered logo on forest green
canvas-$22.50 ➝ Duffel bags: choose bald eagle, bison, coral
reef, polar bears or wolf-$24.95
**NORTH AMERICAN VEGETARIAN
SOCIETY** ♦ *page 138*
➝ Tote bags: -$15
PAWS WITH A CAUSE ♦ *page 148*
➝ Tote bags: beige with teal/maroon logo-$8

LUGGAGE

PROGRESSIVE ANIMAL WELFARE SOCIETY ♦ *page 159*
— Tote bags: black/red animal tracks and names on ivory canvas-$9.50

PURPLE MARTIN CONSERVATION ASSOCIATION ♦ *page 160*
— Tote bags: colorful PMCA logo with gourd on natural canvas-$12.95

SAVE OUR STRAYS ♦ *page 168*
— Tote bags: wheeled-$20

TREE HOUSE ANIMAL FOUNDATION ♦ *page 180*
— Tote bags: "Have A Heart For Animals," pale gray logo on maroon with zipper closure-$16.95

WHALE ADOPTION PROJECT ♦ *page 184*
— Tote bags: large, with navy blue whales, cotton duck-$15.95
— Duffel bags: petite shoulder sling with navy blue whales-$16.95

WILD CANID SURVIVAL AND RESEARCH CENTER ♦ *page 189*
— Tote bags: Keeping The Dream Alive, WCSRC logo and wolf pup, natural canvas-$6

WILDLIFE PRESERVATION TRUST INTERNATIONAL ♦ *page 195*
— Tote bags: red and white dodo logo on black canvas-$12

WOODSTOCK ANIMAL RIGHTS MOVEMENT ♦ *page 200*
— Backpacks: leather look-a-like, black-$38 — Briefcases: leather look-a-like, black-$45 — Shoulder bags: leather look-a-like, flapfront, black-$48 — Tote bags: canvas, Earth Day on

natural or wolf on black-$15 ➞ Duffel bags: iguana, LUGGAGE
black/green-$21.50 ♦ leather look-a-like, black or brown-$18

WORLD BIRD SANCTUARY ♦ *page 201*
➞ Tote bags: WBS canvas logo-$7

WORLD WILDLIFE FUND ♦ *page 202*
➞ Duffel bags: jungle print-$25

Miscellaneous MISC.

Including baskets, fans, humane mousetraps, license plate frames, license plates, key chains/tags, lunch bags/boxes, medicine cards, penlights, umbrellas, wallets

AMERICAN BIRDING ASSOCIATION ♦ *page 20*
➞ Penlights: -$4

AMERICAN RESCUE DOG ASSOCIATION ♦ *page 26*
➞ Key chains: -$7

ANIMAL PROTECTION INSTITUTE OF AMERICA ♦ *page 31*
➞ Lunch boxes: cool-insulated, soft-sided, API logo-$15
➞ License plate holders: "Stand Up For Animals"-$2

ANIMAL RESCUE ♦ *page 32*
➞ Key tags: holds a photo, 2x3-$4.95

ASSOCIATED HUMANE SOCIETIES ♦ *page 38*
➞ Lunch boxes: for children, includes sandwich box and thermos with jungle motif-$15

BROOKFIELD ZOO ♦ *page 208*
➞ Lunch boxes: jungle print, with canteen-$20; sandwich container-$6

MISC. **CARIBBEAN CONSERVATION CORPORATION** ♦ *page 45*

– Key chains: sterling silver sea turtle-$99.95

CENTER FOR MARINE CONSERVATION ♦ *page 47*

– Key rings: pewter humpback whale-$11.50 • pewter penguin and baby-$8 • pewter wolf-$12 • pewter loon-$14.95

ELEPHANT RESEARCH FOUNDATION ♦ *page 66*

– Key chains: silver elephant with ERF insignia-$15

FRIENDS OF THE SEA OTTER ♦ *page 83*

– Key rings: otter face, pewter for $5.25; brass for $5.95

GREYHOUND FRIENDS ♦ *page 88*

– Key chains: leather embossed with GF logo-$4

IN DEFENSE OF ANIMALS ♦ *page 99*

– License plate holders: Act Now-In Defense of Animals, set of two-$6.95

INTERNATIONAL SOCIETY FOR ANIMAL RIGHTS ♦ *page 107*

– Key chains: plastic, "I fight for animals"-$1.50 – Umbrellas: "Too much of a good thing-spay/neuter your pets"-$16.99

MICHIGAN HUMANE SOCIETY ♦ *page 124*

– License plates: MHS logo-$5 – License plate frames: MHS logo-$3

OPOSSUM SOCIETY OF CALIFORNIA ♦ *page 142*

– License plate frames: Opossum Society, choose chrome or black finish with black printing on silver, gold, yellow or ivory background-$10

MISC.

PAWS WITH A CAUSE ♦ *page 148*
→ License plates: beige with teal/maroon logo-$5

PRESERVATION OF THE AMAZON RIVER DOLPHIN ♦ *page 158*
→ Baskets: handwoven from the Shambira palm-$10 to $200
→ Fans: made in the Amazon-$5 to $10

PROGRESSIVE ANIMAL WELFARE SOCIETY ♦ *page 159*
→ Key chains: PAWS logo blue/white acrylic tag-$3.50

SANGRE DE CRISTO ANIMAL PROTECTION ♦ *page 167*
→ Key chains: sterling silver with SdeCAP logo-$25

SAVE THE WHALES ♦ *page 171*
→ Key chains: white heart-shaped Save The Whales logo and message-$2.50

WILD CANID SURVIVAL AND RESEARCH CENTER ♦ *page 189*
→ Wallets: trifold, tan, Wolf Sanctuary logo-$5

WOODSTOCK ANIMAL RIGHTS MOVEMENT ♦ *page 200*
→ Key rings: pewter wolf, dolphin, pig or horse-$13 → Lunch bags: reusable canvas with Velcro closures; choose Save A Tree (fall colors), I Am Saving A Tree (green/red), Recycle (pink/green/blue) or Save The Earth (blue/green)-$7.50
→ Medicine cards: illustrated, includes text-$29.95

WORLD BIRD SANCTUARY ♦ *page 201*
→ Key chains: nail clipper, knife and bottle opener on key chain with logo-$3.50

OUTDOOR
ITEMS

Outdoor Items

Including banners, bat detectors, bat houses, binoculars, bird feeders, bird houses, birding equipment, canteens, compasses, flags, flashlights, garden ornaments and supplies, gourds, mailboxes, naturalists' tools, sports water bottles, suncatchers, wind chimes, wind socks.

AMERICAN BIRDING ASSOCIATION ♦ *page 20*
➝ Binoculars, spotting scopes, tripods and viewing equipment: large selections in all price ranges

BAT CONSERVATION INTERNATIONAL ♦ *page 40*
➝ Bat houses: single-chambered house-$49.95 ♦ do-it-yourself kit-$39.95 ♦ multi-chamber condo-$84.95 ➝ Bat detectors: ultrasonic-$265

CENTER FOR MARINE CONSERVATION ♦ *page 47*
➝ Flags & flag poles: manatee on blue, design on both sides, 28x40 ♦ whale or dolphin on blue, design on both sides, 28x40-$26; flag pole and bracket set-$25 ♦ two penguins on blue background, design on both sides, 28x40-$26; pole and bracket-$25 ➝ Mailboxes: red-eyed tree frog-$89 ♦ sand-carved red cedar with loon design on natural green background-$89

DALLAS ZOO ♦ *page 211*
➝ Kids' canteens: -$7.49 ➝ Kids' binoculars:-$5.99

DAYS END FARM HORSE RESCUE ♦ *page 54*
➝ Sports cups: non-tip, 32 oz.-$4

DESERT TORTOISE PRESERVE COMMITTEE ♦ *page 57*
➝ Wind chimes: ceramic, brown-$10

DOGS FOR THE DEAF ♦ *page 59*
→ Sports tumblers: 46 oz., granite gray with red flip-up lid, straw and logo-$7.50

OUTDOOR
ITEMS

DORIS DAY PET FOUNDATION ♦ *page 64*
→ Sports bottles: red or blue, with straw, 32 oz.-$4.95

HAWK MOUNTAIN SANCTUARY ♦ *page 89*
→ Water bottles: with logo, 21 oz.-$3.95; 28 oz.-$4.95; with detachable belt holster, 21 oz.-$8.95 → Compasses: -$6.95

LOS ANGELES AUDUBON SOCIETY ♦ *page 117*
→ Birding equipment: binoculars, scopes, bird calls, bags
→ Bird and seed feeders: -$9.95 to $47

PEREGRINE FUND ♦ *page 153*
→ Hummingbird feeders: 4 feeding stations, 15 oz. capacity -$6.50; hummingbird food-$2

PURPLE MARTIN CONSERVATION ASSOCIATION ♦ *page 160*
→ Bird houses: over 25 different, for purple martins-$24.95 to $329.95 → Bird feeders: eggshell feeder-$18.95; 5 foot post-$8.95
→ Gourds: many different, natural or plastic-$17.95 to $119.95

TREE HOUSE ANIMAL FOUNDATION ♦ *page 180*
→ Sports bottles: 32 oz. plastic squeeze bottle with straw and flip-top cap embossed with Tree House logo-$4.95

WHALE ADOPTION PROJECT ♦ *page 184*
→ Wind chimes: whales of handmade porcelain-$24.95
→ Wind socks: humpback whale-$24.95

WILDLIFE HABITAT ENHANCEMENT COUNCIL ♦ *page 194*
→ Nest boxes: bluebird-$22 ♦ wood duck-$48 ♦ screech owl-$29.95
→ Hopper feeders: platform feeder, 20x13½ at the base-$48

OUTDOOR ITEMS

WOLF SONG OF ALASKA ♦ *page 199*
➤ Banners: hand painted wolf design on a triangular wood or cloth banner, 19x10-$30

WOODSTOCK ANIMAL RIGHTS MOVEMENT ♦ *page 200*
➤ Kids' gardens: veggie set with pots, tools and seeds-$14.95 ♦ sunflower set-$14.95 ➤ Bat house kits: 6x15x8-$21.95 ➤ Bird house kits: 5³/₄x4³/₄x10-$11.95 ➤ Cedar feeder kits: holds one cup of birdseed-$7.50 ➤ Wood birdfeeder kits: 6x6, age 6 up-$9.95 ➤ Flags: Earth, 3'x5'-$39; 2'x3'-$25

WORLD BIRD SANCTUARY ♦ *page 201*
➤ Bird feeders: recycled plastic in red, blue, yellow or lime green-$6

PERSONAL CARE & GROOMING PRODUCTS

Personal Care & Grooming Products

Including body powders, deodorants, face creams, hair barrettes, hair conditioners, hand and body lotions, hennas, lipstick caddies, makeup, massage oils, perfumes and colognes, pill boxes, purse mirrors, razors, shampoos, soaps, toothbrushes, vitamins.

BALTIMORE ZOO ♦ *page 205*
➤ Soaps: Clean Critters soaps-3 for $9.95

CENTER FOR MARINE CONSERVATION ♦ *page 47*
➤ Toothbrushes: metallic colored dolphins swimming in the handle, three replacement heads-$12.50 ➤ Soaps: glycerin dolphins in assorted pastel colors, 4" long, set of four-$7.95 ➤ Hair barrettes: frogs of antiqued brass-$13.95

SECTION FIVE

PERSONAL CARE & GROOMING PRODUCTS

PEOPLE FOR THE ETHICAL TREATMENT OF ANIMALS ♦ *page 152*

➥ Razors: cruelty-free razor lets you boycott cruelty and get a good shave with the pivoting twin-blade razor system (with ten blades)-$8.85

PROGRESSIVE ANIMAL WELFARE SOCIETY ♦ *page 159*

➥ Soaps: various unpackaged round bars, scented, free of animal ingredients, 3 oz.-99¢ each ➥ Vitamins: 6 preparations available, vegan, no animal ingredients-$6.95 to $34.95

SAVE OUR STRAYS ♦ *page 168*

➥ Pill boxes: flower design-$2.50 ➥ Purse mirrors: kitty design, for purse-$3 ➥ Lipstick caddies: holds 2 tubes-$3

WOODSTOCK ANIMAL RIGHTS MOVEMENT ♦ *page 200*

➥ Soaps: glycerin bar, "rain" scent by Terra Nova, 3.75 oz.-$2.50 ♦ liquid glycerin, "rain" scent by Terra Nova, 8 oz.-$7.50 ♦ scented Woodspirit soaps, 5 different, 4 to 8 oz.-$3.50 to $6 each ➥ Shampoos: biodegradable, by Terra Nova, 8.75 oz.-$7.50; gel, 8.5 oz.-$8.50 ♦ Beauty Without Cruelty, 16 oz., regular and extra body-$4.95 ➥ Hair conditioners: Beauty Without Cruelty, regular and extra body, 16 oz.-$4.95 ➥ Makeup: full line of cosmetics available by Beauty Without Cruelty ➥ Face creams: cleansers, fresheners, moisturizers, masks, eye gels by Beauty Without Cruelty-$6.95 to $12.95 ➥ Hand and body lotions: oil free, 16 oz.-$6.95 ➥ Massage oils: 8.75 oz.-$9.50 ➥ Perfumes and colognes: "rain" scent by Terra Nova, .33 oz. to 2 oz.-$8.50 to $12 ➥ Body powders: "rain" scent by Terra Nova, 3 oz.-$8 ➥ Hennas: eight different shades, 4 oz.-$5.95 each

363

PET CARE **Pet Care Supplies**

*Including cat bowls and placemats, cat and dog grooming products
and tools, catnip, cat toys, dog coats and sweaters, dog collars and
leashes, gift certificates, pet first aid kits, pet foods.*

ALLIANCE AGAINST ANIMAL ABUSE ♦ *page 17*
⤚ Dog sweaters: handmade, of various sizes and colors-$5

**AMERICAN SOCIETY FOR THE PREVENTION
OF CRUELTY TO ANIMALS** ♦ *page 27*
⤚ Cat bowls & placemats: -$20

DORIS DAY PET FOUNDATION ♦ *page 64*
⤚ Pet first aid kits: -$19.95

FELINES ♦ *page 71*
⤚ Cat toys: assorted balls, catnip, etc.

FUND FOR ANIMALS ♦ *page 85*
⤚ Cat bowls: "The Best Cat Ever," ceramic, 5" diameter-$6.00

GREYHOUND FRIENDS ♦ *page 88*
⤚ Dog sweaters: custom knit, plain-$35; greyhound design-
$45 ⤚ Dog coats: heavy nylon with fleece lining, red, blue or
green-$35 ⤚ Dog collars: nylon webbing, choke-$7 • custom
embossed leather-$10 ⤚ Dog leashes: nylon webbing, choke
matching above-$8

LEND-A-PAW RELIEF ORGANIZATION ♦ *page 116*
⤚ Cat care: assorted toys, leashes, catnip-$1 to $15

**PEOPLE FOR THE ETHICAL TREATMENT OF
ANIMALS** ♦ *page 152*
⤚ Cat grooming tools: Sheads All is a durable plastic
grooming tool for cats-$5.50

PET PRIDE OF NEW YORK ♦ *page 154*
➤ Cat care products and toys: $5 to $74.95

SAN FRANCISCO SPCA ♦ *page 166*
➤ Gift Certificates: pet adoptions & grooming sessions

WOODSTOCK ANIMAL RIGHTS MOVEMENT ♦ *page 200*
➤ Animal care products: natural shampoos, dips, powders, deodorizers, coat enhancers, litter treatments, collars-$4.95 to $8.95 ➤ Pet foods: treats and supplements; vegetarian cat/dog food-$1.19 to $23.95

PET CARE SUPPLIES

Stationery

STATIONERY

Including birthday cards, condolence cards, envelopes, foldover notes, greeting cards, note cards, postcards, stationery sets.

ALASKA WILDLIFE ALLIANCE ♦ *page 16*
➤ Postcards: wolf pups-10 for $3.50 ➤ Note cards: wolf designs-8 for $15 ♦ Alaska wildlife-8 for $15

AMERICAN CETACEAN SOCIETY ♦ *page 21*
➤ Note cards: dolphins or whales-10 for $8 ♦ marine life in black and white-10 for $5 ➤ Postcards: whales-12 for $3

AMERICAN LIVESTOCK BREEDS CONSERVANCY ♦ *page 24*
➤ Note cards: illustrations of seven different pig breeds-7 for $5 ♦ William Beebe quote "...when the last individual of a race of living things breathes no more, another heaven and another earth must pass before such a one can be again."-10 for $5 ♦ ALBC logo on ivory paper-10 for $5 ♦ Belted Galloway drawing, choose red or white envelopes-10 for $3 ♦ livestock silhouettes-10 for $5

STATIONERY

AMERICAN SOCIETY FOR THE PREVENTION OF CRUELTY TO ANIMALS ♦ *page 27*
➡ Note cards: two different sets of cards and envelopes-$12 per set

BAT CONSERVATION INTERNATIONAL ♦ *page 40*
➡ Stationery: nectar bat set-$11.95   ➡ Note cards: bat design-$11.95

BEST FRIENDS ANIMAL SANCTUARY ♦ *page 41*
➡ Greeting cards: black and white cat photos-12 for $12.95

BIRDS OF PREY REHABILITATION FOUNDATION ♦ *page 42*
➡ Note cards: assorted raptor drawings-6 for $5

CARIBBEAN CONSERVATION CORPORATION ♦ *page 45*
➡ Note cards: endangered species-6 for $5

CAT CARE SOCIETY ♦ *page 46*
➡ Note cards: "Cajun Caper," 12 designs-$1.50 each or $1.05 each for 12 or more

CENTER FOR MARINE CONSERVATION ♦ *page 47*
➡ Stationery: set for children includes alligator eraser, lion scissors, giraffe ruler, pen-$8

CENTER FOR WHALE RESEARCH ♦ *page 48*
➡ Note cards: marine mammal portraits-10 for $7.50

CHASE WILDLIFE FOUNDATION ♦ *page 49*
➡ Note cards: wildlife of India-12 for $12

CONCERN FOR HELPING ANIMALS IN ISRAEL ♦ *page 53*
➡ Note cards: boy with poodle-10 for $7 ♦ children and animals, royal blue designs on cream paper-8 for $5

DALLAS ZOO ♦ *page 211*
➤ Notepads: gorilla, tiger or wolves-$5.49

DELAWARE VALLEY RAPTOR CENTER ♦ *page 55*
➤ Note cards: assorted, diurnal raptors or nocturnal raptors-$5

DELTA SOCIETY ♦ *page 56*
➤ Note cards: printed or embossed logo-8 for $9.95

DESERT TORTOISE PRESERVE COMMITTEE ♦ *page 57*
➤ Note cards: watercolor, tortoise and hare-10 for $4
♦ tortoise photo-5 for $3.75 ♦ burrowing owl-10 for $2
➤ Postcards: tortoise or foxes-5 for $1.00

DIAN FOSSEY GORILLA FOUNDATION ♦ *page 58*
➤ Note cards: color photos by wildlife photographer-10 for $12

DOGS FOR THE DEAF ♦ *page 59*
➤ Note cards: -10 for $4

DORIS DAY PET FOUNDATION ♦ *page 64*
➤ Note cards: pen and ink drawings of animals-10 for $5.50

ELEPHANT RESEARCH FOUNDATION ♦ *page 66*
➤ Foldover notes: Asian or African elephant artwork-12 for
$5; 40¢ for single sheets

FARM SANCTUARY ♦ *page 70*
➤ Note cards: photo of two Sanctuary pigs nosing the
barnyard gate to greet you and all your friends-20 for $7

FELINES ♦ *page 71*
➤ Note cards: -10 for $3.50

FRIENDS OF THE SEA OTTER ♦ *page 83*
➤ Greeting cards: with removable sea otter magnet-$2.95 each
➤ Stationery: otter designs and envelopes-16 sheets for $6.95

STATIONERY **FRIENDS OF THE SEA OTTER** (CONT)

➤ Note cards: otters on front, FSO message on back-10 for $7.95 ♦ otters in watercolor-8 for $11 ♦ mother and pup-10 for $4.50 ♦ sea otter photo-$1.50 ♦ miniature cards, 3½x5½-10 for $5.25 ➤ Postcards: assorted pen and ink drawings of otters-6 for $1.50

GREYHOUND FRIENDS ♦ *page 88*

➤ Note cards: black & white drawing of greyhound on white paper w/envelopes-10 for $4.50 ➤ Postcards: standing greyhound in full color-10 for $10

HAWKWATCH INTERNATIONAL ♦ *page 90*

➤ Note cards: raptors in color artwork, package of eight-$6 ♦ pen and ink drawings of hawks, set of six-$5 ♦ pen and ink drawings of owls, set of six-$5 ➤ Postcards: six different raptors available-$1 each

HELPING HOMELESS CATS ♦ *page 92*

➤ Note cards: black and white, kitten and teardrop design-10 for $5

HUMANE FARMING ASSOCIATION ♦ *page 97*

➤ Note cards: pigs or cows-12 for $10

IN DEFENSE OF ANIMALS ♦ *page 99*

➤ Note cards: Lincoln and "Animal rights"-12 for $4.95

INTERNATIONAL MARINE MAMMAL PROJECT ♦ *page 103*

➤ Note cards: three dolphins-10 for $12

INTERNATIONAL PRIMATE PROTECTION LEAGUE ♦ *page 105*

➤ Note cards: drawings of gibbons-12 for $10

INTERNATIONAL SNOW LEOPARD TRUST ♦ *page 106*

— Note cards: snow leopard-10 for $8

INTERNATIONAL SOCIETY FOR ANIMAL RIGHTS ♦ *page 107*

— Note cards: pen and ink collage of wild and domestic animals-5 for $6 — Greeting cards: assorted animal scenes for birthdays and other occasions-12 for $9.95

INTERNATIONAL SOCIETY FOR ENDANGERED CATS ♦ *page 109*

— Postcards: assorted wild cat drawings-$1 each
— Note cards: 5 cards of a different wild cat species-$4.50 per pack ♦ mother and baby wildcat designs-4 for $4.50

INTERNATIONAL WILDLIFE REHABILITATION COUNCIL ♦ *page 110*

— Greeting cards: wildlife designs-8 for $5

INTERNATIONAL WOLF CENTER ♦ *page 111*

— Note cards: color photos of Arctic wolf and pup, Mexican wolf or wolves romping-$1.50 each ♦ We Are All One World, with wolf, woman and butterfly-$1.75; the same but with man-$1.50 — Postcards: color wolf photos, two different IWC collections of 22 postcards-$8.95 ♦ IWC resident pack on a postcard-50¢

LEND-A-PAW RELIEF ORGANIZATION ♦ *page 116*

— Note cards: cat design-$1 each — Condolence cards: cat design-$1.25 each or 4 for $5

MOUNTAIN LION FOUNDATION ♦ *page 127*

— Note cards: cougar on recycled paper-10 for $7.95

369

STATIONERY

NATURE CONSERVANCY ♦ *page 131*

➞ Note cards: assorted cards with patterned envelopes-10 for $14.95

NEW ENGLAND ANTI-VIVISECTION SOCIETY ♦ *page 133*

➞ Note cards: six different black and white animal designs-$4 ♦ six different animal color photos-$4 ♦ four different rabbit color photos-$4

OPOSSUM SOCIETY OF CALIFORNIA ♦ *page 138*

➞ Note cards: colorful design of opossum with balloons on 5x7 glossy paper-10 for$12

ORANGUTAN FOUNDATION INTERNATIONAL ♦ *page 144*

➞ Note cards: orangutan drawings-12 for $12

PAWS WITH A CAUSE ♦ *page 148*

➞ Note cards: 12 styles available-$10 per package

PEREGRINE FUND ♦ *page 153*

➞ Note cards: eight different birds of prey in color-$5

PET PRIDE OF NEW YORK ♦ *page 154*

➞ Note cards: design by artist Peter Berg-$10

PURPLE MARTIN CONSERVATION ASSOCIATION ♦ *page 160*

➞ Note cards: set of 25 with martins in textured black ink-$6.95 ➞ Stationery: set of 4 tablets (100 sheets) printed with purple martins-$5.95

RACINE ZOO ♦ *page 223*

➞ Note cards:-$4 per pack

REDWINGS HORSE SANCTUARY ♦ *page 163*
➥ Note cards: watercolors of rescued animals-10 for $7.95
♦ color photos of rescued animals-$2

ROCKY MOUNTAIN RAPTOR PROGRAM ♦ *page 165*
➥ Note cards: six different drawings of raptors (great horned owl, screech owl, red-tailed hawk, bald eagle, American kestrel)-$1 each or pack of 12 for $10

SAVE OUR STRAYS ♦ *page 168*
➥ Notepads: jumbo pads, animal design-3 for $4.50
➥ Envelopes: animal design-5 for $3 ➥ Stationery sets: set of one pad, one pen and 25 envelopes-$3

SAVE THE MANATEE CLUB ♦ *page 170*
➥ Postcards: five each of a manatee mother nursing her calf and two manatee pals surfacing for air-10 for $2.50

SAVE THE WHALES ♦ *page 171*
➥ Greeting cards: Save The Whales, Mary Englebreit design-$1.95each ➥ Note cards: gray whale-4 for $4.95 ♦ eight different marine animals-8 for $13.95

SEA TURTLE RESTORATION PROJECT ♦ *page 173*
➥ Greeting cards: six different species of the sea turtle in color with sea turtle natural history on back-6 for $12

SINAPU ♦ *page 174*
➥ Postcards: black & white wolf photo on recycled paper-4 for $1; 20 for $3

SUTTON AVIAN RESEARCH CENTER ♦ *page 177*
➥ Note cards: bald eagle parent and chick-6 for $5

STATIONERY **TIMBER WOLF PRESERVATION SOCIETY ♦** *page 179*

➼ Note cards: assorted wolf designs-$6.95

TRUMPETER SWAN SOCIETY ♦ *page 181*

➼ Note cards: trumpeter family-10 for $7

UNITED POULTRY CONCERNS ♦ *page 182*

➼ Postcards: drawings and photos of chickens-20 for $4;
40 for $7.50 ♦ Love Is Best-20¢ and 32¢ ♦ Chickens-To Know
Them Is To Love Them-32¢ ♦ Misery Is Not A Health Food-
32¢ ♦ Peaceable Kingdom-20¢ ♦ Re-Searching The Heart-20¢
♦ Turkey & Child: Friends-20¢

VEGETARIAN RESOURCE GROUP ♦ *page 183*

➼ Postcards: Be Kind to Animals - Don't eat Them-10 for $2;
30 for $5 ♦ Be Wary Of Dairy-19 for $2; 30 for $5 ♦ vegan
recipes-10 for $2; 30 for $5

WAKIKI AQUARIUM ♦ *page 228*

➼ Note cards: sea creatures on heavy recycled paper-12 for $14

WILD BURRO RESCUE ♦ *page 188*

➼ Greeting cards: mother and baby burros or herd of running
burros, 100% recycled paper-6 for $10

**WILD CANID SURVIVAL AND CENTER
RESEARCH ♦** *page 189*

➼ Note cards: wolf profile and howling wolf, blue and gray-12
for $18 or $1.50 each ♦ wolf face with wolf border designs at
top and bottom-12 for $18 or $1.50 each ♦ wolf pup and
stalking wolf, black/dark red on tan-8 for $6.50 ♦ wolf pack
howling at the moon on a snowy night-12 for $18 or $1.50
each ♦ two nuzzling Mexican wolves, dark brown and tan

recycled paper-10 for $4.50 ♦ surreal blue and white design of   STATIONERY
a pack of Arctic wolves-12 for $18 or $1.50 each ♦ color design
of wolf with Native American theme-12 for $12 ♦ wolf, moon
and stars in white/taupe/rust-12 for $18 or $1.50 each ♦ wolf
and bear illustration in Native American style-12 for $15
→ Birthday cards: It's Your Day To Howl! Happy Birthday!
howling wolves, fold-out-$1.95 → Postcards: red wolf ink design
on ivory recycled paper-30¢ ♦ Mexican wolf pup photo-30¢

WORLD BIRD SANCTUARY ♦ *page 201*
→ Note cards: assorted raptors-8 for $5 ♦ assorted hawks-8 for
$5 ♦ assorted owls-$5 ♦ assorted eagles/falcons-$5

XERCES SOCIETY ♦ *page 203*
→ Note cards: color reproductions from the Getty Museum featuring invertebrates, fruit, flowers and calligraphy-12 for $13.95

Toys & Games

TOYS
&
GAMES

*Including activity books and sets, animal replica toys, art sets, balls,
bean bag toys, card sets and games, coloring books, educational toys
and games, Frisbees, juggling toys, kites, Make-a-Mug kits, Make-
a-Plate kits, masks, puppets, puzzles, rubber stamp sets and supplies,
sticker sets, stuffed toys, whistles, wooden models*

**AMERICAN SOCIETY FOR THE PREVENTION
OF CRUELTY TO ANIMALS** ♦ *page 27*
→ Coloring books: Big Cats Little Cats-$4.95

ANIMAL RESCUE ♦ *page 32*
→ Coloring books: -$2

ANTI-CRUELTY SOCIETY ♦ *page 36*
→ Frisbees: -$3

TOYS
&
GAMES

BALTIMORE ZOO ♦ *page 205*

━ Balls: Friends of the Forest Earth ball-$21.95 ♦ rain forest inflataballs-2 for $9.95 ━ Stickers: Stick 'n Lift books-2 for $11.95 ━ Wildlife watercolors: 2 paint sets for $8.95 ━ Puppets: penguin-$22.95 ♦ turtle-$15.95 ━ Puzzles: alphabet puzzle-$14.95 ━ Art sets: jungle safari-$24.95 ━ Rubber stamps: rain forest set-$10.95 ━ Card games: Animal Rummy-3 for $10.50

BAT CONSERVATION INTERNATIONAL ♦ *page 40*

━ Card sets: bat fact cards, pack of 25-$1.85

BEST FRIENDS ANIMAL SOCIETY ♦ *page 41*

━ Bean bag toys: frog, gecko, snake or turtle-$15

BROOKFIELD ZOO ♦ *page 208*

━ Art set: art supplies with jungle motif-$22.50 ━ Jumbo crayons: -12 for $3.50 ━ Puppets: spider-$11.50 ♦ bat-$17 ♦ scorpion-$22.50 ━ Wood kits: scorpion or spider-$6.50 ━ Puzzles: frog or turtle-$6.75 ━ Drawing books: endangered animals-$8

CARIBBEAN CONSERVATION CORPORATION ♦ *page 45*

━ Whistles: hand painted ceramic turtle from Nicaragua-small, $5.95; medium, $7.95; large, $14.95 ━ Stuffed toys: non-toxic plush sea turtles, 12"-$22.50; 17"-$54.50; 24"-$86.50

CENTER FOR MARINE CONSERVATION ♦ *page 47*

━ Stuffed toys: sea otter with a stuffed sea shell, 7" long-$13.50 ♦ baby emperor penguin 7" tall-$13.50 ♦ manatee, 15" long-$24.50 ♦ mother turtle with three plush babies inside, mother 10," babies 4"-$17 ♦ white baby harp seal, 14" long 8" high-$16 ♦ 12" mother whale and two babies, 5³⁄4-$17 ♦ baby orca, 12"-$12.50 ♦ dolphin, 16" long-$14.50 ♦ whale with "tooth fairy" pouch, 7½ long-$12.50 ➝ Puzzles: underwater scene pulsing with sea life, 1000 pcs.-$13 ♦ frog slide puzzles, 4" square, ages 5 up-$7.50 ♦ manatee and baby, 1000 pcs.-$16.50 ♦ tropical fish, 500 pcs.-$12.95 ♦ dolphins and sea life, 500 pcs.-$14.95 ♦ portrait of two wolves, 1000 pcs.-$15.95 ➝ Games: Animal Bingo, ages 4 to 11-$15.95 ♦ Ocean Pick-Up Pairs, 96 cards, age 4 up-$8.50 ➝ Rubber stamp sets: 12 sea animal stamps, crayons, ink pad, pencil, eraser, sharpener, carry case, 10³⁄4x7x2-$17.50 ➝ Activity sets: four animals, self inking stamp, 12" sea life ruler, sea life puzzle, pencil, pad, drawstring bag-$14.50

DIAN FOSSEY GORILLA FUND ♦ *page 58*
➝ Stuffed toys: gorilla, 17" tall-$25 ➝ Coloring books: mountain gorilla—$3

DALLAS ZOO ♦ *page 211*
➝ Stuffed toys: 14" gorilla-$34.99 ♦ 9" baby gorilla-$14.99 ♦ Noah's ark with detachable animals-$38.99 ➝ Puppets: 19" full body lion puppet-$52.99 ♦ 30" full body wolf hand puppet-$52.99 ➝ Rainy day activity sets: age 4 and up-$15.99 ➝ Travel box of animals in carry case: -$5.99

DOLPHIN RESEARCH CENTER ♦ *page 62*
➝ Stuffed toys: dolphin, 3"-$3.95; 7"-$9.95; 14"-$20

FARM SANCTUARY ♦ *page 70*
➝ Puppets: pig-$13 ♦ chick-$5 ♦ rabbit-$10 ♦ lamb-$24

Toys
&
Games

FRIENDS OF BEAVERSPRITE ♦ *page 79*
━ Stuffed toys: beaver, 10"-$9 ♦ squirrel, 10"-$9 ━ Puppets:
beaver hand puppet, 12"-$20

**FRIENDS OF THE AUSTRALIAN KOALA
FOUNDATION** ♦ *page 81*
━ Stuffed toys: koala, 10"-$12; 15"-$16

FRIENDS OF THE SEA OTTER ♦ *page 83*
━ Sticker sets: 60 of twelve different aquatic animals-$3.49
━ Rubber stamps: otter-$5.50 ━ Puzzles: sea otter, for age 8
and up-$5.95 ♦ two-sided with sea otter and otter information,
500 pieces, for children and adults-$11.95 ━ Stuffed toys:
otter, 9"-$15 ━ Rubber toys: sea otter family (mom, dad, and
pup) of unbreakable rubber with sea otter information, 2½"-
$3.75 ━ Puppets: sea otter, 11"-$19.99

HAWK MOUNTAIN SANCTUARY ♦ *page 89*
━ Stuffed toys: eagle in three sizes, 6"-$7.95; 8"-$11.95; 20"-$49.95

HUMANE FARMING ASSOCIATION ♦ *page 97*
━ Coloring/activity books: farm animals, ages 3 to 10 or 6 to 14-$3

**INTERNATIONAL FUND FOR ANIMAL
WELFARE** ♦ *page 102*
━ Stuffed toys: whale, 8"-$9.95

**INTERNATIONAL PRIMATE PROTECTION
LEAGUE** ♦ *page 105*
━ Stickers: gibbons and gorillas, five assorted sheets-$5

**INTERNATIONAL SOCIETY FOR COW
PROTECTION** ♦ *page 108*
━ Coloring books: Friends for Life, 48 pages-$5

INTERNATIONAL WOLF CENTER ♦ *page 111*
━ Activity books: Discovering Wolves, wolf biography and

behavior, all ages, 40 pages-$4.95 ♦ Discovering Endangered
Species, nature activity book, 40 pages-$4.95 ─ Coloring
books: The Alaska Wolf, 47 pages-$7.95 ─ Sticker activity
books: Wildlife Create-a-Picture, age 3 up-$6.75 ♦ Baby
Animals Create-a-Picture, young children-$6.75 ─ Rubber
stamps: wolf paw print-$4.50 ♦ timber wolf-$5 ─ Stuffed toys:
howling wolf pup, 12" tall-$24.95 ─ Animal replica toys: brown
timber wolf or white arctic wolf, 3½" tall, plastic, adult-$5.95;
pup, 2½" tall-$2.95; set of two adults and a pup-$14.95 ♦ forest
animals: plastic bear, fox, wolf, lynx, elk and hare-$6.75

TOYS
&
GAMES

JANE GOODALL INSTITUTE ♦ *page 113*
─ Puzzles: four different rain forest scenes, 1000 pieces-$12 each
**NEW YORK TURTLE AND TORTOISE
SOCIETY** ♦ *page 134*
─ Games: The Crazy Turtle Game, match up heads and tails-$5
NORTH AMERICAN BEAR SOCIETY ♦ *page 136*
─ Stuffed toys: teddy bear with "Care About Bears"-$15
OPOSSUM SOCIETY OF CALIFORNIA ♦ *page 142*
─ Coloring books: Cleo the Opossum, personalized book con-
tains six illustrations with text (include child's name when
ordering)-$3 ♦ Cleo & Ben Have an Opossum Adventure, per-
sonalized book contains six illustrations with text (include
child's name when ordering)-$3 ─ Stickers: fuzzy opossum,
panel of four poses-35¢ ─ Puzzles: mother with baby
opossums, wood, 5½x3½-$29 ─ Rubber stamps: single
opossum, ½"x1"-$5 ♦ mother and baby opossum, 1½x1½-$7
─ Hand puppets: squeaking opossum-$18

TOYS & GAMES

PAWS WITH A CAUSE ♦ *page 148*

– Coloring books: Pilot the Service Dog-$5 – Stuffed animals: gold puppy with PAWS backpack-$12

PEREGRINE FUND ♦ *page 153*

– Educational toys: Optic Wonder, when opened makes binoculars, magnifying glass and compass-$5 – Coloring books: Forests-$8.95 – Activity books: Bird Mazes-$1 ♦ Discovering Endangered Species-$3.95 – Stuffed animals: eagle, 11"-$22 ♦ owl, 9"-$17; 6½"-$12; 5½"-$9 – Kites: bald eagle, made of durable tyvek, assembled-$60; unassembled-$50 ♦ osprey, made of durable tyvek, assembled-$25; unassembled-$20 – Make-A-Plates: create a design, send it in a pre-addressed envelope and receive a melamine plate-$10 – Make-A-Mugs: create a design, send it in a pre-addressed envelope and receive a 10 oz. mug-$5

PURPLE MARTIN CONSERVATION ASSOCIATION ♦ *page 160*

– Coloring books: A Field Guide To The Birds-$5.95

RAPTOR CENTER AT THE UNIVERSITY OF MINNESOTA ♦ *page 161*

– Coloring books: birds of prey-$2.95

RAPTOR EDUCATION FOUNDATION ♦ *page 162*

– Coloring books: 44 North American raptors with color reference plates-$5

SAVE THE MANATEE CLUB ♦ *page 170*

– Stuffed toys: manatee, 24"-$31.95; 18"-$21.95; 12"-$13.95; 10"-$9.95

TOYS
&
GAMES

SAVE THE WHALES ♦ *page 171*
— Stuffed toys: dolphin, penguin, Beluga whale, polar bear or sea otter; an educational hang tag included, 5" to 6"-$3.95
— Puzzles: jigsaw puzzle of marine mammals, 550 pieces, 18x24-$9.95 — Coloring books: marine life, 32 pages, drawings with text-$6.95

SUTTON AVIAN RESEARCH CENTER ♦ *page 177*
— Coloring books: Birds of Prey-$4.95

TIMBER WOLF ALLIANCE ♦ *page 178*
— Activity books: Discovering Wolves, 40 page workbook-$4.95

TREE HOUSE ANIMAL FOUNDATION ♦ *page 180*
— Stickers: set of 99 one inch high stickers with Tree House logo in purple with red heart-$2.50

VEGETARIAN RESOURCE GROUP ♦ *page 183*
— Coloring books: The Soup To Nuts Natural Foods Coloring Book-$3 — Activity books: I Love Animals And Broccoli-$5

WAIKIKI AQUARIUM ♦ *page 228*
— Stuffed toys: turtle, 11"-$16.25 ♦ orca, 10"-$14.25
♦ dolphin, 15"-$18.25

WHALE ADOPTION PROJECT ♦ *page 184*
— Stuffed toys: white baby harp seal of 14"-$19.95 ♦ gray humpback whale of 20"-$17.95 — Games: The Whale Game, family board game-$19.95 — Stickers: 6 puffy whale stickers, 3" long-$3.45

TOYS & GAMES

WHALE MUSEUM ♦ *page 186*

▬ Stuffed toys: orca, 24"-$20.95; orca calf, 6"-$4.95; both-$22.95 ▬ Games: The Whale Game, board game of strategy, age 8 up-$19.95 ♦ Task, board game of learning to live in harmony with nature, age 10 up-$24.95 ♦ 50 Tails for 50 Whales, matching puzzle game, age 6 up-$12.50 ▬ Card games: Ocean Lotto, learn to identify 36 ocean creatures, four games in one, age 3 up-$8.95 ♦ Ocean Pick-Up-Pairs, memory game with 96 cards, age 4 up-$7.95 ♦ Ocean Quiz, 250 questions and answers-$7.95 ♦ Ocean Animals, six games, matching clues to animals, age 7 up-$9 ▬ Puzzles: Whales, 22 whale species, age 6 up-$9.95 ♦ Pollution Patrol in Our Oceans, assemble and locate hazards, 300 pcs.-$11.95 ♦ Water's Edge, underwater scene with over 50 sea creatures, age 8 up-$11.95 ♦ North American Marine Wildlife, 1500 pcs.-$24 ♦ Fragile Earth, animals of the earth in a spiral, 1200 pcs.-$17.95 ▬ Wooden models: laminated with mounting stand, age 8 up, bottle nosed dolphin, blue whale, shark or orca-$6.95 ▬ Coloring books: whales, dolphins or marine mammals-$2.25 ▬ Activity books: The Ocean Book, 113 pages-$12.95 ♦ Marine Mammals, Salmon, Endangered Species-$3.95 ♦ Adventures in Greater Pugent Sound-$3.95

WILD CANID SURVIVAL AND RESEARCH CENTER ♦ *page 189*

▬ Stuffed toys: howling wolf-$70 ♦ small Mexican timber wolf-$5 ♦ wolf doll dressed in fake sheep pajamas with lace trim and pink ribbon, 28" tall-$100 ▬ Masks: wolf, plastic

with elastic band-$3 → Puppets: squeaking wolf pup with tail- TOYS
$20 ♦ Wolfgang-$15 → Card games: plastic-coated playing   &
cards with six gold wolves on red or white-$5 ♦ double deck   GAMES
playing card set, one white and one red-$10 → Puzzles:
napping wolf puppy, 8x10-$5 → Rubber stamps: howling
wolf-$4 ♦ full length howling wolf-$6 ♦ large paw print-$4
♦ small paw print-$3 ♦ endangered grey wolf-$6

WILDLIFE PRESERVATION TRUST INTERNATIONAL ♦ *page 195*

→ Stuffed toys: ring-tailed lemur, 12"-$28 ♦ black-footed
ferret, 12"-$24

WOLF SONG OF ALASKA ♦ *page 199*

→ Activity books: Who lives here?...Forests, educational col-
oring guidebook-$4.95 ♦ The Alaska Wolf-$7.95 ♦ Discovering
Wolves-$4.95 ♦ Wolves for Kids-$6.95 and $14.95 ♦ The Big
Good Wolf-$4.95 ♦ Looking at the Wolf-$4.95

WOODSTOCK ANIMAL RIGHTS MOVEMENT ♦ *page 200*

→ Juggling toys: tossed salad or Earths-$14.95; orcas-$13.95
→ Stuffed toys: squirrel, 8"-$21 ♦ hedgehog, 10"-$19.95
♦ dolphin, 18"-$21 ♦ whale, 24"-$42 ♦ penguin, 11"-$19; 19"-$42
♦ iguana, 40"-$76 ♦ elephant, 15"-$58 ♦ fox, 13"-$29 ♦ owl, 11"-
$25 ♦ cow, 12"-$29 ♦ tiger, 14"-$42 ♦ wolf, 12"-$25 ♦ pig, 21"-
$48 → Hand puppets: octopus, 13"-$21 ♦ frog, 13"-$15
♦ glowing firefly, 10"-$14 ♦ lizard, 22"-$22 ♦ grasshopper, 10"-
$14 ♦ cockroach, 10"-$15 ♦ ladybug, 9"-$14 ♦ bee, 8"-$14
→ Rubber animals: snake, 72"-$8.95 ♦ iguana, 12"-$7.50

TOYS & GAMES

WOODSTOCK ANIMAL RIGHTS MOVEMENT (CONT)

➞ Rubber stamps: 10 different messages to make a difference in the world-$4.25 to $6.75 ➞ Rubber stamp sets: World Of Difference, 11 stamps, color indexing stickers, case-$13.95 ◆ Rain Forest, eight stamps of rain forest inhabitants, ink pad-$7.95 ➞ Ink pads: child safe, 8 colors-$3.50 each

WORLD BIRD SANCTUARY ◆ *page 201*
➞ Activity books: Bald Eagle-$6

XERECES SOCIETY ◆ *page 203*
➞ Coloring books: Butterflies East and West, 80 pages-$6.75

TRAVEL & EXPERIENCES

Travel & Experiences

DOLPHIN RESEARCH CENTER ◆ *page 62*
➞ Dolphin Encounter: swim with the dolphins in an educational workshop, age 5 and up-$90 ➞ Dolphin Insight: a half day interactive program with the dolphins, age 12 and up-$75 per person ➞ Dolphin Lab: spend an educational week at the Dolphin Research Center, age 18 and up, includes room and board and ground transportation-$1050

OCEANIC PROJECT DOLPHIN ◆ *page 140*
➞ Whale Watch gift certificates: full-day trip from San Francisco, Dec.-Apr.-$48; three-hour trips from Half Moon Bay-$32 ➞ Farallon Islands cruise gift certificates: full day, from San Francisco, June through November-$58

WILD HORSE SANCTUARY ◆ *page 191*
➞ Weekend pack trips: $235 per person for two days; $335 for three days; $435 for four days

Tree Plantings
ORANGUTAN FOUNDATION INTERNATIONAL ♦ *page 144*

Videos, Audio Cassettes & CDs
ALLIED WHALE ♦ *page 18*
⬅ Videos: *Marine Mammals of the Gulf of Maine*-$20

AMERICAN BIRDING ASSOCIATION ♦ *page 20*
⬅ Videos: large selection on birds and birding-$24.95 to
$39.95 ⬅ Audio Cassettes and CDs: large selection of bird
calls and sound recordings-$9.59 to $75.00

AMERICAN MUSTANG AND BURRO ASSOCIATION ♦ *page 25*
⬅ Videos: *America's Wild Horses*-$24.95

AMERICAN VEGAN SOCIETY ♦ *page 28*
⬅ Videos: over 100 videos on nutrition, animal rights, animal-
free shopping, health, religion, vegan and vegetarian cooking,
the environment, ethics-$12 to $23 ⬅ Audios: over 30 tapes
on lectures from various conventions-$6

ANIMAL PROTECTION INSTITUTE OF AMERICA ♦ *page 31*
⬅ Videos: *Eyes of the World*, Harp Seals-$5

ANIMAL WELFARE INSTITUTE ♦ *page 34*
⬅ Videos: animal welfare topics-$5

BAT CONSERVATION INTERNATIONAL ♦ *page 40*
⬅ Videos: *The Secret World of Bats*, documentary-$41.95
♦ *Bats of America*-$19.95 ♦ *Bats: Myth and Reality*-$19.95
♦ *Very Elementary Bats*-$17.95

TREE
PLANTINGS

VIDEOS,
AUDIO
CASSETTES
& CDs

VIDEOS, AUDIO CASSETTES & CDs

CENTER FOR MARINE CONSERVATION ♦ *page 47*

➤ Videos: set of two for children, *The Great Barrier Reef and Dolphins, Our Friends From The Sea*, 30 min. each-$16.95 ♦ set of three for children, *Creatures of the Sea, Ocean Life, Penguins*-$25 ♦ *Watching the Whales*, 30 min.-$29.95 ♦ *Baby Animals Just Want To Have Fun*, ages 2 to 8-$15 ♦ *Animal Alphabet*, 30 min.-$14.95 ♦ *Return of the Great Whales*-$29.95 ♦ *Life on Earth* by David Attenborough, a natural history of earth and its creatures, four hours-$39.95 ➤ Audio cassettes: *The Singing Humpbacks*-$7.50 ♦ *Killer Whale Songs*-$7.50 ♦ *The Sounds of the Arctic*-$7.50 ♦ *Sounds of the Dolphins*-$5.95 ➤ Compact discs: *Sounds and Songs of the Humpback Whales*, 60 min.-$9.99 ♦ *Peaceful Ocean Surf*, 63 min.-$9.99 ♦ *Sounds of the Dolphin*-$9.95

DALLAS ZOO ♦ *page 211*

➤ Audio cassettes and CDs: safari sounds on CD-$17.99; on cassette-$11.99

DOLPHIN ALLIANCE ♦ *page 60*

➤ Audio cassettes: Dolphins-$12

DOLPHIN RESEARCH CENTER ♦ *page 62*

➤ Audio cassettes and CD's: wild spotted dolphin vocalizations to classical music, cassette-$12; CD-$20 ➤ Videos: dolphins with meditative calming music, 25 minutes-$29.95 ♦ *Talbot: The Video*, film sequences of dolphins and orcas by renowned marine photographer, Bob Talbot with the ethereal music of Mannheim Steamroller & Ray Lynch, 30 minutes-$26.95

DORIS DAY PET FOUNDATION ♦ *page 64*

➤ Audio cassettes: Doris Day music-$15 ➤ Videos: Doris Day movies-$19.95

EARTHTRUST ♦ *page 65*

➙ Videos: *Where Have All the Dolphins Gone?*-$20 ♦ *Whalesong*, video of the plight of the whales-$20 ♦ *Hawaii's Humpback Whales*, video of whale watching on Maui-$20 ♦ *Fall of the Ancients*, video of the plight of the sea turtles-$20

FARM ANIMAL REFORM MOVEMENT ♦ *page 69*

➙ Videos: *Healthy, Wealthy, and Wise*, introduction to vegetarian lifestyles-$20 ♦ *A Diet For All Reasons*, illustrated lecture on vegetarian health-$20 ♦ *Food For Thought*, environmental damage done by animal agriculture-$20 ♦ *Fit For Life*, food preparation demonstrations by Marilyn Diamond-$25

FRIENDS OF BEAVERSPRITE ♦ *page 79*

➙ Videos: *My Forty Years With Beavers*, award-winning filmstrip-$15

FRIENDS OF THE SEA OTTER ♦ *page 83*

➙ Videos: *The World of the Sea Otter*-$29.95

GREAT BEAR FOUNDATION ♦ *page 87*

➙ Videos: *Biggest Bear*-$15 ♦ *The Great Bears of North America*-$29.95 ♦ *The Great Bears of Yellowstone*-$14.95

HUMANE SOCIETY OF THE UNITED STATES ♦ *page 98*

➙ Videos: *Guide to Cat Behavior and Psychology*-$20 ♦ *Guide to Dog Behavior and Psychology*-$20 ♦ *Dog Care*-$15

IN DEFENSE OF ANIMALS ♦ *page 99*

➙ Audio cassettes and CD's: a benefit compilation by major recording artists-Pearl Jam, REM, Michael Stipe, Primus, Concrete Blonde and others, cassette-$12.95; $14.95 for CD

VIDEOS, AUDIO CASSETTES & CDs

VIDEOS, AUDIO CASSETTES & CDs

IN DEFENSE OF ANIMALS (CONT)

→ Videos: *Talbot: Dolphins and Whales*, cinematography and music without narration-$24.95

INTERNATIONAL FUND FOR ANIMAL WELFARE ♦ *page 102*

→ Videos: *Peace On Ice: Journey To The Winter Wonderland Of Baby Seals!* 25 minutes-$19.95

INTERNATIONAL MARINE MAMMAL PROJECT ♦ *page 103*

→ Videos: *Where Have All The Dolphins Gone?*-$29.95

INTERNATIONAL PRIMATE PROTECTION LEAGUE ♦ *page 105*

→ Videos: *Forgotten Apes*, starring Beanie and the IPPL gibbons-$29.95

INTERNATIONAL SOCIETY FOR COW PROTECTION ♦ *page 108*

→ Videos: *Training Oxen By Voice Commands*-$20

INTERNATIONAL WOLF CENTER ♦ *page 111*

→ CDs and audio cassettes: *Classical Wolf*, classical music blended with howling wolves, CD-$15.95; cassette-$9.95 ♦ *Wolf Talk*, wolf howls and other natural sounds, CD-$15.95; cassette-$9.95 ♦ *Howling Harmonies*, CD-$15.95; cassette-$9.95 ♦ *Wolves and Humans*, educational tape with wolf vocal-izations, cassette only-$13.95 ♦ *Timberwolves in Tall Pines*, CD-$15.95; cassette-$9.95 → Videos: *Wolves* narrated by Robert Redford, 60 min.-$19.95 ♦ *Return of the Wolves*, Yellowstone documentary-$19.95

386

INTERSPECIES COMMUNICATION ♦ *page 112*
━ Audio cassettes: *Orcas Greatest Hits,* music between musicians and wild whales-$11 ♦ *A Fish That's Song,* for children-$12

JANE GOODALL INSTITUTE ♦ *page 113*
━ Videos: *National Geographic Presents Jane Goodall: My Life With The Chimpanzees,* one hour, color-$30 ♦ *National Geographic Presents: Among The Wild Chimpanzees,* one hour, color-$30 ♦ *Chimps So Like Us,* 30 min., color-$20

LEND-A-PAW RELIEF ORGANIZATION ♦ *page 116*
━ Videos: *Catnip*-$15

LOS ANGELES AUDUBON SOCIETY ♦ *page 117*
━ Audio cassettes: bird songs, sounds, calls-$9.95 to $79.95
━ Videos: bird identifications-$25 to $39.95

NATURE CONSERVANCY ♦ *page 131*
━ CDs & audio cassettes: soundscapes from Costa Rica, Australia, New Guinea or the jungles of Borneo, CD-$14.95; cassette-$9.95

NORTH AMERICAN LOON FUND ♦ *page 137*
━ Audio cassettes: loon calls-$9.95 ━ CDs: loon calls expanded-$14.95 ━ Videos: *Solitudes-Loon Country by Canoe*-$24.95 ♦ *Loons*-$24.95

ORANGUTAN FOUNDATION INTERNATIONAL ♦ *page 144*
━ Videos: *Orangutans: Grasping the Last Branch*-$20

PRESERVATION OF THE AMAZON RIVER DOLPHIN ♦ *page 158*
━ Videos: rare pink dolphin footage narrated by Lindsay Wagner-$25

VIDEOS, AUDIO CASSETTES & CDs

VIDEOS, AUDIO CASSETTES & CDs

PURPLE MARTIN CONSERVATION ASSOCIATION ♦ *page 160*
→ Audio cassettes: *Purple Martin Dawnsong*-$10.95

ROAR FOUNDATION ♦ *page 164*
→ Videos: *Roar*, 1961, the 47 minute action adventure film that started the Shambala Preserve, stars Tippi Hedren and her daughter Melanie Griffith-$55

SANGRE DE CRISTO ANIMAL PROTECTION ♦ *page 167*
→ Audio cassettes: Robert Hoyt sings of political and social causes-$10 ♦ *Metalheart (Rock Against Furs)*-$5 → CDs: Robert Hoyt sings of political and social causes-$15

SAVE THE DOLPHINS PROJECT ♦ *page 169*
→ Videos: *Where Have All The Dolphins Gone?* narrated by George C. Scott, 48 minutes-$29.95

SAVE THE MANATEE CLUB ♦ *page 170*
→ Videos: *The Best Of The Manatees*, 30 minutes, includes a message by Jimmy Buffett-$24.95

SAVE THE WHALES ♦ *page 171*
→ Videos: *Dolphins and Orcas*, 30 minutes-$24.95 → Audio cassettes and CDs: *Songs And Sounds Of Orcinus Orca*, killer whale vocalizations ♦ *Jonah's Journey*, relaxing instrumentals with humpback whale sounds ♦ *Songs And Sounds Of The Humpback Whale* ♦ *Pacific Blue*, orca sounds combined with instrumental background ♦ *Beneath The Waves*, humpback whale recordings with music; cassettes-$9.95; CDs-$15.95

SUPRESS ♦ *page 176*
→ Videos: *Hidden Crimes*, a comprehensive film on the subject of animal experimentation, 78 mins.-$27

SUTTON AVIAN RESEARCH CENTER ♦ *page 177*
➥ Videos: *On A Wing And A Prayer*, 30 minute documentary on the Sutton Center Bald Eagle Restoration Project-$19.95

TIMBER WOLF PRESERVATION SOCIETY ♦ *page 179*
➥ Audio cassettes: wolf howls with narration-$15

TRUMPETER SWAN SOCIETY ♦ *page 181*
➥ Videos: *Trumpeter Blues*, swans of Yellowstone-$25

WHALE ADOPTION PROJECT ♦ *page 184*
➥ Audio tapes: humpback sounds and songs-$9.95 ➥ Videos: *Beyond Belief: The Humpback Whale*-$31.95 ♦ *Best of Provincetown Whale Watching*-$31.95

WHALE CONSERVATION INSTITUTE ♦ *page 185*
➥ Videos: *In The Company Of Whales*, by WCI and Discovery Channel, 90 minute documentary-$24.99 ➥ Audio cassettes: *Songs Of The Humpback Whale*-$10 ♦ *Whales Alive*-$10 ♦ *Deep Voices*, right whale, blue whale and humpback sounds-$12
➥ CDs: *Songs Of The Humpback Whale*-$12 ♦ *Whales Alive*-$12 ♦ *Deep Voices*, right whale, blue whale and humpback sounds-$12

WHALE MUSEUM ♦ *page 186*
➥ Videos: *Orca: Killer Whale Or Gentle Giant?*, excellent coverage of family structure, pod dialects and behaviors of Northwest orcas, 30 min.-$29.95 ♦ *Killer Whales-Wolves of the Sea*, National Geographic, 60 mins.-$19.95 ♦ *Magnificent Whales & Other Marine Mammals of North America*, Smithsonian, 60 mins.-$36.95 ♦ *Watching The Whales*, Marine Mammal Fund, 12 species of whales and dolphins, 30 min.-$29.95 ♦ *Dolphins & Orcas*, Mannheim Steamroller soundtrack

WHALE MUSEUM (CONT)

with wild dolphins and orcas footage by Bob Talbot, 30 mins.-$30.95 — Audio cassettes and CD's: *Orca's Greatest Hits*, hydrophone recordings of orcas' response to musicians-$12 ◆ *Killer Whales & Friends*, wild orca vocalizations-$10.95 ◆ *Beneath The Waves*, wild humpback vocalizations, tape-$12.50 ◆ *Pacific Blue I and II*, instrumentals with wild whale vocalizations, tape-$10.95 each; CD-$19.95 each ◆ *San Juan Suite*, Michael Gettel's music with wild whale vocalizations, tape-$12.50; CD-$22

WILD CANID SURVIVAL AND RESEARCH CENTER ◆ *page 189*

— Audio cassettes: *Howling Harmonies*, 60 minutes of wolf howls-$9.95 ◆ *Wolves And Humans-Wolf Vocalizations*-$13.95 ◆ *New Age Wolf*-$9.95 — CDs: *Howling Harmonies*, 60 minutes of wolf howls-$15.95 ◆ *New Age Wolf*-$15.95 — Videos: *Cry Of The Wild*, timber wolf, 80 minutes-$19.95 ◆ *The Wolf: A Howling In American's National Parks*, narrated by Robert Redford, 30 minutes-$24.95

WOLF HAVEN INTERNATIONAL ◆ *page 197*

— Audio tapes: *Howlin'/ True Story Of Little Red Riding Hood*, from the wolf's point of view, with 10 minutes of songs-$9.95

WOLF SONG OF ALASKA ◆ *page 199*

— Audio cassettes and CDs: *Wolf Talk*, sounds of the pack in chorus; *New Age Wolf* ◆ *Howling Harmonies* ◆ *Wolves & Humans* ◆ *Jazz Wolf* ◆ *Classical Wolf* and others, audio cassettes-$9.95; CDs-$15.95

WOODSTOCK ANIMAL RIGHTS MOVEMENT ♦ *page 200*

VIDEOS, AUDIO CASSETTES & CDs

➼ Audio cassettes: 10 different nature recordings-oceans, wolves, loons, frogs, birds, thunderstorms, jungles-$9.95 to $10.95

➼ Compact discs: 10 different nature recordings -oceans, wolves, loons, frogs, birds, thunderstorms, jungles-$15.95 ➼ Videos: *Diet For A New America*, John Robbins, 60 minutes-$19.95 ♦ *A Diet For All Reasons*, Dr. Michael Klaper, 90 minutes-$24.95

**CENTER
FOR MARINE
CONSERVATION**
Ceramic dolphin box
♦ $12.50

**CENTER
FOR MARINE
CONSERVATION**
Lead crytal dolphin
bowl ♦ $225.50

**CENTER
FOR MARINE
CONSERVATION**
Sea life teapot
♦ $32.50

Achor, Amy Blount. *Animal Rights: A Beginner's Guide*. Yellow Springs, Ohio: WriteWare, 1992.

Chapin, Alice. *The Big Book of Great Gift Ideas*. Wheaton, Illinois: Tyndale House Publishers, 1991.

Coats, C. David. *Old MacDonald's Factory Farm: The Myth of the Traditional Farm and the Shocking Truth About Animal Suffering in Today's Agribusiness*. New York: Continuum, 1991.

Corrigan, Patricia. *Where The Whales Are: Your Guide To Whale-Watching Trips in North America*. Chester, Connecticut: The Globe Peguot Press, 1991.

Erickson, Brad. *Call To Action: Handbok For Ecology, Peace and Justice*. San Francisco: Sierra Club Books, 1990.

Folzenlogen, Darcy & Robert. *A Guide To American Zoos & Aquariums*. Littleton, Colorado: Willow Press, 1993.

Global Tomorrow Coalition. *The Global Ecology Handbook: What You Can Do About The Environmental Crisis*. Boston: Beacon Press, 1990

Goodman, Billy. *A Kid's Guide To How To Save The Animals*. New York: Avon Books, 1991.

Heintzelman, Donald. *Wildlife Protectors Handbook: How You Can Help Stop The Destruction of Wild Animals*. Santa Barbara: Capra Press, 1992.

King, Judith. *The Greatest Guide Ever*. Cincinnati: Betterway Books, 1993.

Koebler, Linda with the ASPCA. *For Kids Who Love Animals.* Los Angeles: Living Planet Press, 1991.

Koebler, Linda. *Zoo Book: The Evolution of Wildlife Conservation Centers.* New York: Tom Doherty Associates, 1994.

Lanier-Graham, Susan D. *The Nature Directory: A Guide To Environmental Organizations.* New York: Walker and Associates, 1991

Living Planet Press. *The Animal Rights Handbook.* New York: Berkeley Books, 1993.

Makower, Joel. *The Nature Catalog.* New York: Vintage Press, 1991

Marshall, Anthony D. *Zoo: Profiles of 102 Zoos, Aquariums, and Wildlife Parks in the United States.* New York: Random House, 1994

Miller, Louise. *Careers For Animal Lovers and Other Zooogical Types.* Lincolnwood, Illinois: VGM Career Horizons, 1991.

Newkirk, Ingrid. *Kids Can Save The Animals.* New York: Warner Books, 1991.

Newkirk, Ingrid. *Save The Animals: 101 Easy Things You Can Do.* New York: Warner Books, 1990.

Nilsen, Richard. *Helping Nature Heal: An Introduction To Environmental Restoration.* Berkeley, California: Ten Speed Press, 1991.

Nyhuis, Allen W. *The Zoo Book: A Guide To America's Best*. Albany, California: Carousel press, 1994.

O'Brien, Tim. *Where The Animals Are: A Guide To The Best Zoos, Aquariums, and Wildlife Sanctuaries in North America*. Old Saybrook, Connecticut: The Globe Pequot Press, 1992

Robbins, John. *May All Be Fed: Diet For A New World*. New York: William Morrow and Company, 1992.

Sequoia, Anna with Animal Rights International. *67 Ways To Save The Animals*. New York: Harper Collins, 1990.

Seredich, John. *Your Resource Guide To Environmental Organizations*. Irvine, California: Smiling Dolphins Press, 1991.

Silverman, B.P. Robert Stephen. *Defending Animals' Rights Is The Right Thing To Do*. New York: Shapolsky Publishers, 1992.

Singer, Peter. *Animal Liberation*. New York: Avon Books, 1990.

Singer, Peter. *In Defense Of Animals*. New York: Harper & Row, 1986.

Sperling, Susan. *Animal Liberators: Research & Morality*. Berkeley, California: University of California Press, 1988

Walls, David. *The Activist's Almanac: The Concerned Citizen's Guide To The Leading Advocacy Organizations in America*. New York: Simon & Schuster, 1993.

Weil, Zoe. *Animals In Society: Facts and Perspectives on Our Treatment of Animals*. Jenkinown, Pennsylvania: The American Anti-Vivisection Society, 1991

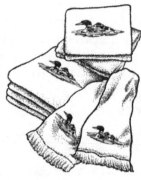

CENTER FOR MARINE CONSERVATION
Loon towels,
green or ivory
bath ♦ $18.50
hand ♦ $14.50
fingertip ♦ $9.50

CENTER FOR MARINE CONSERVATION
Toothbrush holder ♦ $13.50
Tissue box cover ♦ $37.00
Soapdish ♦ $13.50
Pump dispenser ♦ $16.50
Wastebasket ♦ $60.00

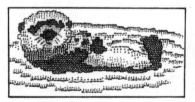

FRIENDS OF THE SEA OTTER
Sea otter
needlework
♦ $10.95

(Bolded page numbers indicate illustrations)

gifts from
  godparents 7
  grandparents 7
Gifts That Make A Difference 3
glasses **viii**, **4**, 47
  see also crystal
goats 29, 94
golf hats 146
  see also caps
golf shirts 228
Gorilla Foundation 86
gorillas 15, 58, 86, 105, 236
gourds 160
Great Bear Foundation 87
Great Danes 125
Greater Los Angeles Zoo Association 214
greeting cards 41, 83, 107, 110, 127, 171, **173**, 188
  see also birthday cards, condolence cards, holiday cards
Greyhound Friends 88
greyhounds 88

H

hand and body lotions 200
hand puppets *see puppets*
Happy Hollow Park Zoo 214
hats 50, 51, 62, 88, 136
  see also caps
Hawk Mountain Sanctuary 89
hawks 29, 42, 73, 90, 142, 165
  see also birds
Hawkwatch International 90

hair conditioners 200
Helen Woodward Animal Center 91
Helping Homeless Cats 92
Hemlock Hill Farm Sanctuary 93
hennas 200
hens *see poultry*
hip packs 31, 62, 64
holiday cards 42, 70, 82, 83, 123, 142, 149, 159, 163, 195, 206
holiday items 328-330
Honolulu Zoo 215
Hooved Animal Humane Society 94
Horse Power Projects 95
horses 17, 22, 25, 50, 54, 67, 91, 94, 95, 163, 191, 237
housewares and home accessories 331-341
Humane Education Committee 96
Humane Farming Association 97
humane societies 237-238
Humane Society of the United States 98

I

In Defense of Animals 99
Indianapolis Zoo 215
ink pads 200
International Bird Rescue Research Center 100
International Crane Foundation 101
International Fund for Animal Welfare 102
International Marine Mammal Project 103
International Osprey Foundation 104
International Primate Protection League 105

GIFT LIST

Name	Item	Page No.

GIFT LIST

Name	Item	Page No.

GIFT LIST

Name	Item	Page No.

GIFT LIST

Name	Item	Page No.

GIFTS THAT MAKE A DIFFERENCE: HOW TO BUY HUNDREDS OF GREAT GIFTS SOLD THROUGH NONPROFITS was also written by Ellen Berry. This book profiles 165 nonprofit organizations of all kinds and the gifts they offer for sale to raise funds for causes that help the environment, animals, children, historic preservation, Native Americans, third world people, emergency relief, the hungry, the homeless, disease research, etc. If you would like your nonprofit organization to be included in another book in this series, please send the appropriate information to:

Foxglove Publishing
P.O. Box 292500
Dayton, Ohio 45429-0500
USA

▲

To order a copy of *GIFTS THAT MAKE A DIFFERENCE*, please send $7.95 plus $2.00, handling and shipping, to:

Foxglove Publishing
P.O. Box 292500
Dayton, Ohio 45429-0500
USA

If you would like your organization to be included in another book in this series or if corrections should be made to current text for an updated edition of *GIFTS THAT SAVE THE ANIMALS: 1001 GREAT GIFTS SOLD BY NONPROFITS THAT PROTECT ANIMALS*, please send the appropriate information to:

Foxglove Publishing
P.O. Box 292500
Dayton, Ohio 45429-0500
USA

To order a copy of *GIFTS THAT SAVE THE ANIMALS: 1001 GREAT GIFTS SOLD BY NONPROFITS THAT PROTECT ANIMALS*, please send $9.95 plus $2.00, handling and shipping, to:

Foxglove Publishing
P.O. Box 292500
Dayton, Ohio 45429-0500
USA